DOUBLE
ACT

Also by Michael Denison

Overture and Beginners

(*with Dulcie Gray*)
The Actor and His World

DOUBLE ACT

Michael Denison

Michael Joseph   London

First published in Great Britain by Michael Joseph Ltd
44 Bedford Square, London WC1
1985

British Library Cataloguing in Publication Data

Denison, Michael
  Double act.
  1. Gray, Dulcie   2. Denison, Michael
  I. Title
  792'.028   PN2598.G66/

ISBN 0 7181 2290 9

Phototypeset by Alacrity Phototypesetters,
Banwell Castle, Weston-super-Mare
Printed and bound in Great Britain by
Biddles Ltd, Guildford, Surrey

For Dulcie

CONTENTS

Acknowledgements		viii
List of Illustrations		ix
Author's Note		xi
Prologue		xiii
I	The Fifties	1
II	The Sixties	97
III	The Seventies	197
Stop Press		275
Epilogue		281
Chronological Chart		284
Index		298

ACKNOWLEDGEMENTS

The author and publishers would like to thank the following for their kind permission to reproduce material in the book:

The Executors of the Estate of Maurice Baring for the quotation from his *Collected Poems* on page 281.

Victor Gollancz Ltd for the quotations from *The Actor and His World* by Michael Denison and Dulcie Gray on page 39 and from *Overture and Beginners* by Michael Denison on page 57.

A. D. Peters & Co Ltd for two extracts from *Dragon's Mouth* by Jacquetta Hawkes and J. B. Priestley on pages 33-4 and the letter from Rebecca West to Michael Denison on pages 243-4.

Weidenfeld & Nicolson for the quotation from *Confessions of an Actor* by Laurence Olivier on page 40.

And lastly to Richard Attenborough, Gerald Croasdell and Laurence Olivier for permission to quote themselves on page 138 and to Derek Nimmo for permission to quote his letter to Equity on page 147.

Every effort has been made to trace the copyright holders of both the quotations in the text and of the illustrations. However, the publishers would like to apologise for any omissions or inaccuracies, which will be remedied on any future reprints.

LIST OF ILLUSTRATIONS

Between pages 34 and 35

Let Them Eat Cake, 1959 (Angus McBean)
Michael with Dorothy Tutin in *The Importance of Being Earnest*,
    1951 (The Rank Organisation Plc)
Dulcie with Jack Hawkins in *Angels One Five*, 1951 (THORN EMI
    Elstree Studios Limited)
The Fourposter, 1950 (Denis de Marney)
The White Knight and the White Queen, 1955 (Frances
    Charteris)
J. B. Priestley (Jacquetta Hawkes)
Michael with Vivien Leigh in *Twelfth Night*, Stratford 1955
    (Angus McBean)

Between pages 162 and 163

Boyd QC (1956-63) (Associated-Rediffusion)
Candida, 1958 (with Jeremy Brett) (Kenny Parker)
Dulcie with Keith Baxter in *Where Angels Fear to Tread*, 1963
    (Angus McBean)
With Robert Flemyng and Gillian Raine in *Happy Family* and
    On Approval, 1966 (Houston Rogers, Theatre Museum,
    V & A)
Rebecca West (BBC Hulton Picture Library)
At Chalet Coward, September 1966

Between pages 242 and 243

At home with the Rolls, early 1970s (Universal Pictorial Press
    and Agency Limited)

Mrs Alving, 1972 (Alec Russell)
Miss Marple, 1977 (Sir Peter Saunders)
Pooh-Bah on stage (E. J. Connolly)
Pooh-Bah with the Three Little Maids, 1975 (Doug McKenzie)
Eileen Leahy
Prospero (Declan Thompson)

Between pages 274 and 275

A Song at Twilight, 1983 (Freddie Feest)
See How They Run, 1984 (Michael J. Gell)
Cold Warrior, 1984 (BBC Enterprises Ltd, 1974)
Lady Sneerwell (Saturday) and Mrs Candour (Monday), Duke
    of York's, 1984 (Zoë Dominic)
Investiture, 1983 (B. Broadway)

AUTHOR'S NOTE

In 1973 J. B. Priestley wrote to me about *Overture and Beginners*, my first attempt at the difficult art of combining biography and autobiography. I had sent him a copy, as an old friend and mentor who had played a crucial and beneficent part at the outset both of my career and of my marriage.

To my delight he praised the book as being 'easy' and 'lively', and then went on: 'If I have a complaint – and of course I always have – it is that you might have enlarged your limits, and gone rather deeper into your two characters, and the nature and the art of the Theatre. Yours Ever, Jack.'

In my reply I suggested that if anyone were to write about the theatre in those terms it should be he. After all, had he not made of that forbidding title *Literature and Western Man* a book that one can't put down? I sidestepped the criticism that I should have delved deeper into our characters.

But the challenge I dodged twelve years ago has not been forgotten; and although I am no better qualified today than I was then to measure up to it, it has been continuously at the back of my mind while writing this book.

Given my character, the only solution open to me lies in the hope that an account of the long and varied careers of two very different people, who happen to be married, may provide, en route, some insights into the 'art and the nature of the Theatre' in which they have worked for more than forty-six years; and that from our activities and our reactions to people and events, rather than from any deliberate self-exploration, there may emerge two portraits, hopefully of interest, certainly honest. For if a man cannot say what he thinks at the age of seventy, there is something wrong with the man – or with the society in which he lives.

The reader should be warned however that, though what I think may be a surprise now and again, it is unlikely to be in the category of a box-office sensation. I have a built-in antipathy to amplified sound, whether it proceeds from a discothèque or from the beating of breasts.

In *Overture and Beginners* I told our stories – particularly Dulcie's, which was far the more interesting – from birth to Film and West End stardom. Her early background included: birth in the Police Officers' Mess in Kuala Lumpur, though neither parent was in the police or under arrest; boarding school in England before her fourth birthday, with a working knowledge of arithmetic – since mislaid; a school teacher and journalist in the jungle at seventeen; receiving innumerable proposals of marriage, but nevertheless working her passage home to England looking after a child on a cargo ship; arriving with £10 and starving her way through art and drama schools; marrying for money – her overdraft of 6/7d to my credit balance of £30.

All this was helpful to my determination not to write just another book of theatrical memoirs. This time, though my determination is unchanged, the task is much harder. I shall therefore escape whenever possible from a recital of professional successes and disasters into other aspects and interests of our lives – painting, cricket, architecture and landscape, the intrusion of politics into the theatre, Equity, the Arts Council, travel, dogs, butterflies, old Rolls-Royces, etc. etc. – above all, the friendships, by no means all theatrical, which have meant and mean so much to us.

If this results in a cascade of names – some of them famous – I am unrepentant. Dulcie and I have never found hero-worship difficult or diminishing. The names are not dropped for the effect on the reader; they are there out of gratitude for the effect they have had on us. For instance Jack Priestley, whom we loved and mourn, gave me my first London contract and then permitted me to break it to marry Dulcie.

There will inevitably be many absentees from the index – colleagues and friends whom I would wish to celebrate, but cannot, from lack of space not lack of affection. Present or absent, may they all forgive me.

Michael Denison

PROLOGUE

My reverie in front of the first of many sheets of virgin paper was interrupted by a knock. 'Come in.' 'Good evening, sir. This is your half-hour call.' 'Thank you, John.'

I was sitting, in February 1983, in my dressing-room at the Haymarket – that last London haunt of the call-boy – with Dulcie next door; we were involved (even though on this occasion we didn't exchange a word on stage) in our twenty-fifth joint starring appearance in the West End, a highly successful revival of *The School for Scandal*.

What more could we ask? Just this. That our luck should last as long as our energies; and our energies as long as life itself.

I The Fifties

I have chosen to begin my account of the Fifties in 1949. For one thing it *was* the fiftieth year of the century; for another my previous book of revelations carried our joint and separate stories to 1948.

It was a decade of shifting patterns for us, in which the eclipse of our film careers was fortunately followed by an increasing volume of work on television, culminating for me in the long-running series, *Boyd QC*, and for Dulcie, after a painful period of frustration, in a number of memorable character studies in the new medium. There was also our fluctuating struggle to live down our film-star images and to be accepted in the theatre – important milestones on this path being *Dragon's Mouth* by J. B. Priestley and Jacquetta Hawkes, *Candida* for Frank Hauser at Oxford, and my season at Stratford with the Oliviers.

It saw the start of my long, absorbing and sometimes hazardous years on the Council of Equity; and of Dulcie's successful secondary career as a writer, in which she soon switched decisively – and, I fear, irrevocably – from plays to novels. (From her Public Lending Right figures – which reveal hundreds of thousands of library borrowings – it is clear that she has a large and faithful public.)

It brought us our first London home and our first ancient Rolls-Royce. Work took us jointly to South Africa; and Dulcie alone to Australia, and on round the world.

I
1949

First London house – Queen Elizabeth Slept Here – *an outstanding director* – *our 'discovery' of Audrey Hepburn* – *Equity and British films*

1949 was a year of important and varied beginnings for us – of our first London house, my first election to the Council of Equity, our first blockbuster of a success in the West End. It was also the year in which *The Glass Mountain* was on general release – a film which apparently still has many friends and thereby causes us gratification and embarrassment in equal measure when it is periodically shown on the box. (The last time I saw it I thought it unlikely that my tempestuous composer would have *one* girl after him – let alone two!)

The house was a miraculous acquisition, the first of three remarkable bargains which in turn have been our homes ever since. It was a large and potentially elegant Nash house in Regent's Park – the sort that is currently on the market in the four to five hundred thousand bracket – but was acquired, with some effort on our part, for two thousand five hundred. I say 'potentially elegant', because the elegance of a dwelling depends to some extent on the furniture and fittings, and the proud owners of 39 Chester Terrace had little of either. True, there was an Elizabethan fourposter and some more humdrum items – the product of an inspired shopping spree by Dulcie on tour in Inverness while I was still overseas in the army – but the austere grace of our three-windowed drawing-room, with its tantalisingly oblique view of the park through a great Corinthian arch, was displayed to our visitors in what can only be called the nude.

An early visitor was Ivy Every, wife of Sir Edward, a gentle, genial and civilised baronet, who owned Egginton Hall, a decaying Georgian mansion in Derbyshire, and lived serenely, among beautiful furniture, silver and pictures, in a cottage at its

5

gates. In contrast to her husband, Ivy was a dynamic organiser who in her long life succeeded in organising everyone except her much-loved husband. 'It's very bare, isn't it' she said, contemplating the open spaces of our drawing-room. 'We've got some pictures and Regency furniture rotting away up at the Hall. I'll ask Squire if we can't lend you some of it. I'm sure he won't mind.' Nor did he. And soon the house began to glow with seventeenth-century portraits and a beautiful set of black and gold Regency chairs – the latter admittedly somewhat dilapidated, but last seen by us (years later and after some restoration) adorning the window of Mallett's in Bond Street.

With these glories around us we couldn't wait to give a house-warming party and to invite my boss Robert Clark, then production chief of Associated British Pictures, to whom I was under long-term contract. Mr Clark – he did not become Robert to us for many years – was (and no doubt still is) an enigmatic Scotsman of considerable wealth and power. His wealth was not, I am sure, derived from British films, but from some less hazardous source. Films were important to him nevertheless, for he had immortal longings in him; though sadly, from my point of view, these seemed too often to be snuffed out by the inhibiting hand of caution. He and his wife, May, were clearly amazed by the splendour of Chester Terrace; he knew what he was paying me – I think it was currently £40 a week – and must have assumed that we had considerable private means. 'Dulcie,' he said, 'I would like to live in a house like this.' Dulcie mentioned that there were two or three available in the terrace. 'I'll go and ask May,' he said. He came back deflated. 'No. May says, and she's quite right, "How would we ever keep the ceilings clean?"' I can only say that in the thirteen years we lived there we never bothered – they were, after all, fifteen feet up.

Mr Clark was a bewildering and at times frustrating employer; but then I, after six years away from my beloved theatre during the war, was something of a reluctant film star, and must have bewildered and frustrated him. There was nevertheless respect and affection on my side, and I believe on his. He gave me my first great opportunity in films, casting an unknown in the leading role of *My Brother Jonathan* opposite a far from unknown Dulcie – no undue caution there; and, as we shall see, he was also responsible in a characteristic manner for giving me, five years later, my last great opportunity in films – to date. *Jonathan* put me fifth in 'The Picturegoer Gold Awards' for 1949 – a choice made by the public not the industry – behind Laurence Olivier, Michael Wilding, Robert Donat and Alec Guinness and ahead of Ralph Richardson, Gregory Peck and Alan Ladd. I have every reason to be grateful to Robert Clark.

During the early months of 1949 I was filming Nevil Shute's story, *Landfall*, at Elstree, without Dulcie. I remember little about it, except that it won the author's approval (as indeed *Jonathan* had Francis Brett Young's) – and that was important to me. It also brought about my first meeting with a great hero of mine, A. E. Matthews – the fabled 'Mattie'. Mattie, then in his eighties, had one day on the picture as an air-raid warden; and, so, despite sixty or more years in the business, did not rate his own chair on the set. I fixed that, and had it put next to mine. 'My boy,' said Mattie, 'I very much enjoyed that picture of yours about the doctor.' (*Jonathan*.) I looked at him suspiciously. He returned my gaze steadily. 'I don't believe you saw it.' 'No I didn't.' 'Then why did you say you did?' 'My boy,' he said, 'I'm lucky enough to have a young wife, and she told me that's what you'd want to hear. I can see now that I needn't have bothered.' He chuckled and a firm friendship was established. Later that day he painted for me an unforgettable picture of what life was like for a young actor at the turn of the century. He and Gerald du Maurier were together at Wyndham's at seven pounds a week – on which Mattie was able to keep a manservant and two ponies at his cottage in Devonshire Mews. du Maurier said he'd always wanted to ride, and Mattie mounted him on the quieter of his ponies – the one on which he used to go shopping in the West End. They reached Rotten Row without incident and Mattie, having given basic instructions on the way, then cantered on. When he pulled up there was no sign of Gerald. Knowing that the other pony was totally safe, Mattie continued his ride and went home. Half an hour later the other horseman returned. He had been taken on Mattie's usual route down Bond Street and back up Regent Street with visits to the bank, Robinson and Cleavers, etc. Gerald was of course much recognised and at the various unexpected stopping places he tried to entertain his public with funny stories. The pony made its own decision as to when to move on – more often than not just before the punch line.

Our joint career was resumed in the summer, at the Strand

Theatre, with *Queen Elizabeth Slept Here* – an anglicisation of *George Washington Slept Here* by Kaufmann and Hart. It was a broad and mechanical farce about the horrors of country life for a young couple unused to it. It was a far cry from the Chekhovian dying fall of Peter Watling's *Rain on the Just* in which we had first played together in the West End a year previously and which had won golden opinions but failed to run. *Queen Elizabeth* ran for a year, but sadly disappointed our intellectual supporters, who had included Somerset Maugham, Edward Marsh, Michael Redgrave and many critics. Considering that we were then 'film stars', and therefore by definition unable to act, the critics had been remarkably friendly about *Rain on the Just*. In our farce, Ivor Brown said we were 'not natural clowns' but the headlines proclaimed 'Noisy Night for the Denisons', 'You Won't Sleep Through This'. And the box-office staff were at full stretch for months – nowadays it might well have been for years.

Richard Bird directed. It was Dulcie's fourth experience of his skills – the first having been in *Brighton Rock* in 1943, in which her performance of Rose, the little Cockney waitress, literally brought her overnight stardom. For me it was the first and last. A highly successful actor in the Thirties, he turned to directing while the 'Star System' still held sway in the West End, as well as on the touring circuit – where it still does. (So much nonsense is talked and written about the Star System – I have seen members of the avant garde go puce in the face at even hearing the words – that a down-to-earth definition is called for. Technically, a star is a performer (in whatever medium) whose name is considered important enough to put above the title of the production in letters at least as big as any other member of the cast. On the day this first happens to you you become a Star; when it ceases to happen, you are one no longer. By and large the public is unaware of this technicality; they take longer to recognise stardom, but they remain faithful for longer too. Opponents of the Star System like to believe that stars impelled by vanity are forever blackmailing managements impelled by greed into letting them play quite unsuitable parts. This is to disregard the passage of a hundred years; the arrival of cinema and television, whose 'documentary' approach to casting has spilled over into the theatre; and, last but not least, the common sense of modern managements and even of the stars themselves.)

But back to 'Dickie' Bird. For my money – and Dulcie's – he was a model director. He had done his homework on the script before rehearsals began; he had basic movements planned; he had both a sense of comedy and a sense of humour – which, strangely, are not synonymous; he was firm but not blinkered. Above all, when he was our only audience at rehearsals, and therefore the focus of our hopes and fears, he gave unmistakable signs of approval when things were going right, and was ready with constructive advice and demonstration when they weren't. And when the play was successfully launched and he was drawing his percentage, did he disappear, as, I fear, the majority of his present-day successors do? Never. He was there, unannounced, every two or three weeks of the year's run, giving notes to cast and stage management, if necessary calling rehearsals, and, needless to say, doing the same for all his other productions. In 1948-9 he had five big successes in London simultaneously.

Our choice of *Queen Elizabeth*, and its success, may have cast doubts on the height of our brow in some quarters, but it was an important piece of theatrical education for us. Physically, if not intellectually, demanding, it required us, week in and week out, to make ordinary folk laugh (*faire rire les honnêtes gens* – Molière's goal, it may be remembered); and we discovered how hard and how satisfying it was to win such laughter legitimately, and without condescension.

Our guests on the first night were Bob and Kay Lennard (he was casting director of my film company and my doughty champion throughout my contract) and Richard and Sheila Attenborough. We took them on for supper to Ciro's nightclub, where we had seen a girl in the cabaret chorus whose style was quite exceptional; we wanted to see how our quartet, unprompted, would react. It was exactly as we had hoped. Four pairs of eyes had already locked on to her when she was doing her chorus routine with the others; but when she had her 'spot' as Ma'mselle de Paris, their excitement was intense. How right we all were! Her name was Audrey Hepburn.

Bob, as we had hoped, put her under contract immediately and gave her a tiny film part as a cigarette girl in a restaurant. Then, for British films, an all-too-typical tragedy. There had been talk for some time of a re-make of *The Good Companions*, with Dulcie as Miss Trant and myself as Inigo Jollifant. One day I asked Bob why the project seemed to be hanging fire. 'We can't find the girl for the Jessie Matthews part,' he said. 'But Bob,' I said unbelievingly, 'we found her for you, and you've got her under contract – Audrey.' 'I know,' he replied, 'but the Board says, "We want a star name. And in any case how do we know that she can act?"' Within a year the world knew, when they saw her in the enchanting *Roman Holiday* co-starring with Gregory Peck, and lost for good to British pictures.

And so to Equity. For the previous couple of years there had been a growing anxiety in some theatrical circles that the actors' trade union was moving more and more to the Left. I was one of those, by no means all of the Right (for instance, Richard Attenborough, an avowed socialist, was another), who were drafted to stand in the annual Council election pledged to put a stop to this. As I understood my mandate – a highly congenial one – it was to help restore the non-party-political equilibrium of the union, making it possible for men and women of all political faiths, and indeed of none, to sit together at the Council table and on its committees, not always agreeing of course, but finding a common motivation in what was good for performers, rather than toeing conflicting party lines. 1949 produced a landslide victory for this point of view. In the following twenty-eight years, which spanned my Council experience, there were naturally backslidings from this Utopian ideal, but the Councils (and there were many) where it came nearest to realisation were the happiest and most productive. Gordon Sandison, the brilliant General Secretary, who had been chosen after the war for his left-wing credentials and who died in harness at the end of the Fifties, was adroit and devoted enough to ride the sea-change of 1949 (which included a damaging, painful, and I believe baseless witchhunt against him) and eventually even to enjoy its consequences. On one rail journey to Manchester where he and I were to address the Trades' Council on British films, he said to me, 'It's fascinating at Equity nowadays. You never know how any vote is going to go – not even on topics with a political content.' I took this as a generous and important admission that Equity was, for the moment, on course again.

The new Council was soon plunged into a major campaign (of which the Manchester trip was part) to preserve the British film industry. There were many elements, domestic and foreign in the crisis, which made it difficult to resolve. The most crucial was undoubtedly the feebleness of the Quota legislation, designed to ensure the showing of a minimum proportion of British films on British screens (45 per cent in 1949, reduced to 30 per cent a year later) but more honoured in the breach than the observance by many cinema owners. As I told the trade union audience in Manchester:

The quota defines as British a film made in a British studio by a British company with 75 per cent of the cost going to British labour. In assessing this percentage, the salaries of one artist or one technician may be excluded (permitting therefore a foreign star or director to be employed). The loopholes are legion. For instance a film could be shot by a British company exclusively on location in Italy with American stars, a French director, a Greek scriptwriter and a few British supporting actors and technicians and yet qualify for the British quota.

The main threat to our industry's independence comes from the vast production capacity of Hollywood, supported by a world market for its international stars, but I want to emphasise that Equity is not anti-American and that all we ask is that, in order to qualify for British nationality, a picture should have, within its 75 per cent labour costs, at least one British star. The advantages would be great, and not only to British pictures. American-financed pictures made in our studios would not be damaged by the loss of British nationality, since they already have the entrée into 70,000 of the world's 90,000 cinemas; and if they were no longer British, Equity could no longer raise objections to the star casting. (*There had been much justifiable agonising over the casting of Gregory Peck and Virginia Mayo in the 'British' film,* Captain Horatio Hornblower R.N.) More positively, a British star, teamed with an American in a British picture, would be seen all over the world, and hopefully thereby enhance not only his or her reputation, but, crucially, that of British films as well. (*This in fact happened to Richard Todd in* The Hasty Heart, *when he was cast with Patricia Neal – and Ronald Reagan.*)

We had confidential evidence, Dulcie and I, from an important American film producer, that Hollywood was not unsympathetic to the idea. Sadly, the other unions in the British industry, fearing that American film-makers would be driven away from British studios, with a consequent loss of jobs to their members, were less than helpful to Equity's campaign. As a result, by the middle Fifties serious British film production was in decline; studios large and small were closed or closing; had it not been for the resolution of a few independents – notably the Boulting brothers – and the providential expansion of BBC television and the advent of ITV, job losses would have been even more severe, many of them on the highest level of technical and artistic skills. Furthermore, the profits of Rank and ABC came from showing pictures in their two cinema chains, and only rarely from making them. (For instance, in 1950 Rank's cinemas had a trading profit of £3½ million, his film production a loss of over half a million.) Not surprisingly their shareholders and other cinema owners were more interested in stepping up the flow of no-risk American product than supporting the home article, which, if it were authentically British, had little or no chance of wide distribution in America – and too small a home market to pay its way.

In pointing all this out pretty forcefully to my Manchester audience and also at a London press conference in which I led for Equity and was followed by Dulcie and Laurence Olivier, and in rebutting a *News Chronicle* leader entitled 'Inequity', I was criticising Arthur Rank and Robert Clark, as well as the other trade unions. I sent Robert a copy of my Manchester speech, which had been widely reported in the press. He was very nice about it, but coming only a year after I had turned down a star part for Otto Preminger in Hollywood, because I thought the script was awful, it can hardly have helped my image as a docile contract artist. Looking back, I am frankly appalled at the risks I took; and for poor loyal Dulcie it was a sore trial. But the cause was a good one and, had we won, it might have been at Pinewood and Denham and Elstree, not Hollywood, that Vivien Leigh, James Mason, David Niven, Richard Burton, Elizabeth Taylor, Rex Harrison, Audrey Hepburn and many others would have had their best opportunities.

In attempting to serve my profession through Equity, when I was for the moment a big name in films, I was following an honourable tradition. The action which gave the infant union teeth had been taken in 1934, when, in order to establish 100 per cent membership in the West End, Dames Marie Tempest and May Witty gave a luncheon at the Savoy and invited a number of leading lights of the profession to sign a pledge that they would not work with non-members of Equity. This was done specifically to give support to the Drury Lane Chorus, who were in a membership dispute, and it was swiftly instrumental in creating the London Theatre Council, consisting of equal delegations of the managers and of Equity, which administers the London theatre to this day. Traditionally the motivation to make a union effective develops upwards from among the most exploited; Equity is not least extraordinary in that in its early years the process was frequently reversed. The (temporarily) secure, the (temporarily) established, put their livelihoods at hazard in the interests of those with less bargaining power, receiving from the latter the resolute support necessary to make idealistic gestures effective.

On the periphery of our professional lives there were a number of memorable incidents. One was a week-end invitation to Dorset from our agent, Jack Dunfee, the former Bentley boy – second at Le Mans in 1929 and winner of the 500 mile race at Brooklands in 1931. Jack was an engaging character with a most distinctive nasal drawl (which I used, effectively I hope, for the Duke of Bristol in *On Approval* some years later). He believed in matrimony, but on his own terms, which resulted in his spirited and attractive wives leaving him – usually for the peerage, and always to his surprise. He had bought his way into the agency, largely, I suspect, to bring himself closer to a supply of 'market' (his term for the beautiful girls who were always in his company), and arriving late on his first morning to frosty looks from his two partners, he enquired with much solemnity, 'I say, am I late for prayers?'

On the Friday of our visit, as we approached Melplash Court (a name straight out of Dornford Yates, though our 9 h.p. Wolseley certainly was not), I said to Dulcie, 'We must remember that we employ Jack, and that we are the boss and his wife visiting our employee's country cottage.' We topped a rise, and there, in a hollow of the hills, was a great stone manor approached by an avenue of chestnuts, the prize heifers on one hillside, the prize turkeys on another, the prize hunters in the paddock and a couple of Bentleys by the porch. 'The boy's doing all right,' said Dulcie.

At the time Jack was between wives; and, out of respect for the stultifying respectability of our marriage, he had forbidden his intended to arrive until breakfast on the Saturday, by which time he hoped, I suppose, to have softened us up. Alas for the delicacy of his plan, we arrived before our host, and the butler, with our tea, had given us the early edition of the *Evening Standard*. On the front page was the headline: '*Harry Roy and Jack Dunfee cited as co-respondents in same divorce.*' After reading the story (which involved yet another lady) we put the paper on a low stool by the fire, where Jack's eagle eye saw it the moment he arrived. 'You've seen that, have you?' he twanged. 'I can't say I'm mad about the billing. Anyway I only took her out every Monday.' (Didn't Mondays count, I wondered?) During dinner a telegram from Warwick Castle was brought in. Silently Jack passed it to us. It read: 'KNOWING YOU AS WE DO CONVINCED OF YOUR INNO-CENCE. WARWICK.' We were softened up indeed, if not quite as Jack had intended.

Another very special occasion was due to the friendship of Lady Annaly. We had met her because of her enthusiasm for *Rain on the Just* and had received many kindnesses from her in the interim. One of the Queen Mother's greatest friends (Lavinia Annaly had been a Lady in Waiting when she was Duchess of York), she now invited us to drinks to meet Her Majesty (then the Queen), explaining that she had already obtained permission for us to leave first, because of our performance. The party began with semi-formal presentations – during which a very tall American film producer who was standing next to three ladies (and was as excited as we were to meet the Queen) followed their example and did a bob instead of a bow. We were summoned first to talk to her, and fell completely under her spell – where we remain. 'What is the play you are doing, Miss Gray?' Her Majesty asked, and Dulcie had to reply, '*Queen Elizabeth Slept Here*, ma'am.'

There were two other royal occasions later in the year. The first was the Irene Vanbrugh Memorial Matinée at Drury Lane attended by the Queen and the two Princesses. There were some informal presentations on stage afterwards, and Sir Kenneth Barnes, Dame Irene's brother and then Principal of RADA, presented me as 'Mr John Clements'. Her Majesty clearly knew he was wrong, but there was a tacit decision between us not to embarrass him. He was not spared for long. John was further down the line. (It was the first of many cases of con-fusion between us. Dulcie and Googie Withers have a similar problem.)

The second occasion was the Royal Film Performance. In those days the film was always followed by an under-rehearsed and blush-making stage show in which such indifferent plums as were going went to our American visitors and the British contingent played the bit parts. This particular year was better than some, because that marvellous dancer/choreographer/director Wendy Toye put us through our paces in a barn dance, in which much energy was expended. Up in the Royal Circle Robert Clark was heard to enquire of his neighbour, 'Is Denison drunk?'

II
1950

The Franchise Affair - *learning to swim* - The Fourposter - *Robert Clark*, The Importance *and John Gielgud*

Jimmy Hanley and Rosalyn Boulter successfully took over our parts at the Strand in the early summer of 1950, releasing us to film *The Franchise Affair*, from the marvellous thriller by Josephine Tey. Making his film debut in the tiny part of a garage mechanic was Kenneth More. (Years later Kenny told us that when he first went to Hollywood, with *Reach for the Sky* and other sterling performances behind him, he was given the full treatment – a house which appeared to have a swimming pool outside every window and a bar and television set in every room. When he was left alone, he gave himself a drink, put his feet up and switched on the nearest television. To his amazement the Big Star saw himself in black and white emerging from under a car in *The Franchise Affair*. 'Thank God, I was alone,' he said, with that distinctive chuckle.)

The location for the picture was in the exquisite little Cotswold town of Chipping Camden. And there we found in the same hotel George Kaufmann, the author of *Queen Elizabeth*, with his actress wife Leueen MacGrath. They thanked us most warmly for the success of the play in London, which had enabled them to have a European holiday; we thanked George Kaufmann for writing it, and thereby enabling us to have our first summer holiday together. 'Where are you going?' asked Leueen. 'Oh, a tiny little place in the South of France. You wouldn't know it,' I replied. 'And you?' 'Oh the same sort of thing,' she said. We ended up, not only in the same hotel, but in neighbouring rooms with *Private Lives*-type balconies.

This was where I learned to swim – after a fashion. A puny child, who was hardly expected to survive, I had been forbidden by the family doctor (Celia Johnson's father) any immersion in cold water. For this I was sincerely grateful on winter mornings at

16

Harrow, where, for others, the day began with a cold 'tosh'; but having survived thirty-five years including a world war, and having a wife whose favourite element was (warm) sea water, I thought it was time to take the plunge. It required a good deal of courage, moral if not physical, because I was constantly being recognised, from *Jonathan* and *La Montagne de Verre*, and much curiosity was aroused by my first faltering steps towards a breast stroke – which was precisely what they were. Even when after a week or so I became regularly water-borne, a sudden request for an autograph would cause me to sink.

The holiday was a blissful one, which was just as well, for as we drove homeward across France in the elegant black Triumph saloon which had superseded the little Wolseley, we knew we were facing the consequences of one of the bravest (or most foolhardy?) decisions we had yet taken.

We had agreed to appear in *The Fourposter* by the Dutch playwright, Jan de Hartog. It was the story of the marriage of Michael and Agnes, told in six scenes spread over fifty years and requiring us to age from fifteen years younger than we were, via one happy episode for which we were right casting, and on into old age. But that was not all. It was a two-character play, with lightning-quick changes of costume and make-up; and it had already been published in hardback – which for a play which has never been performed is a sort of respectable burial.

Now a highly successful novelist, living I believe in America, Jan had written the play (in English) when hiding from the Gestapo in an old women's hostel in Amsterdam. He had had to leave the manuscript there when he escaped, and had collected it two years later, after the war. Perhaps because of the tension under which it was created, he described the play as written 'with the passionate sincerity of a suicide note to posterity.' In 1950 he, Peter Ashmore the director, and we were still close to the grim days of war and inevitably we looked at *The Fourposter* through Jan's eyes – as a dramatic thesis on LIFE and LOVE. (Indeed the last line of the play as originally printed is 'God is Love.') It took our first audiences to show us that what we had in the first four scenes was a charming comedy, which was moving gradually into deeper waters but remaining both funny and true.

The final scene – in Jan's view the *raison d'être* of the play – which showed me as an aged man alone in a garret, visited by ghostly memories of happier days (Dulcie, in a tutu!), was the first casualty; the previous scene also was considered too melodramatic. Alas, in their place, Jan wrote a moving but down-beat scene in which each of the characters knew that Agnes was terminally ill, and at last came to face the situation together. We sent our audiences out into the street moved perhaps, but certainly deeply depressed.

But this is to anticipate. During rehearsals we were asked by the management if we could help with a little capital. We helped with *all* our 'liquid assets' – £400 – thereby ensuring that the frail craft reached its launching at Cambridge.

In spite of all problems we had an extremely successful tour, not creeping round intimate playhouses but brazening it out in the Manchester Opera House, Royal Court Liverpool, King's Edinburgh and Glasgow, Theatres Royal Newcastle and Nottingham, Grand Leeds, New Cardiff, etc., etc. It has almost a ring of one of Shakespeare's lists: 'Harry the King, Bedford and Exeter, Warwick and Talbot, Salisbury and Gloucester ...' (though none of these is a No. 1 date).

It was an extraordinary experience to be alone on stage with Dulcie in those vast theatres, and to know that from curtain up to curtain fall the responsibility was ours and ours alone. Undoubtedly many people came to see film stars in the flesh – as though we were strange exhibits at a zoo; but it has never worried either of us why people come to the theatre, only what sort of experience they have when they get there. We were audible at least, unlike some film stars; and although nowadays many distinguished actors and companies are squeamish about taking straight plays to the big provincial houses, we found them actually helpful to *The Fourposter*. For an odd reason. Among its qualities, which fortunately included much excellent dialogue, was what Jan described as the 'keyhole' nature of the play. Michael and Agnes were to be observed without mawkishness or prurience on their wedding night, at her first pregnancy, his first adultery, her change of life. These commonplaces of life's pattern were watched by audiences in those great theatres with Olympian sympathy. There we were, two tiny mortals at grips with a world far 'bigger than both of us'. It was a scale which exactly suited the play.

Once we moved to London, things became more difficult. The management, assuming, I suppose, that there should be a logical relationship between the size of auditorium and the size of cast, chose for us the West End's smallest theatre – the Ambassadors. There the audience were almost in the bedroom with us; and

Michael and Agnes appeared larger and therefore less vulnerable. A small theatre has a further disadvantage on an opening night: the proportion of press to public is higher. In this connection there had been an unfortunate development before the first night. A journalist came to visit us at Chester Terrace and the crucial part of the interview went like this:

Q: Do you always work together?
A: No.
Q: But you like working together?
A: Yes.
Q: Like the Lunts?
A: Oh please, not 'Like the Lunts'!
Q: Why? Don't you like the Lunts?
A: We think they are absolutely wonderful. But they are at the top of the ladder; we are beginners. Please don't mention us in the same breath.

The Sunday before we opened there appeared the following: 'Behind a yellow front door in Regent's Park lives a young couple whose *secret ambition it is* [my italics] to be the English Lunts.'

There can be a wide gulf between intention and result. I am prepared to believe his intention was to write 'a nice little piece about us' – because it was in those terms that he reminded me of it when we met ten years later. I had to disabuse him, and tell him that in the small world of the theatre it had taken us most of the decade to live it down. The Ivy (then the top theatrical rendez-vous) must have hummed with it, and the Ivy was just across the road from the Ambassadors.

Nevertheless *The Fourposter* made many friends, though not enough to prolong the run beyond nine weeks. During this period there were protracted negotiations for us to take the play to New York. They foundered eventually because the American impresario, aware that there was considerable risk in presenting two unknowns in an unknown two-character play, required us to agree to stay eighteen months, in case it were a success. Reason-able enough, as was the refusal of my film company to release me for more than six. Within a day of the breakdown, the American rights were acquired by that brilliant couple, Jessica Tandy and Hume Cronyn; José Ferrer was engaged to direct, and the three of them, less affected than we had been by Jan's declared motiva-tion for writing the play, prevailed upon him to forget about death and write a touching but comedic final scene which even managed to re-introduce 'God is Love'. This transformed the play – as we later found when we toured the American version in South Africa – and it became an enormous success on Broadway, was filmed in Hollywood by Rex Harrison and Lilli Palmer, and eventually converted into a popular musical *I Do, I Do*. All this has been watched with rueful pride by the two 'reckless fools' (Jan's words) who were the first prepared to perform it as written, and but for whom, as they say, perhaps none of this would have happened.

Remembering the commitment of our liquid assets to the enterprise, the reader might assume that at least we had considerable financial compensation for these disappointments. Alas, no. Our tiny percentage of the London manager's share of the New York run resulted quite quickly in the return of our £400. He then went bankrupt, after losing heavily on a terrible play which he offered us and we refused; and it then transpired that he had used the Broadway *profits* – ours as well as his – to finance it. So that was *The Fourposter*. Recollected thirty-five years on, I am glad we helped release it into the theatre from its hardback prison; nor shall we forget the response of our audiences, particularly on the road.

On 1 December 1950, during our London run, I received a remarkable telephone call from Robert Clark. 'Denison,' said the familiar Scots voice, 'I thought you'd like to know that I have taken your advice and today registered with the BFPA (British Film Producers' Association) *The Importance of Being Earnest*.' I was incoherent with gratitude. *The Importance* was a subject very close to my heart; and I had for a year or two been trying to persuade my employer to include, among his production plans, films of some of the great classics of the British theatre. (Was it because I hoped thereby to become more easily reconciled to film stardom?) This was Mr Clark's first tangible reaction to my arguments.

Characteristically, having made his decision, he proved 'the quickest draw' in the BFPA. Wilde had died in Paris on 30 November 1900, so on 1 December 1950 *The Importance* came into public domain. By registering the title, Mr Clark ensured that no other film company could make it. 'I would like you to approach Mr Gielgud with a view to directing it. Goodbye.'

This was an awesome responsibility to have thrust upon us; it was also an exciting challenge. So we invited John to sup with us at the Ivy.

I have always considered John Gielgud to be the 'founding father', whose genius gave to almost all the great British acting talents of the last fifty years crucial opportunities to build or establish their reputations. Olivier, Evans, Frangcon Davies, Ashcroft, Redgrave, Guinness, Scofield – all owed him a special debt. I exclude Richardson, not to belie his stature but because they began and continued as friends. (Professionally, their paths divided during Gielgud's period of maximum influence – John remaining with the classics as actor/director/impresario, Ralph content to remain an actor, but ready to risk his reputation in the works of new playwrights, notably J.B. Priestley.) And what a joy it is today to see that John, after a period of partial eclipse when the time seemed out of joint for him, has, as Ralph did, triumphantly and serenely come to terms with the contemporary scene.

In 1950, for all his great achievements of the Thirties and Forties, John was still desperately shy – except at work in the theatre, or at ease with his intimates. Dulcie and I were not of that company. True, he had been, unwittingly, the most important element in my decision at Oxford in 1936 to turn aside from the family insurance business and become an actor; and in 1943 he had directed Dulcie in an unlikely part in *Landslide* – in which she had to commit suicide to protect the religious vocation of her lover. But neither of these contacts seemed likely to be much help to us in our delicate assignment. Dulcie and I react to the shyness of others by becoming tongue-tied (or desperately garrulous) ourselves; and that evening at the Ivy the pauses between the three of us would have done justice to Macready. Eventually with the coffee I blurted out the substance of Robert Clark's proposal. Speaking very fast in reply John said, 'Oh no, I don't think so. I seem to have been doing the play for years. In any case I don't think it would make a picture, do you?' A thoughtful pause – then, 'Of course it might be rather fun to do it Chinese.'

And after another long silence he took his leave. I sadly reported his rejection to Mr Clark, omitting the final suggestion, which I felt was unlikely to commend itself to him. For the moment the matter remained unresolved.

III
1951

Film Festival in Uruguay – Angels One Five – The Importance *surrendered to Rank – Dulcie excluded – my anxieties about her career – Dulcie in revue –* The Importance *filmed*

After these mental and physical exertions we were in need of a break; and we got it in the most exciting manner. We were invited to be part of the British delegation to the first ever South American film festival in Uruguay. Our colleagues were Phyllis Calvert and her delightful scholarly actor husband, Peter Murray Hill; Glynis Johns with her husky voice and pale blue eyes; the rugged Robert Beatty and his wife; John Sutro, who had co-produced *The Glass Mountain*; and critics Freda Bruce Lockhart and Matthew Norgate.

We set off ahead of the rest, to have a few days in Madrid, to see the Prado, the Escorial under snow, and Toledo; and also something of the city's night life, in the friendly company of Bryan Wallace (son of Edgar), who had arrived there as an escaped prisoner of war in 1943 and had stayed on the embassy's pay-roll ever since – quite indispensable to incoming ambassadors because he knew the local scene so much better than the career diplomats with their short periods en poste.

In those days, though never a regular diarist, I used to write accounts of notable journeys and holidays. Their style grew marginally more adult between 1934 (the first) and this one (the last), but considered from the summit of my present sophistication they appear to oscillate between technicolour travelogue and failed attempts at 'fine writing'.

Just occasionally, however, a description hits the spot. At Madrid airport we walked across to the Customs. 'The swing doors opened and we were immediately engulfed in a warm wind, bearing in a highly concentrated form that intoxicating smell of all Continental railway stations, compound of cleanliness and unopened windows, of garlic, old tobacco and older uniforms, of

22

generous applications of floor polish, and – since our bath towels at the hotel smelt of it too – of soap, we assume and hope.'

I will spare the reader my descriptions of the Prado and of El Greco's house in Toledo, and move on to our introduction to flamenco. 'I had understood that flamenco meant "Flemish", from the days of the Spanish Netherlands, but the sounds we heard were pure Arab. A song is begun with a fairly well-defined melody, then suddenly the singer goes off into a wailing Oriental cadenza while dancer, musicians and audience wait with growing excitement for his return to earth. When it is clear that he has found his way back through his chromatic labyrinth, the audience gives a thunderous "Olé" (Allah?), the dancer gives an ecstatic stamp and the musicians resume operations. Sometimes, in their eagerness, part of the audience shouts "Olé" too soon and is then hissed by the rest before hissing back in self-justification. A fascinating evening.' (Years later we had the joy of working with Gladys Cooper in her last long London run. Sometimes in her later years a little uncertain of her words, she was impeccable in *Out of the Question*, with the exception of one speech which was a solo tour de force lasting perhaps two minutes, and spoken without interruption to the whole cast. It varied from night to night, to our great fascination, but always got to its correct destination. One night at the end of a particularly convoluted version I murmured 'Olé', and had to explain to Gladys her connection with flamenco.)

From Madrid the delegation went on together, from winter into high summer. There were stops at Dakar, and at Recife in Brazil for breakfast after an all-night South Atlantic crossing in a tropical thunderstorm. Everyone but Dulcie was panting in the humidity; for Dulcie, the old Malaya hand, it was almost a homecoming. But by midday at Rio in a welter of newsreel cameras and interviews and a shade temperature of 100° Fahrenheit, the British party in their winter tweeds looked, and felt, a pretty scruffy 'constellation'.

On arrival at Montevideo we were met by Sir Douglas Howard, the Ambassador – a cousin of Gladys Boot, our beloved lodger at Chester Terrace – and as we all approached the terminal, 'we were greeted with loud applause and cries of "Cuba, Cuba". This was puzzling. Were we being recommended to get to Cuba out of there? This seemed unlikely in view of the applause. Had we been mistaken for the Cuban delegation? Unlikely too. Or had the presence of the British Ambassador been made the excuse for a demonstration in favour of the return of Cuba to Uruguay? Or of Uruguay to Cuba? The explanation was simpler. Following us off the aircraft was the Cuban basketball team.'

After a day of pleasant junketings in the capital we set off for Punta del Este, the scene of the festival. We were installed in the San Raphael hotel – a large pink Uruguayan-Elizabethan structure looking out on to the South Atlantic across a beach which stretched northwards to infinity. 'You will find it very English', we had been told. The festival itself took place in the Cantegril Country Club – a luxurious complex of buildings, swimming pools and sporting facilities set among the prevailing pinewoods.

We were there for eleven days (or, rather, nights which lasted till breakfast).

'Highlights in this exhausting routine were the films *Domani e troppo tarde* and *La Ronde*, and the more than generous reception given to *The Glass Mountain*; meeting Claude Nollier and Gérard Philippe; and one of the many parties. It was at a house deep in the woods and we had been dancing to a local band in a strange open-air first-floor room reached from the garden by a long flight of steps. Suddenly we became aware of lanterns winding through the trees and of negro voices singing. It was the relief band; as they approached, the South Americans moved to the head of the stairs and started to descend, meeting the negro musicians on the way up. Neither melody nor rhythm ever faltered and by the time the newcomers were installed, the lanterns of the outgoing band were fading into the wood. We continued dancing as in a dream.'

Soon after our return to England, we started work on *Angels One Five*, which provided Jack Hawkins with, surprisingly, his first starring role in pictures, as Tiger, an RAF Station Commander during the Battle of Britain. I had a reasonable though not particularly exciting part (my third in RAF uniform) as one of his Squadron Leaders; but for Dulcie – and therefore for me – the picture was a great let-down. She was persuaded to accept a small part on the understanding that a scene would be added which would enable her, as a service wife, to do for the RAF what Celia Johnson did so memorably for the Navy in Noël Coward's *In Which We Serve*. The promise was honoured, to the extent that the scene was written and shot, and very moving it was. It was then however cut entirely, on the grounds that the film was overlength, leaving Dulcie with nothing to justify her presence – or her star billing.

Worse was to follow. Robert Clark now told me that he had decided to release *The Importance* to Rank, but had made it a condition that I should be in it. Apologetically he said he could not make the same condition about Dulcie (who was to have played Gwendolen in the Associated British version) as she was not under contract to him. My feelings about all this were, literally, mixed. I was depressed by the surrender of the subject by 'my' film company; touched by Mr Clark's condition, but embarrassed too in case Antony Asquith, the Rank director, should think I was wrong for it. Above all I was horrified by the hatchet job I appeared to be doing on Dulcie's career. Just consider. When I returned from the Middle East in 1945, Dulcie was the darling of the public and the critics, both in films and theatre; in 1945-46 she starred in five pictures and four plays and came out of them all with personal credit whether they were successful or not. But in *Jonathan* (1947), which I would never have been given but for her, her character was more worthy than exciting; in *The Glass Mountain* she was the abandoned wife; in *Rain on the Just* she played an indifferent part from top of the bill to enable me to star for the first time in the West End. True, she had perhaps slightly the better part in *The Fourposter*; but now there had been this double blow for her in films.

Fortunately, while I was busy making a ghastly movie, *The Tall Headlines*, with a very distinguished cast – Flora Robson, Mai Zetterling, André Morell – she was invited with her greatest friend in the business, the lovely, funny and lamented Anne Crawford, to represent the old country at the Venice Film Festival. No substitute for a good part of course, but at least there were meetings and junketings with Winston Churchill, the Duff Coopers, Orson Welles, Beatrice Lillie and many lesser luminaries. She has one particular memory of Sir Winston. He was alone, tucking into a substantial meal by the large window of a restaurant on the Lido (Anne and Dulcie were nearby), when he saw a little ragged urchin watching every mouthful from the other side of the plate glass. 'Bring that child to my table,' he commanded; and soon the small boy and the saviour of the West were side by side, enjoying their food with equal satisfaction – but in complete silence. After all, they were neither of them linguists.

*　　*　　*

Some time during the summer I was taken by my casting-director ally Bob Lennard to meet 'Puffin' Asquith – on approval. Mercifully, embarrassment didn't last long. Puffin and I got on immediately; and I learned that when *The Importance* began at Pinewood in October I should be joining Edith Evans, Michael Redgrave, Margaret Rutherford, Miles Malleson, Joan Greenwood and a girl new to filming, Dorothy Tutin.

Dulcie's autumn engagement could not compare with this in glamour, but it was historic in its way and gave her rich opportunities to display her versatility. It was Sandy Wilson's first complete show, an intimate late-night revue, *See You Later*, at the tiny Watergate Theatre at Charing Cross. The inspiration to invite her was not Sandy's, but Chris Hewett's – the leading man in the show. Not surprisingly Dulcie was fed-up with her current image; her suicidal roles of the Forties had at least had some meat in them but, as we have seen, her recent characters (apart from *The Fourposter*) had been dim indeed. By contrast, her sketches in the revue included (her own idea, this) a milk-and-water Miss tending her garden in a Kate Greenaway costume to a milk-and-water tune and then with a dramatic change of rhythm revealing that her borders were filled with indian hemp, cocaine poppies, hemlock and every conceivable noxious plant; a fourposter number entitled 'Michael Denison Slept Here – it's all right, it's perfectly legal'; and – my own favourite – a raddled and decaying French singer 'Mlle Suzy Sans Doute' in spangled leotard and fishnet stockings and a deep baritone voice. All great fun for the audience and a marvellous therapy for Dulcie. Even Ken Tynan (not yet a critic) was so impressed that he asked her to appear simultaneously in a Grand Guignol season which he was directing at the diminutive Irving Theatre. She couldn't do it – it would have meant twenty changes of costume in two theatres per night – but he seemed much affronted by her refusal. What is sad is that a projected transfer of *See You Later* to a West End theatre didn't come off – all the sadder because the critics were once more virtually unanimous in their praise of her. One example only, from John Barber, then of the *Express*: '*In her first revue, Dulcie sings and dances with venom, but reserves real bitterness for the dillwater dolls she acts in films. This revue may go into history for its discovery of the demon in Dulcie as well as . . . for Sandy Wilson, who writes words worth hearing to songs worth cheering.*'

Well, the second part of this prophecy was fulfilled by *The Boy*

Friend, but Dulcie's auspicious debut has not – as yet – been followed up by any management. A pity, though no surprise to Dulcie, who had after all been sacked by Gainsborough Pictures the morning after receiving the best film reviews of her career. It would shortly be no surprise to me either, for my film career was about to come to a virtual end with my best performance in my most successful picture. These are facts deserving of record. If they surprise the reader, I can assure him or her that they have long ceased to concern us, not because we have become cynical over the years, but because we find the present more interesting than the past, and the future, hopefully, more interesting than either.

Fortunately I was unaware that for me the writing was on the walls of Pinewood when I arrived in high excitement for my first day's shooting on *The Importance* – which was in fact the long opening duologue between Michael Redgrave as John and myself as Algy. We arrived at the studios together and were shown into well-worn neighbouring dressing-rooms, identical even to the patches of hair oil above the divans, where no doubt had rested many famous heads. There was first a lengthy session for each of us with make-up and wardrobe, and I was back in my room going over my words when Michael's secretary invited me across the passage for coffee. The twin room was transformed. A beautiful tapestry obscured the hair-oil, a beautiful rug the tatty carpeting; the divan had a luxurious covering and a mass of cushions. Michael was in an exquisite dressing-gown, and coffee – such coffee! – was served out of Spode breakfast cups.

I worked happily with Michael on the picture. It was not easy for either of us, perhaps because I was a great fan of his and no doubt showed my awe (which is the reverse of Algy's attitude to John Worthing). But I never felt that I really got to know him. His shyness put up a barrier even more impenetrable for me than John Gielgud's. At least when John came to utterance it came in a flood; Michael's small talk was monosyllabic.

Dulcie – as usual in our lives – was more successful than I in breaking down Michael's resistance, for which he was clearly grateful, for he was at heart a warm and civilised man, but that is not to say that success was always complete. One day, after a rapturous theatrical embrace, they looked at each other in silence.

'Good luck with the play,' hazarded Dulcie hopefully.

'Thank you,' said Michael. 'And good luck with the film.'

'Thank you,' said Dulcie – then, apologetically, 'Actually mine's a play.'

'Ah,' said Michael. 'Well actually mine's a film.'

Apart from the joy and privilege of being inextricably connected on celluloid with Edith Evans' Lady Bracknell – and indeed of watching it at close range being meticulously recreated for the screen – my chief memory of an outstandingly happy picture was of escorting Dorothy Tutin to her first rendezvous with the film camera, and watching her take to the strange business with truth and assurance. Far more so than my other distinguished 'débutante' of four years previously, Claire Bloom; but then as Cecily, Dorothy did have a much better part than poor Claire, who had been the cardboard juvenile of an awful film.

Dorothy lived in those days up on Putney Heath with her parents, and used to begin her journey to the studios on the dark autumn mornings on her bicycle, leaving it at Shepherds Bush station and getting as near to Pinewood as she could by Underground and bus – a hideous prologue (and epilogue) to a long working day. I used to pick her up at Shepherds Bush when we were both called together, and I shall never forget the contrast between the diminutive figure with shining morning face, thick sweater, ski-ing trousers and heavy boots waiting for me on the pavement, and 'my little cousin Cecily' two hours later in her elegant muslin, arranging the roses which Algy thinks she so much resembles.

The year was almost over before Dulcie and I appeared together. It was for BBC television in *Milestones* – a spin-off from *The Fourposter*, I suppose, for the age span demanded was as wide or wider. Television drama was live in those days – major plays being done on Sundays, and repeated, with no more than a technical run-through, on Thursdays. How the costume and make-up changes in *Milestones* were coped with in a transmission which then lasted two hours (and would now be allocated two or three days of recording) was indeed a miracle. Thank God it was soon to become an unnecessary miracle – but not yet. The strain, particularly on performers and director, was appalling. One example from the transmission of *Milestones*: we had reached the bustle period of the story and Dulcie was sporting a pronounced example of that bewitching style. During the scene we were performing, we were due to sit on a delicate little Victorian love-seat. As Dulcie manoeuvred to sit, her bustle sent the love-seat flying. ('Cut' they would cry today amid laughter. 'Let's go again.' Not in 1951.) Dulcie recovered from her half-sit – it must have looked as if she were curtseying to me – and the viewers didn't see what had happened, merely heard the crash, and probably noticed expressions of panic and hysteria quite inappropriate to the scene appear on our faces. We had perforce to remain standing but we knew that when the camera pulled back to enable us to leave the room, the wreckage wrought by the bustle would be seen by ten million people. To our rescue there came a hero doing a sort of breast stroke across the studio floor, out of sight of viewers of course, but not to us. He grasped the seat by one leg, managed to set it on its feet and swam away again, with Dulcie and me acting away above him with what we hoped looked like conviction.

IV
1952

Dragon's Mouth, *J.B. Priestley and Jacquetta Hawkes – Dulcie's 'death sentence' – end of my film contract – Sweet Peril and the libel threat – Dulcie's 'reprieve' and collapse*

1952 was to be the last year for some time in which we did an appreciable amount of work together – and a strange mixed bag it was. It began on a high note with exciting parts for us both in the first dramatic collaboration between J.B. Priestley and Jacquetta Hawkes, the archaeologist, who was soon to become his wife.

Jack was a good friend of mine, having given me two important parts in London during my brief pre-war career, and having then permitted me to break my contract with him to get married to Dulcie; he had also welcomed me back from the wars with another excellent part in *Ever Since Paradise*; but until *The Fourposter* he had never, I believe, seen Dulcie on stage. He had been complimentary about our performances in the two-hander, and some time early in 1952 asked us to come and see him at his chambers in Albany (B4, the same address as John Worthing in *The Importance*) where he solemnly handed us two yellow scripts inscribed *Dragon's Mouth, A Platform Drama in Two Parts*. 'It's the best thing I've done,' said Jack, 'though I can tell you I have been very lucky with my collaborator, Mrs Hawkes.'

He went on to explain in that sombre West Riding manner of his, which so often overlaid an intense inner excitement, that the idea had been born the previous autumn in New York when he had seen the famous recital of Shaw's *Don Juan in Hell* performed by Charles Laughton, Cedric Hardwicke, Charles Boyer and Agnes Moorehead. Jacquetta had seen it too, and they had agreed that the only thing wrong with it was that the material had been written as part of a conventional play, and was not therefore tailor-made for the heightened style in which the quartet were performing it. It had however stimulated them both far more than any of the conventional plays they saw in New York, and they agreed there and then, much encouraged by Laughton, to collaborate on a piece written specifically for this new medium; Jack, the experienced playwright, would contribute the plot, and they would divide the four characters between them – one man and one woman each. We were being offered the two written by Jacquetta, subject, we understood, to a satisfactory meeting between her and us, and of course to our liking it sufficiently to want to do it. Jack conceded that the proviso about the meeting was unusual, in that it came after the offer, but diplomatically explained that Dulcie's role of Nina – the relaxed accepter and lover of the physical world – was, in part, a self-portrait of Jacquetta herself. At this time we had only seen her once, dining with Jack at the Caprice, wearing a sombrero and a cloak, and smoking a cheroot. Dulcie fell in love with the character of Nina, but, as the most conventionally feminine of dressers herself, she was naturally anxious as to how she would measure up in the eyes of Nina's creator. She needn't have worried. There was an immediate and enduring rapport between us and Jacquetta.

The plot of *Dragon's Mouth* concerns four people on a yacht in the Caribbean. One of the crew has died from a violent tropical disease, and our four are awaiting the result of blood tests to see whether they have been infected. While they wait they talk, and each proclaims, confidently and entertainingly, the superiority of his or her attitude to life over that of the others. Apart from the danger of their situation, what gives their conversation bite and colour is the widely differing natures of the protagonists. Matthew (played here by Norman Wooland), Nina's husband and owner of the yacht, is a powerful, but still power-hungry tycoon; Harriet (Rosamund John) has denied her womanhood to win a reputation for efficiency in a man's world – and paid the price; Stuart, my character, is a tense intellectual perfectionist. With Nina, as an attractive example of the *femme moyenne sensuelle*, they were planned to represent the four 'functions' of Jung – sensation, intellect, intuition and emotion – but the great psychologist-philosopher's name was never mentioned, and few members of our audience can have been aware of his connection with the enterprise (none of our critics either, to judge from their reviews).

In the second part of the play, news has come that one of them is infected, and therefore doomed – but the radio breaks down before the identity of the victim is revealed. The protagonists' arrogant confidence is transformed into clear-eyed and moving self-examination, from which emerges the Jungian theme (with Nina as its spokeswoman) that what is needed is a balance between – or even a fusion of – their dominant characteristics. We never learn who is to die.

'A Platform Drama in Two Parts' sounds a pretty ponderous affair. But *Dragon's Mouth* in performance belied its authors' description. For its cast it was a great challenge joyfully accepted, and it won from many if not all our audiences and critics the sort of response which made us feel that we were indeed, as our authors intended, extending the boundaries of the drama. We had some funny moments with it too. Jack directed, and Jack was a very good director, with a respect for actors unusual among distinguished playwrights. But in every show there are rehearsal days when nothing goes right, when the goal which seemed attainable at the first reading is suddenly further off ten days later. We had one such day in the appropriate brown gloom of the St Pancras Town Hall. Jack was making some matching dark brown comments on our efforts, when there suddenly materialised among us a little frail old man.

'Excuse me,' he said in a respectful, quavering, Cockney voice, 'but is this where you get death certificates?'

'No,' said Rosamund John, 'but I know where it is,' (she was already Mrs John Silkin), and she led him gently back into the shadows.

'You know,' said Jack when they had gone, 'I invented him.' And he laughed delightedly at his own little joke.

One weekend during rehearsals Jack invited us down to his home on the Isle of Wight. His marriage (to his second wife) had by now broken down, and he had told her to take whatever furniture she wanted. 'But she won't have done it yet,' he added.

But she had. And when, after a long journey by train and boat and taxi, he flung open the front door of Brook – which looked like Colditz but had a sensational view towards the Needles – it was to reveal monumental reception rooms containing only a billiard table and a pianola. Jack could be an awkward guest, but he was an inspired and inspiring host, and never in our experience had his gifts of hospitality been more hilariously displayed. Food I suppose came with us, and there was certainly drink; but the high spot of the evening was Jack accompanying the pianola as a dancing 'cellist without a 'cello.

The only rift between us on the tour was in the matter of the bus. Jack had planned for us an itinerary (mostly playing city halls) of twenty-two one-night stands in four weeks, starting in Malvern and extending as far north as Newcastle and as far south and west as Swansea and Weymouth. The travelling would be in a private bus, which he saw romantically as a unifying symbol of the new Good Companions. Dulcie was the first to shatter the image. She was still prone to travel sickness in those days and she offered Jack the stark alternative. 'I'll come in the bus if you insist, Jack, but I may well be sick in it or delay you all while I'm sick in the ditch – *and* I may not be well enough to perform when we get to our destination. Or I'll go with Michael in our car, and be all right!' Jack capitulated with an ill grace.

We had other advantages, often leaving an hour after the bus and still having first choice of rooms at the other end – a situation made worse for the others by the bus driver's shortcomings as a map-reader. Soon Jack admitted defeat and withdrew to Brook in high dudgeon to console himself by entertaining a string quartet – including a real 'cellist, I presume.

He rejoined the column when we reached Bournemouth, but, arriving late for the performance, encountered a Bournemouth colonel and his lady beating a premature retreat. 'Ah, sensible fellah,' said the colonel, 'see you're leaving too.' It was Jack who told us of the encounter.

We played a respectable seven weeks in London in a most unsuitable theatre, the Winter Garden, and in a mixed press won golden opinions where it mattered to us most. Dulcie's Nina, to my intense delight, was singled out for praise. John Barber called her 'Superb'; Ken Tynan, now launched on his career as a critic, hated the show but admitted 'furiously' (his word) that it contained 'several flights of the best rhetorical prose I have ever heard on the stage'. Chief among these, by common consent, was Nina's extraordinary idyll of a woman lying alone under an umbrella on a beach in the South of France, sensuously at one with her surroundings, when quite suddenly a seagull makes a dive at her:

'Its eyes were pale and fierce and utterly without thought; its bill was wide open – screaming. I felt as though I had been assaulted, as though a steel dart had been thrown into the very centre of all my nerves and senses. In a way it was agonising. My tongue knew what it was to be the tongue in that bird's hard narrow bill, and my muscles shared in the pull on its wings and yellow legs. Of course it only lasted an instant, leaving me with a sharp aerial image of a woman in a bathing dress lying under a green and white umbrella ...'

A glimpse only. There is much more than that, for the speech played nearly five minutes, and was usually greeted with the silence actors dream about, followed by applause. Not, however, on one occasion. We were playing the City Hall of Southampton and, as Dulcie began, so did the city clock, immediately above our heads. It chimed slowly. It struck nine even more slowly. It then played a complete verse of 'O God our help in ages past', the final reverberations of which coincided with the end of a quite inaudible speech.

Towards the end of the play, Nina has this to say:

'I find myself strangely willing to die. I am ready, even eager to be your Ipheginia, to be the sacrifice that will allow the rest of you to set sail from Dragon's Mouth. Perhaps it is because I have so much desire for shapeliness, for perfection of form, that I want to cut short my life before it blurs – to die while I am still in possession of the rose, while heads still turn in the street ...'

I did not know, because she did not tell me, that on 30 June, during our London run, and when she was speaking those words every night, Dulcie had been to a specialist who had told her that she was mortally ill, with an expectation of seven to eight months.

It was a particularly lovely day, she remembers, and she felt a most un-Nina-like anger against the world and all its works. I was playing golf, the diary tells me, and by the time I returned, Dulcie had decided – most unwisely I can't help feeling – to keep it to herself. When she eventually told me, long after the diagnosis had been proved false, and I asked her why she had kept silent, she said she had not wanted to worry me, and that she had had a picture of herself looking her last on all things lovely every hour and accepting her fate with gentle resignation. 'Actually,' she went on, 'if you remember, I was an absolute shrew for those eight months and taut as a bow-string.'

What I remember was not in those terms, but I became progressively more anxious about her as the year progressed – a year in which we were busier than ever.

Dragon's Mouth was followed, with rehearsals overlapping, by a revival of *The Fourposter* for John Counsell at Windsor; then

Let Them Eat Cake, 1959

above Michael with Dorothy Tutin in *The Importance of Being Earnest*, 1951

below Dulcie with Jack Hawkins in *Angels One Five*, 1951

above *The Fourposter*, 1950

below The White Knight and the White Queen, 1955

above J.B. Priestley

below Michael (second from left) with Vivien Leigh in *Twelfth Night*, Stratford 1955

by our last film together, *There Was a Young Lady* (in which Dulcie was my super-efficient secretary who had to get kidnapped by a smash-and-grab gang before I realised I loved her). That in turn was followed by *Sweet Peril*, which eventually came to the St James's. Somewhere among all this we did *Desert Island Discs* – the first married couple to be cast-aways – and chose records we would choose still, ranging from Fats Waller and Sinatra to the letter duet from *Figaro* and the Creed sung by the Russian Choir in Paris. And I became Vice-President of Equity, presumably in recognition of my abortive efforts for British films.

In saying that my film career virtually ended with *The Importance*, I have been less than fair to the many friends involved with us in *Young Lady*, and indeed, if memory serves, to the finished article. It was a small-budget picture. The script, which I have just re-read and find light-hearted and ingenious, was by John Jowett, an ebullient young friend of ours whose considerable comic talent was at war all his short life with chronic idleness and expensive tastes. The producer was Dick Rawlinson, my understanding Commanding Officer at a crucial moment for my (civilian) career, at the end of the war; another firm friend directed – Laurie Huntington, with whom we had so much enjoyed working on *The Franchise Affair*; and the cast included two brilliant newcomers to films: Geraldine MacEwan as a coy and flustered typist, and Kenneth Connor as an ancient rustic, blood brother to his Mr Kimber, who had been such a success in *Queen Elizabeth*.

The little picture did not rate a West End showing on its own, but it was chosen to accompany the Coronation film on general release in 1953.

Earlier in the year I had come to a parting of the ways with Associated British and Mr Clark. I had not made a picture for them since *Angels One Five*, and had been unhappy about that on my own account as well as Dulcie's; so when they proposed a variation in my contract after *The Importance* and apparently had no firm plans for me, I decided to make the break and stake my future in films on what I hoped – with reason, as it turned out – would be a personal success as Algy. (The success was there; the future in films was not.) We parted amicably – my letter from Robert was the warmest I have ever had from him. 'So great is my appreciation,' he wrote, 'that it leads me to hope that notwithstanding the non-existence of a contract, our relationship will continue for a long time to come.'

It didn't. The blight we had foretold was now settling over British film production, and I could not have chosen a worse moment to fly solo. Since *Young Lady* I have only made three pictures, and none at all since 1959. It is true I was offered a part in *Gandhi* by Dickie Attenborough in 1964 when we met in an aeroplane flying to Rome; but despite his heroic efforts the film, as we all now know, was not shot until 1979-80, by which time I was no longer suitable casting. Dulcie's record has been no better, though she did make one picture in the middle Sixties. But if we had unwittingly taken major strides away from the 'filmstar image', we had for a while nothing comparable to put in its place. It was to be a long struggle before I could gain, and Dulcie could regain, any serious recognition in the theatre – and ironically, when it came, it came from television.

Sweet Peril, our fourth joint enterprise of the year, an American play set in Cornwall, did little to help; although, when the curtain fell to cheers on the opening night at the St James's in early December, and the Oliviers were enthusiastic (he was then running the theatre), it seemed that it might.

I had been attracted to the play by the opportunity of playing an anti-hero – a self-pitying and hard-drinking Old Harrovian – a welcome contrast to the stiff-upper-lip heroics which, apart from Algy, had been my lot in films. Dulcie was my staunch, practical wife – a best-selling writer whose work I looked down on from Olympian heights of idleness.

Throughout the highly successful preliminary tour, Dulcie was becoming most untypically tearful and exhausted – the reader now knows why – but Marie Löhr, who played my mother in the play, did her best to mother Dulcie off-stage. We had never met Marie before, and were horrified to find that the management had billed a star of her magnitude and seniority below us. At the end of the first reading, I asked Dulcie to explain to her that the billing was not our idea – which she did very shyly. 'Ah, my dear,' said Marie in her rich booming voice, 'I can see you're emotional. So am I. I'm so emotional I cry when I send my carpets to be cleaned.'

During the tour there was a historic meeting in Birmingham. We were playing the old Theatre Royal, and, at the Alexandra, Dickie and Sheila Attenborough were on the prior-to-London tour of *The Mousetrap*. They came to our matinée, and said *Sweet Peril* would run for ever; I went to theirs – Dulcie was not well – and had to take refuge in saying that it was not really my sort of play, but that they were splendid in it. How wrong we all were about what was to come.

The end of *Sweet Peril* was perhaps the most dramatic thing about it. Just after Christmas, the management – the Daniel Mayer Company – arrived en masse, dressed for a smart cremation, and informed us that they had no option but to withdraw the play, because they and the co-authors had been threatened with a libel action. The plaintiff, I learned to my astonishment, had been with me in the same house at Harrow, though two years my senior; I had not seen him since, and there was certainly nothing in the play to make me think of him twenty years on. However, one of the two American playwrights had apparently written to him saying, 'Do go and see Michael Denison in the play we've written about you,' or words to that effect. Given all the circumstances, there could be no defence in the courts against that.

More or less simultaneously with this débâcle Dulcie, on the basis of a second opinion, learned that the earlier medical diagnosis was mistaken. The relief, coming after so long a period of tension, provoked a total collapse – a breakdown, which brought exhaustion, depression and insomnia in its train. They were a vicious trio indeed, each feeding on the others to deepen the hell through which she was living, and from which she would emerge only slowly and with many backslidings over the next few years. I knew a lesser hell – the hell of the spectator who is impotent to help. Behind any façade of success, it was a difficult time for both of us.

V
1953

The Bad Samaritan – *dissertation on critics – Denis Compton,
Terence Rattigan and my return to cricket –* What's my Line? –
Dulcie and Maurice Teynac – Alice Through the Looking Glass –
cure for singing sharp

Dulcie began 1953 with some weeks in hospital, where enforced
sleep was, I suppose, of some benefit. She struck up a firm
friendship with Dr Tredgold, the hospital psychiatrist, encouraged not least by his frank assertion that she didn't need his
services. (In years to come she gratefully consulted him on the
behaviour patterns of psychopaths, etc., when writing her crime
stories.)

Meanwhile the rent had to be paid, and luckily I was very busy.
First was a television production of Behrman's *The Second
Man –* and a wonderful part, famous as one of only three not
written by himself which Noël Coward played after becoming an
established playwright. Then came my introduction to William,
Rachel and all the Douglas Homes in *The Bad Samaritan*, in
which I played the son of an Anglican Dean (George Relph) who
abandoned his own girlfriend (Heather Stannard) in order to do
the decent thing by the pregnant girlfriend of his holy brother,
who had developed a vocation for the Church of Rome (Virginia
McKenna and Ronald Lewis). 'Nearer to Ruby M. Ayres than
Ibsen' said one headline. Many miles from either, I would say.
Marvellous opportunities for performers and marvellous entertainment for audiences can spring from unlikely story-lines
(consider what goes on at Stratford and in opera houses the world
over) and certainly *The Bad Samaritan* was a delight to play, and
appeared to give much pleasure, if not to the majority of the
critics.

The critics! In 1964 Dulcie and I collaborated on *The Actor and
His World*. It was a book for the young, but what I wrote about

38

critics was not geared exclusively to the young reader. I said:

> My profession is not unique in finding it difficult to live with
> its critics ... But among the arts our position vis-à-vis our
> critics is I think the most difficult, not because we are the most
> vain of artists but because we are the most vulnerable. The
> painter, the writer, the composer can stand back from his work
> and look at it shoulder to shoulder with his critics; however
> much of himself he has put into it, it now has its own
> independent existence, and even its creator can achieve some
> detachment in judging it. But the actor's art is himself – his
> appearance, his mannerisms of speech and movement, his
> background, his imagination and sense of humour. These are
> the things about which every human being – even a critic – is
> absurdly sensitive ... Hence the actor's hope, particularly in
> the theatre, where they are at their most important, that the
> critics will provide fair and expert comment not only on the
> play but on his contribution to it.
>   ... The profession is choosey about its critics. Those in
> whom we can detect a love of the theatre as warm and as
> discriminating as our own, albeit from a different angle ... who
> have catholic tastes and the capacity to be fair to something
> well done even though it doesn't appeal to them personally,
> and who can perform the minor miracle of expressing their
> views in a concise and stimulating manner against their papers'
> deadlines – to these, managements and players will listen with
> respect, however stern their verdicts. But there are, and pro-
> bably always will be, critics, whose main equipment seems to
> be a journalistic flair for the sensational ... and who manage to
> give the impression, with varying degrees of subtlety, that they
> and their opinions are of more importance than what they
> criticise.

Dulcie and I are not regular browsers among the chaos of our
press cuttings – for twenty years or so we have renounced albums
and press-cutting agencies – and when I began researching for this
book it was the first time in many years that I had studied the
evidence of our activities in the Fifties. It has been a considerable
surprise to see how well-disposed towards us were most of the
press; even when we disappointed them, they showed more
sorrow than anger. Harold Hobson, Ivor Brown, Philip Hope
Wallace and John Trewin were among the more important of
those who found virtues in our work.

There were of course exceptions; there was one arch-exception, Ken Tynan. As Olivier put it in his recent memoirs, his 'destructive weapons were deadly, strengthened by the scintillating quality of his writing ... I told him that he had been directly responsible for at least one of Vivien's nervous breakdowns.' I would not claim that he had any responsibility for Dulcie's, but he certainly loomed over our professional lives for ten years or more – perhaps we should have been honoured to share the target area with Vivien and others – and as late as 1960 John Gale, who put on our revival of *Candida* as his first solo managerial venture, felt constrained to tell us on the first night that Tynan was not in front, when he was. Was this just neurosis on our parts, induced by a feeling of inadequacy when facing the most powerful critic of the day? No – it was the conviction, which the evidence supports, and which I know Vivien shared, that 'the scintillating quality of his writing' would be used primarily to express his scorn for us as people; as for our work, we were guilty before the curtain rose. In mitigation of this most 'uncritical' behaviour, one must remember that Ken was a revolutionary who in the early Fifties was still awaiting his revolution (signalled by *Look Back In Anger* in 1956); and that he saw us and our life-style, and, by extension, our work-style as no more than objects of ridicule, unworthy of a place in his brave new world.

To return to more congenial topics. I have so far appeared in four of Willie Douglas Home's plays (and resisted his considerable powers of persuasion in the case of four more) and from the outset have been made aware of his very proper concern for the rhythms of his dialogue – in particular the iambic pentameter. After a hard-fought game of golf with him on the prior-to-London tour of *Bad Samaritan*, I delivered myself of the following:

> Of his golf clubs a golfer at Lytham
> Remarked I can do nothing with 'em;
> I fret and I fume
> And I want to go Home;
> But whatever I've not, I've got rhythm.

On my return from the army I had developed a passion for watching cricket, not least because I was no longer required to play it. During the summer terms of my schooldays I had had to play six days a week, and cricket is a nightmare for the untalented, among whom I was to be numbered. Boredom, panic and humiliation are almost sure to be your lot – they certainly were mine. (How different is golf, where even a rabbit can hole a putt that Nicklaus can miss and where your humiliations are unlikely to be so public.) Living in Regent's Park I naturally gravitated to Lords and became a devoted supporter of Middlesex. It was a good time to form such an allegiance – oh my Compton and my Edrich long ago (to adapt Francis Thompson), to say nothing of my Robertson, my Murray and my Titmus – and many happy hours I spent around the Tavern and the free seats.

One day in the summer of 1953 I was rung up by Terence Rattigan, with whom I had been at school. 'Oh Michael,' he said, 'I'm organising a charity cricket match at Tichborne next Sunday and I wondered whether you and Dulcie would come.' 'We'd love to, but I haven't played for seventeen years,' I said. 'Oh not to play,' he went on smoothly, 'just to sign autographs and so on. And wear white flannels if you will – it'll look more festive.' Smelling no rat we drove down to Hampshire to be greeted by Terry with: 'Michael, I'm putting you in first.' And so it was that I found myself in the middle with my great hero Denis Compton. We put on fifty together thanks to some charitable bowling in my direction; and later, an opposing batsman was dismissed, c. Compton b. Denison, by a high full toss dropping out of the setting sun.

A firm friendship ensued; and through Denis, Dulcie and I were introduced to many great cricketing figures. Dulcie was a bit diffident, the first time we went to a Compton party for a visiting Test side. 'I know nothing about cricket. What shall I talk to them about?' I did my best to reassure her, and was amused to see her within minutes the centre of an animated group. 'You seem to be doing all right,' I said when she joined me. 'Yes,' she said, 'you see, the dialogue was quite familiar. They were all discussing their critics. And they have them at every performance – not just first nights, poor things.'

At about the time of *The Bad Samaritan*, I was invited to join the panel of *What's My Line?*, then television's top parlour game. With me there came, as a new girl, Lady Isobel Barnett JP – a darling woman, funny, relaxed, knowledgeable, intuitive and courteous. (Given those gifts, her success on the programme was assured; given those gifts, what an appalling and unnecessary waste was the self-inflicted punishment – so far from fitting the crime – which eventually ended her days.) I was less well suited to the enterprise, though I could scarcely have refused. To join Gilbert Harding, Barbara Kelly and an Eamonn Andrews only marginally more youthful-looking than he is today, was then the equivalent of being invited to play TV for England. My trouble was that though I have always been able to answer questions fluently, whether accurately or not, I become very inhibited when required to ask them, which was of course the point of *What's My Line?* This trait, which stems I think from nursery training in good manners, had been a handicap when interrogating German prisoners during the war, but at least then the questions were in German and directed towards an enemy, which distanced them from the nursery. Now, before an audience of millions, I was called upon to pry into the jobs of strangers – in English! Not cricket. Mind you, I got results; but my agony was so apparent that the whole thing became a tribunal rather than a game. The producer was surprised and disappointed – he had recently seen me endowed with the humour of Wilde, Behrmann and Douglas Home and had perhaps thought it was mine. Robert Morley came for one transmission, and said to a dithering blonde, 'Don't worry, darling, your secret is safe with me.' How I envied his wit – and his departure. I was soon, thankfully, to follow him.

Dulcie's life, despite the breakdown, had been equally full. True, she had had a month's convalescence in France at our familiar haunt, the Colombe d'Or at St Paul de Vence – something that was still financially possible until its comforts and its prices soared together – but at my insistence she had taken with her Millie, our beloved Cockney housekeeper, partly to look after her, and partly as a reward for seven years' devotion to 'the Mr and the little Mrs', as she called us. The excursion was not quite the success we had hoped. Millie had never been abroad before and didn't much like it. An excellent cook and mistress of all the domestic arts herself, she managed, without a word of French, to communicate her disapproval of a wide range of French methods and their results. This made for difficulties with the staff of the Colombe – most of them old friends of ours – and Dulcie was hard put to it to preserve the peace.

Back from France, Dulcie was soon involved in two television plays, playing a Marie Tempest part in one and a mermaid in the second (*A Fish in the Family*), and went straight from the latter into *The Distant Hill*, in which she was the wife of an eccentric puppeteer, played by a distinguished French actor, Maurice Teynac.

Maurice brought with him his new bride, Françoise – most attractive but inclined to be jealous. And who could blame her? For Maurice was both susceptible to female charms, and accident-prone. One day, on tour in Peterborough, Dulcie received from me a copy of the first number of a (short-lived) new national newspaper, which was full of hilarious misprints. Dulcie decided to share the joke with Dermot Walsh, who was in the next room, at the intensely respectable hour of noon. They were laughing away, with the door open, when Maurice came along the corridor and saw Dulcie. He stopped dead and beckoned her forcefully to join him. He then led her back into her own room and gave her a lecture. 'In France,' he said, 'to be seen in a bedroom of someone of the opposite sex means only one thing. Please be careful.' At which moment, Françoise came along the corridor – and stopped dead. Another time, at supper in Southsea, Françoise had gone to the Ladies, and Dulcie was telling a story. With an over-animated gesture she knocked a full bottle of red wine over the trousers of Maurice's smart pale grey suit. 'Salt!' she cried. 'We must put salt on it, and it will take away the stain.' And when Françoise returned, there was Dulcie on her knees salting Maurice's crutch.

Despite good performances from Dulcie, Maurice and Dermot, the play was not thought strong enough for the West End; but 1953 had not yet finished with me. I was approached by Toby Robertson, just down from Cambridge, where he had contributed to that remarkable theatrical flowering which has given us Peter Hall, John Barton and Trevor Nunn – not to mention the *Beyond The Fringe* quartet. He invited me to play Humpty Dumpty, Tweedledee and the White Knight in a musical version of *Alice Through the Looking Glass*, devised by his mother, the playwright Felicity Douglas. (Having myself been at Oxford towards the end of the period when that university had a considerable influence on the nation's serious theatre, while Cambridge was more concerned with sport and, disastrously, with politics, it has been fascinating to see the theatrical pendulum swing towards Cambridge at much the same time as success in the boat race – for any Oxonian of my generation, a lost cause indeed – began to be an Oxford monopoly.) My reply to Toby's offer, 'I'm afraid I don't sing' was answered by 'That doesn't matter' – an exchange which has preceded all the four musicals in which I have appeared. It was explained that the engagement was to be for six weeks in the Dolphin Theatre Brighton (since demolished) and that my co-stars would be Margaret Rutherford and Binnie Hale (as the White and Red Queens), and Wally Crisham, an old friend, who had been the West End's resident American dancer in revues and musicals for more than twenty years, and whose talent, kindness and abrasive sense of humour were all on a par. There was no question, I was assured, of a London run or of national press coverage; so I agreed.

The Brighton run was exhausting. There were seven of us, each playing two or three parts, in the male 'star dressing-room'; there was also our corgi, Bonnie, and Wally's dachshund, Miss Dutch, who providentially didn't fancy each other. We played twice daily, so that meant six costume and make-up changes – a regime from which my face has never recovered; and we were the most enormous success. Inevitably, and to my horror, we were offered a London theatre. 'No thank you,' I said, thinking of one particular critic, who shall remain nameless. 'In that case we won't take it in,' they said.

We had a number of highly talented and very young dancers in the show, who, after my decision was known, never said anything, but just looked at me with eyes made enormous by ballet make-up. Within forty-eight hours I had capitulated; and almost immediately I began to sing sharp; what was worse, I knew it but could do nothing to stop it. To the rescue came Binnie Hale, with whom I was working for the first time. A quintessential professional with a lovely voice, she now showed herself a true friend.

'Go and see John Musgrove,' she commanded. 'He'll put you right – I'll give him a ring, he's an old friend of mine.' And so the scene was set for the first of many consultations at 34 Wimpole Street, always at moments of crisis and always successful, of which the last was only months before his death in 1979. By a cruel irony, John, the restorer of speech to countless actors and singers, was by then speechless himself with cancer of the throat; but even so his skill and his style never deserted him. He was short and dapper, and treated you immediately as a friend; he listened most carefully to what you had to say, and then, before the examination, pressed a switch which closed the curtains across his tall windows – a reassuringly theatrical beginning. By the time the switch was pressed again and daylight came flooding back into that elegant room, confidence was restored and the cure was under way. On this first occasion, the diagnosis was solemnly impressive. 'You're suffering from a neuro-muscular spasm, old boy. Take this.' And he handed me a prescription. Secretly and shamefully I had thought that my complaint was no more than blue funk at the prospect of singing in the Metropolis. As soon as I heard I had a neuro-muscular spasm I was cured, and back on the note. When I thanked Binnie for the introduction and told her the good news, her smile was enigmatic. Then the penny dropped. 'Neuro-muscular spasm' was John's polite way of saying 'blue funk'.

VI
1954

Painting – Olympia, *Stephen Harrison and Martita Hunt* – The Fourposter *and* Private Lives *in South Africa*

From the garden of our cottage in Essex (a diminutive bolthole owned since 1947), we could hear the locals greeting each other in the lane as they passed on foot or on bicycles – 'Funny old day' – 'Funny old day'. For us, 1954 was a funny old year. It contained a bewildering variety of work and other activities – more engagements in fact than in any other year of the decade – and yet requires more prompting than usual from the diary to bring them to mind, perhaps because there was no long run among them to give the year a shape.

After the end of the *Alice* season in London (in which my White Knight was likened to A. J. Balfour and my Humpty Dumpty to Noël Coward) we set off in our new car, an Austin Atlantic, for a brief holiday in St Paul. The car, bought on the advice of Jack Dunfee, was indeed fast, but ugly and shoddy, and eventually repaid our dislike in a dramatic manner. Meanwhile it transported us uneventfully to Provence.

Holidays are a well-known source of matrimonial friction, particularly where, as in our case, one partner is for lying on a beach and the other for walking in the mountains. As the years pass the walker (skier, golfer) comes ever closer to the beach, where the beachcomber has become totally and happily immobile. But back in '54 Dulcie did still occasionally accompany me, even on the golf course; so, waking to a spring morning in St Paul, fragrant with wood smoke and mimosa, and of such splendour that leaf and bud and blossom seemed to be unfolding before one's eyes, I suggested a walk. 'No darling,' said Dulcie. 'I'm still exhausted after the journey. But if you look in the boot of the car you'll find something that might interest you, I think.'

And there I found a box of oil paints and half a dozen small canvases. Dulcie knew that both at Harrow and at my prep

46

school Art had been an 'extra', and that the masters concerned, after seeing my attempts to draw a vase or a table, had recommended that my parents be spared the additional outlay.

'You know I can't draw,' I remonstrated. 'Why should you think I could paint? And in oils too!'

'The way you talk about the countryside makes me think you might enjoy trying to record it. You'll learn all you need to know about drawing by painting. And oil is much the best medium for a beginner. Easier than pencil and far easier than watercolour.'

She spoke with authority. She had, after all, won a scholarship to a London art school and sold everything she had done there – until the theatre and, later, writing submerged in her any desire to paint.

The Colombe d'Or has a long artistic tradition; on its walls to this day are pictures by Picasso, Braque, Matisse, Modigliani, Marie Laurençin, Léger, our great friend Manfredo Borsi, who was then usually there for a midday drink, and the patron, M Roux, himself no mean painter.

I sat myself down on the hotel terrace with my six-inch-square canvas, facing the valley to the east of the village – then (before the advent of vast greenhouses for growing carnations) an unspoilt idyll of olives and old houses and little dusty tracks and terraced crops. Ravishing – but requiring a Segonzac at least to cope with its detail, or a Cézanne to reject detail in favour of a sculptured whole. I should, I suppose, have felt embarrassed at painting my first picture in such surroundings, but it never occurred to me. I was gripped by a concentration more intense than I had ever known. It took me three hours in the hot sunshine to cover my minuscule canvas – and myself – with paint. The laughter and chatter of the midday drinkers, who included Dulcie and the Borsis, floated out to me from the bar – I didn't hear it. A waiter was hoping to lay for lunch the table at which I was working. I didn't notice, and eventually M Roux, another amused spectator, unobtrusively called him off. My right arm became severely sunburned. I was unaware. At last Op. 1 was finished, and so was I. Embarrassment now came flooding over me. I tried to escape with the object, but the bar and its occupants were in my path.

The canvas – we have it still (in a cupboard) – looks like the work of a retarded, if optimistic, child faced with an African rain forest on a sunny day. '*Ah, mais voilà,*' they cried, crowding round it. '*C'est tellement sauvage. C'est primitif, vous savez.*'

And much-needed drink and food was pressed upon me, to be followed by a much-needed siesta.

The next day I was off early in the car to find an easier and more private subject. The result was without artistic merit, but had at least moved from the Congo to the Alpes Maritimes. 'Not bad,' was the off-hand verdict on Op. 2 by the Critics' Circle in the bar; their enthusiasm was reserved for Op. 1.

And so, thanks to Dulcie, there began a period of heightened awareness of the world around me which has lasted to this day. For the first ten years or so nothing was safe from my brush; then, gradually, output was restricted to holidays; and the discovery of quick-drying poster paint made me less of a threat to my surroundings and my wardrobe. Another rich bonus was the opening of my eyes to real painting, and in particular to those masters whose subject matter was the same as mine. Respect gave way to excitement and wonder before the skies and trees and fields of Constable, the rivers of the Impressionists, the last watercolours of Turner. I was the true *amateur* in this new activity, truer I believe than those amateur actors who know nothing of and care less for the professional theatre and rest complacently on the laurels provided by friends and relations. Unlike them I have never had any illusions about the artistic value of the end product, and have found my satisfaction and justification in the battle – usually a losing one – to set down what lay before me. As Shakespeare says: 'Joy's soul lies in the doing.'

It was, I believe, because of this attitude that I was befriended and encouraged by two distinguished professional artists – Maurice Codner, whose portraits were his bread and butter but whose love was landscape, and Ted Seago, as much cherished by the public as he was inexplicably underrated by the critics. The former took me painting with him in Suffolk and at Stratford, comparing notes afterwards on our two versions of the same scene; and Ted painted a Venetian canal-scape for me as I sat with him in his studio at Ludham, so that I could watch the whole process, and learn.

Before we had gone to France we had committed ourselves to a play, *We Must Kill Toni*, which read well and had a glamorous central role for Dulcie – something that was long overdue. There was to be a long provincial tour before London, and this effectively prevented Dulcie from appearing with Peggy Ashcroft in *Hedda Gabler*. To add insult to this injury, *Toni* only ran a few weeks – it quite signally failed to translate from script to stage. Equally forgettable was my part as a customs officer in a film called *Contraband Spain*.

Then things looked up a bit. Dulcie was splendid as Mrs Pooter with George Benson in *The Diary of a Nobody* directed by Basil Dean. But even this was frustrating, for it was only for a season at the Arts Theatre and did not transfer for a commercial run.

Next we appeared together on television in *Olympia* by Molnar, directed by Stephen Harrison. Stephen, who to the sorrow of his friends in the profession retired at fifty-five, was one of the BBC's top directors. He had, among other gifts, the disconcerting habit of making personal remarks about your performance or appearance with such courteous, constructive, scientific directness that it was impossible to take offence. (For instance, to one young actor of chiselled profile and crisp golden curls, which their owner with reason thought of as his crowning glory, Stephen suddenly said at rehearsals, 'We're going to have to do something about your hair, aren't we?' 'My hair?' said the young man in alarm. 'Yes,' said Stephen. 'With a chubby face like yours, we'll have to fluff it out a bit.')

Playing Dulcie's mother, an Austrian Archduchess, in *Olympia* was that marvellous actress and eccentric, Martita Hunt, whom we were meeting for the first time. She was known to be temperamental – though this would not have impinged on Stephen – and it was her first television. Not only would the transmission be live, but in those days there were rarely more than two cameras available for a scene, unlike the four or more which are on hand today. One effect of this was the 'tight eight-shot' – the necessity, towards the end of a sequence, of getting as many members of the cast as possible into a sort of family group on Camera 1, while Camera 2 trundled away to the next set. Martita was of course unaware of these technicalities. Stephen had arranged for Dulcie, Martita and me to be together on a settee with only one camera available. 'I feel cramped here,' said Martita at rehearsal in her grandest manner, which was very grand indeed. 'There's a perfectly good chair there. I should be happier in that.' 'Oh,' said Stephen, re-marking his camera script, 'Very well. I was going to come in to a close-up of you but I'll make it a two-shot of Dulcie and Michael instead.' It was not said in order to bring her to heel – though that was the result; he was simply explaining the technical solution to the problem she had created.

Waiting for Gillian, another television, followed for me, in which I had the joy of working with Annie Crawford again and with Patrick Barr for the first time. It was also memorable for my favourite notice, which came from the critic of *The Tailor and Cutter*. He took the BBC to task for the clothes worn by Patrick and myself – unjustly, in fact, for we were wearing our own. Scorn was poured on Patrick's suit for having two slits in the jacket, and then: 'Mr Michael Denison, adopting a negligent posture at the mantelpiece, demonstrated the inadequacies of his central vent.' Of what went on above that level there was not a word.

In November there was one of our treasured and all-too-rare meetings with Noël Coward. He was in London for the last of his famous cabaret engagements at the Café de Paris, and we were all three appearing in the Royal Variety Performance at the Palladium. (How *we* got on to the bill I can't imagine.) We were sitting with him in the stalls, waiting to run through our various contributions and listening to an American singer whose appearance, if not his name, has lingered in the memory. He had a square head accentuated by a blond crew cut, enormous square shoulders (or his suit had) and very short legs. He had a very big voice, which he used sparingly (most of the work was done by an invisible backing group), and he was sweating profusely.

'That character gets £5000 a week,' someone whispered in Noël's ear.

'Really,' said Noël. 'And he has everything against him, hasn't he?'

'Why don't you come to South Africa?' said Denis Compton's wife, Valerie, one day. She was just sailing on a Christmas visit to her native Durban. We explained that nobody had asked us. We were off to Dublin for a week with *The Fourposter*. (Dublin is a remarkable city. We knew nobody when we arrived, but by the Friday night we had twenty-three people on first-name terms in the dressing-room, only two of whom we have ever seen since.) While we were there we were asked to take the play to South Africa; and after a flight to Johannesburg and a thousand-mile drive over the Great and Lesser Karoo to Cape Town we were able to send a cable to an astonished Valerie, still at sea, inviting her to lunch with us at the Mount Nelson Hotel when her ship docked.

We much enjoyed the South African visit. It began with six weeks or so in Cape Town in the high summer of Christmas. The play (with the American happy ending) went outstandingly well, and we made many friends – notably our employer Brian Brooke and his bright-eyed, energetic little wife Petrina, so inappropriately known as 'Tweets'. (Who, apart from a canary, wouldn't be inappropriately known as 'Tweets'?) Then there were Bernard and Fredagh Podlashuk, owners of the Bellingham wine farm with its superb white seventeenth-century Dutch house near Paarl, who invited us whenever we could get away: one of the most beautiful properties I have ever seen, in a green valley with a backdrop of dark blue mountains, it was the subject of numerous Denison paintings.

From Cape Town we drove to Port Elizabeth, where we added *Private Lives* to our repertoire, directed by Tweets and with Brian and a local girl making up the quartet. This move meant leaving the four Brooke children behind, including one-year-old twin boys. In charge were two large cheerful black Mammies. This seemed odd in view of Brian's frequent assertions that the black races were composed of happy-go-lucky children, unable to shoulder any serious responsibility.

Not surprisingly we found most white people defending apartheid as a sensible and realistic way of dealing with the facts of South African life. We remained (and remain) unconvinced. We enquired whether we couldn't give performances for black and coloured audiences. 'No point,' said Brian. 'They wouldn't come. Wherever we play a City Hall like Port Elizabeth they are entitled to come, as local taxpayers, but as you see they don't.' 'Because they can't afford it?' I suggested. 'Because they wouldn't understand it,' he replied. This was unanswerable, and the subject was dropped but – as will be seen – not forgotten.

In the wide spaces of the Eastern province of the Cape, it must be said that the obnoxious nature of apartheid was not intrusively apparent to two visitors who were after all there to act, not to carry out a sociological enquiry. We played a number of one-night stands to full houses, travelling by car and stopping for picnic lunches by rivers or the sea, which gave me a chance to paint while the others swam. Any natives we met smiled happily – apparently reinforcing Brian's relaxed paternalism.

Heading north for Durban on a day of heavy rain, we came

round a corner to see the scenery lorry on its side in the ditch and the fourposter, surrounded by props and costumes, upside down in a field. 'Oh dear, oh dear,' said Brian phlegmatically and set about organising the rescue with the calm efficiency which was his way of dealing with the thousand natural shocks which come the way of a one-man touring management. (He was soon to build the Brooke Theatre in Johannesburg as the headquarters of his organisation, the realisation of a long-term dream.) The virtues of his calm are not always apparent to Tweets, who is a dynamic worrier. One evening when they were bringing us home from the theatre she exploded with rage at the front door. 'Brian, you bloody fool, I've left the key behind!'

After Durban, where we visited Valerie at her family home of Issipingo, we played a couple of nights in Pietermaritzburg, and then Brian took us on a short visit to 'Otterburn' (an Anglicisation, we were told, of the Zulu for 'home of the eagle'), where his brother was growing wattle. Set high above the Insusi river, the primitive corrugated-iron farmhouse looked out on rolling hills of vivid green on which lilies and red-hot pokers grew wild. In the foreground were the attractive thatched 'rondavels' of the Zulu settlement. Of course I tried to paint Alan Paton's 'Beloved Country', and of course I failed to do it justice; but I shall always carry its beauties in my mind's eye. The Zulu children screaming and splashing in the sparkling river, the women singing as they worked in the fields or prepared their evening meal. And the men? The men were in the Johannesburg mines, absent from their homes and families for months at a time and for years on end. Only so could they earn enough to keep wives and children – a realisation which dimmed the beauty of that lovely place.

We moved on to Johannesburg, but did not perform there, as the Brooke Theatre was still a hole in the ground. Despite much overflowing hospitality we were not happy there either. The iron bars on windows, the pass laws, the enforced separation of black couples acting as servants – all this spoke of implacable confront-ation, and made us glad to leave, though sorry to say goodbye to Brian and Tweets.

VII
1955

Stratford – the Shakespeares and James – John Gielgud and Aguecheek – death of Lavinia Annaly – a motor accident – the Oliviers in Macbeth *– Peter Brook's* Titus Andronicus *– Audrey Cameron and the Ellen Terry performances – Dulcie's* Love Affair *in Birmingham – bought by Henry Sherek – Dulcie in* Alice

Some time in 1952 we had had a visit at Chester Terrace from Tony Quayle and Glen Byam Shaw, then co-directors of the Shakespeare Memorial Theatre at Stratford (it was not yet the RSC) to discuss a possible joint engagement for the following year. We expressed great enthusiasm for the idea, and were the more disappointed to learn later that they could not after all come up with a suitable line of parts. It remained a goal for us both, however, and when it was announced in the summer of 1954 that the Oliviers were to lead the company in 1955 I had gone to see Larry to ask him to put in a good word for us. It was something I would not normally have done, but we had been seeing each other regularly on the Equity Council and he had more than once expressed his appreciation of the work I was doing for the profession. I explained our longing to get our teeth into the classics and he promised to talk to Tony and Glen.

The outcome was an offer to me to join the company; but, with Angela Baddeley, Joyce Redman and Maxine Audley already contracted, there was nothing suitable for Dulcie. As with *The Importance*, this removed much of the gilt from the gingerbread but we agreed that it was too good an opportunity for me to miss. The parts, as originally offered, were not exactly exciting – Bertram in *All's Well*, surely the most unattractive 'hero' in Shakespeare; Fenton in *The Merry Wives*, a vapid juvenile; and Lucius in *Titus Andronicus*, whose only distinction is that he survives the holocaust at the end. There was the added embarrassment that I was to play three twenty-year-olds at the age of forty. Glen had directed me in an Oxford Richard II

53

twenty years before; did he suppose that for me, if for no one else, time stood still?

We had gone to South Africa partly to fill in the gap before the Stratford rehearsals began, and partly to have the pleasure of working together in excellent parts before what was clearly going to be a long professional separation. Domestic arrangements for a nine-month season away from home are particularly important, and are not made easier by the need to maintain a large house in Regent's Park and a cottage in Essex – all on a net salary of £36 a week. (Larry and Vivien were each getting only £20 more. The pursuit of glory can be expensive in the theatre.)

I was very lucky in my digs – the Old Ferry House, on the river bank, a stone's throw from the theatre. It was owned by the only Mr and Mrs Shakespeare in Stratford – he a fine-looking old boy with the domed forehead of his ancestor, she a monumental but cosy Midlands matron, who, if memory serves, was rarely to be seen without a hat. Running the establishment was James, Mr Shakespeare's batman from World War I, who in appearance and temperament resembled Happy of the Seven Dwarfs. The house is built into a low cliff so that, from my first-floor bedroom, I had a French window into the walled garden at the back and a bay-window overlooking the Avon.

The Shakespeares were much taken with Dulcie, who came camp-following whenever she could, and one day over morning coffee asked if we would do them a great favour. 'We call you Michael and Dulcie. It seems wrong that you should call us Mr and Mrs Shakespeare. Please call us Uncle and Auntie Shake.'

So much for the background of my Stratford life.

Work began with two weeks' rehearsals for *All's Well* – I suppose because it was to follow *Twelfth Night*, the opening play, so quickly – and it was during those two weeks that I had my first pleasant surprise. Glen asked me if I would like to play Aguecheek. There had to be a reshuffle, as Brewster Mason had been forced to withdraw from the season on medical grounds; Alan Webb would now take his place as Sir Toby, leaving a vacancy as Aguecheek. I was of course thrilled, though nervous too. After all, the greater the opportunity the greater the risk.

I decided that I must read the play as if I had never read or seen it before, and that, above all, I must erase from my mind memories of any previous Aguecheeks. This last proved quite impossible: it is obvious from the text that Aguecheek is downcast at his first appearance – he has spent a lot of money and got nowhere with Olivia, and declares his intention of going home – yet all the Aguecheeks of my recollection had bounced on as cheerfully as Ralph Lynn in a Ben Travers farce. There were no more revelations in my reading of the play, but I kept my one idea to myself with growing difficulty and excitement until rehearsals began.

John Gielgud directed; Larry was Malvolio, Vivien Viola, Maxine Audley Olivia, Keith Michell Orsino, Angela Baddeley Maria, William Devlin Antonio. The first reading had the same sort of tension that precedes the first ball of an England-Australia test series.

John addressed us briefly and at his usual lightning speed: 'Now I'm not sure what I shall have to offer you in this lovely play, so let's see first of all what you've got to offer me. We'll read it without a break, shall we? Keith, you're Orsino aren't you, will you begin?'

Keith cleared his throat portentously.

'If M ...'

'No, no, no. If *Mu – u – sic* ...' fluted John, in the first of many interruptions.

Two days later we got to the first actual rehearsal involving Aguecheek.

'Michael, where are you?'

'Here, John.'

'Now you know what the set looks like. There's a little pavilion in the middle with a low wall on either side. I want you to appear up left, see Toby and Maria, and wave to them cheerfully – "Woo-woo" – then go behind the pavilion and go "Woo-woo" again when you reappear.'

I was aghast. I saw my one ewe lamb being strangled at birth.

'Yes I see, John,' I said with desperate politeness. 'The only thing is, it seems to me that he should be sad. After all ...'

'Sad? Sad? No. Terribly gay. Terribly gay.' And so I loyally went 'Woo-woo' and we worked slowly through to the end of the scene.

Rehearsals took place in the old theatre, which had a strange horseshoe staircase which started at floor level and returned thither with no intervening destination. Whatever its original purpose, it was used in my day as a convenient place to sit out during rehearsals. Deeply embarrassed I sat on the nearest tread, and was suddenly aware that I was sharing it with Larry.

'You're perfectly right, you know,' he whispered. 'Would you like me to try and do something about it?'

'I would,' I replied fervently.

Lunch was reached and Larry, Vivien and John went off together. Sharp at two they returned.

'Michael, Michael, where are you?' cried John, bubbling with enthusiasm.

'Here.'

'Larry's had a marvellous idea – that you should be sad at the beginning of that scene.'

I was just about to claim paternity for the ewe lamb, when I caught sight of Larry's warning look behind John's shoulder.

'Oh yes. That'll be a great help. Thank you, John.'

'Don't thank me, thank Larry,' said John, with Olympian modesty. And thank him discreetly I did.

The definitive description of the joys and hazards of being directed by John Gielgud is, I think, to be found in Edwin Richfield's *Letters from An Actor*, on the subject of Richard Burton's Hamlet. Put briefly, the joys are in being in contact with that incomparable source of theatrical taste, experience and enthusiasm; the hazards spring from John's unchanging humility, which leads him to question and often reverse his decisions at the eleventh hour or later. (I owe to our dear friend Robert Flemyng a story which illustrates this perfectly. He was appearing with John in *Love for Love* in Washington. At the end of the play John had arranged a formal dance involving the whole company, in the course of which John and Bobby met centre stage and bowed to each other with many flourishes. In the middle of his bow one matinee Bobby heard John whisper urgently 'Go down stage right.' 'Now?' enquired Bobby in astonishment. 'Yes. Now.' So Bobby set off self-consciously past mystified colleagues to an open space down right where he improvised a sort of *pas seul* until the curtain fell. In reply to his questioning look as the company trooped off stage, John said, 'I thought it would be better, but it wasn't.')

Twelfth Night had a mixed bag of reviews, but it seemed that I won my spurs with Glen and Tony, for I was relieved of Fenton – one of my dreaded juveniles – and given instead that fizzing Frenchman, Dr Caius, who was much more to my taste. But *The Merry Wives* was still three productions away. Meanwhile Bertram had to be endured. The sets and costumes were on the most lavish scale – my three pairs of Cavalier suede boots had cost £200, the wardrobe proudly informed me. I would gladly have settled for one pair and the rest in cash.

That summer we suffered a great loss by the death from lung cancer of Lavinia Annaly. She and her family had made a unique contribution to the fun in our London lives. As I wrote of her in *Overture and Beginners*:

> She loved the arts and artists, and having the instincts of a patron without the means to fulfil them as she would have wished, she put to their service her marvellous gifts as hostess and friend. Her cramped little flat was filled with painters, dancers and actors – often the younger ones – together with a sprinkling of high society. Sometimes the highest. We had the honour to be there on three or four occasions when the Queen Mother (then the Queen) came to drinks or supper. Lavinia by some magic made the flat larger for these parties. She even provided cabaret by Beatrice Lillie – and they were looked forward to and enjoyed by us all with the highest excitement.

A Memorial Service was arranged for Friday 13 May, and as *Macbeth* was now in rehearsal and I was not in it, it was possible for me to drive up for the service and be back for the evening performance of *Twelfth Night*. I had negotiated the everlasting bottleneck of High Wycombe on a wet morning and was picking up time between Beaconsfield and Gerrards Cross when I saw a car-transporter lorry on a bend ahead of me. 'I'll get in behind him and overtake after the corner,' I thought. Too late I realised he was stationary. I came to, some twenty minutes later. From Beaconsfield Police Station I rang Dulcie, alarming her considerably by saying in slurred tones, 'It's all right, darling. Don't worry. I know who you are. I even remembered our telephone number.' My head was X-rayed at the local hospital, and I was allowed to return to Stratford by taxi, bruised and lightly concussed but apparently otherwise unhurt. Bonnie our corgi was also unscathed; and it was almost a relief to learn in due course from the insurance company that the car was a write-off and they would pay me cash.

Everyone was most solicitous on my return to Stratford – particularly Vivien, with whom of course I had to fight the comic duel. I was determined to play that night, and in fact all went well until the duel. Suddenly I experienced a searing pain, and wondered for a moment whether Vivien had run me through. A fuller X-ray next morning revealed a cracked rib.

There was one other important consequence of the accident, though its significance did not become apparent for another ten years. Apart from the obstruction of High Wycombe – the M40 was still far in the future – I now had even stronger reasons for disliking the standard Stratford-London route. The next time I drove Dulcie to town (in a self-drive car) we went by Banbury, Aylesbury, Wendover and along the pleasant Misbourne valley towards Amersham. Suddenly Dulcie cried out, 'Michael, stop. Just look at that house.'

There was a lake with a wooded island below the road to the right, and on a green hill above it, flanked and backed by woods, was an austerely formal white Palladian mansion fronted by a noble Corinthian portico. From our years at Chester Terrace we were already 'heavily into' Corinthian, and this seemed a dream house indeed. 'We'll live there when we win the pools,' said Dulcie.

Next came a grief which can only be trivial to those who have never owned and loved dogs. Bonnie died of a heart attack early one morning. He had been an integral part of our lives for eight years – appearing in *The Glass Mountain, Angels One Five, There was a Young Lady* and *The Tall Headlines* – and when not 'working' himself, was always to be found backstage with us on tour and in the West End, establishing the custom which still holds, despite warning notices at stage doors, that 'the Denisons always bring their dog with them'. Had my accident, I wondered, contributed to the end of this dear amusing character, who appeared to enjoy acting as much as we did? Anyway, we were desolate.

Patrick Wymark, after commiserations, mentioned that at the farm where he was living with Olwen and the children there had just been a litter of Labradors. 'Oh, I wouldn't want a Labrador,' I said. 'In fact I'm not sure I want another dog.' 'I quite understand,' said Pat, 'but they really are awfully sweet. Bring Dulcie out for a drink on Sunday just to see them.' This Machiavellian invitation had the result Pat envisaged. Mother was black, father unknown, and of the eight offspring four were black, two yellow and two – one of each sex – were off-white. We found the white male irresistible, paid £1.50 for him, and christened him Titus since he would be ready to leave his mother during the week that *Titus Andronicus* opened. Keith Michell acquired one of the yellows and called him Duff, and Andrew Faulds, not yet a politician, took the white girl and called her Honey. Both Duff and Titus appeared in London – Duffy giving a sensational performance and having to take an individual curtain call in *Two Gentlemen of Verona* at the Old Vic, and Titus, more staidly, with us in *Let Them Eat Cake* at the Cambridge. In view of his progeny's records perhaps that unknown father was a canine strolling player.

Larry and Vivien, as the Macbeths, gave the crowning performances of the season. His very first line – 'So – foul – and – fair – a – day – I – have – not – seen' – spoken slowly with that strange spacing of the words he can use so effectively, was like the first announcement of a Beethoven theme and foretold the battle within the man himself. I have never seen so clearly the relentless growth of the scorpions in Macbeth's mind; indeed, the only respite came in the glittering black comedy of his interview with the murderers of Banquo. Finally, cornered and alone and exhausted, he found again, movingly and excitingly, the soldier's dignity which he had betrayed.

Vivien perfectly complemented this performance. For once a Lady Macbeth had the beauty to send her Lord spinning into the abyss to satisfy her lust for power, and the scorn to keep him to her purpose until it became his own – a scorn more terrible and effective because she still enslaved him sexually.

Disintegration from a position of assured success was, as is now well known, already a recurring nightmare of Vivien's life. Actors use a combination of experience and imagination to portray the emotions of their characters – the proportions varying according to the relevance of the experience and the depth of the imagination. How the proportions worked out in Vivien's Lady Macbeth no one can tell, but the result was one of the finest performances of her career, producing in this spectator the authentic pity and terror required of a tragic character.

Of course those critics committed to the view that Vivien was no more than a beautiful woman clinging to Larry's coat-tails and impeding his triumphant progress, dismissed her as usual. The knowledge that she could never win against this relentless prejudice, despite her dedicated professionalism, must have added greatly to the dangers of her precarious emotional condition.

Let me declare an interest here: I was a fan. I had first met her in 1936, when we both appeared in *Richard II* for the OUDS in a production directed by John Gielgud and Glen Byam Shaw, and she had come to lunch with me at Magdalen in the springtime of her beauty. She had welcomed Dulcie to the West End stage with a charming gift and letter in 1942; and now, at Stratford, she and Larry discharged their duties on stage impeccably, and their self-imposed obligations of hospitality to us all with grace and generosity. There were straws in the wind which suggested that she was overtaxing her strength, and Larry's workload was phenomenal – playing Malvolio, Macbeth and Titus and super-intending the dubbing of his film of *Richard III*; but that she was sick in mind as well as body, and that he was at breaking point, there was no public sign whatever. I salute them both.

There were always company parties after each first night, which Vivien adored, and from which Larry used to slip away. 'Could I come along to the Ferry House and sit there quietly for a while with a drink?' he asked us after *Macbeth*. Of course we agreed, and it became a custom. We returned from the *Titus* party to find we had very special guests: Noël ('in the chair'), Emlyn and Molly Williams, Johnny and Mary Mills, Irene Brown, Vivien's parents and Larry. *Titus* had been a triumph – on the morrow, Larry was to be hailed as the greatest actor of the English-speaking world – and the atmosphere was very festive. Noël was at peak form with those marvellously economical stories, and the even more staccato comments, which seemed to come too quick for conscious thought and to surprise and delight their author as much as his listeners. Into an infinitesimal pause Larry managed to insert, rather nervously, the start of an anecdote, which he directed straight at Noël. His verbal style is more literary, more decorated and slower moving than was Noël's – but the punchline won delighted laughter from us all. When conversation became general, Dulcie said to him quietly, 'It really mattered to you, didn't it, that Noël should laugh at your story?' 'Well, after all,' he said, 'he was my first leading man. And the gap never closes.'

Titus Andronicus is a terrible play, with passages of sublime poetry. The smart audience, coming to giggle over the sons in the pie, were enthralled – the word for once is to be taken literally – by the alchemy practised by Olivier and Peter Brook. Brook had designed the set and the costumes; had composed the strange atmospheric sounds that transported cast and audience into a nightmare world of blood; and, as director, had exerted his ageless authority to win from his cast, and in particular from Larry and Tony Quayle (as Aaron), performances which matched and enhanced the intensity of his vision. Giggles, if any, were left in the bar.

It has been my only experience of working with Peter Brook. His next assignment was to direct Paul Scofield in *Hamlet*. The production came to Birmingham en route to Moscow and we all went to see it in high excitement on our various nights off. Dulcie and I were bitterly disappointed, and admitted as much to Larry and Vivien who had invited us to supper. 'Yes,' said Larry. 'Peter was trying to save *Hamlet* too, wasn't he?'

By common consent the theatre today is dominated by star directors rather than star actors. As a general rule, the better the material the more brightly shines the star actor. Does the star director, by contrast, come most surely into his own when the material is indifferent – when all his skills are needed to save it? A fascinating subject for debate.

1955 had provided little fascination and less work for Dulcie since our return from South Africa. The diary shows her commuting between London and Stratford with occasional visits to the cottage; turning the ground floor of Chester Terrace into a flat for Janet Brown and her husband Peter Butterworth, to make some money; helping me entertain the stream of friends who came to the Ferry House for a couple of nights to see the plays. It doesn't show that she was writing a play, *Love Affair* – set in a small London art school run by an eccentric Frenchman – which had echoes of her student days with Amédée Ozenfant at his Ecole des Beaux Arts in the Warwick Road. The only acting that came her way that summer was an unpaid appearance with me in the annual Ellen Terry performance, and we grabbed the opportunity with both hands.

Every July, on the Sunday nearest the date of her death, there was a theatrical pilgrimage to the great actress's last home at Smallhythe near Tenterden in Kent. The barn next to the house had been turned into a tiny theatre by her daughter Edith (Edy) Craig, and performances were given there annually throughout the Thirties and again after the war. After Edy's death, the shows were organised by her great friend, Audrey Cameron – who as a small girl had appeared as a small boy with Ellen – and they continued until there was hardly anyone left who knew Ellen well. It was through Audrey that we first became involved with the Smallhythe performances – we appeared in them three or four times – and it was through that involvement that our friendship grew and deepened, until today we can all three look back on thirty-five years of a relationship which has been a mutual blessing. Working with Audrey at the BBC had been, very properly, a serious business – she won an MBE for her contribution to radio drama – but laughter was never far away; and the fun we always have when we relax in her cottage home at Haddington in East Lothian is enhanced by a serious perfectionism of hospitality on Audrey's part. Every egg, every fish, every cutlet has been the object of exhaustive scrutiny and meticulous preparation on behalf of her fortunate guests. The wine list is comprehensive, the Glen Moranjie apparently on tap, and the talk of theatre, television, politics and cricket is no less stimulating. Dogs are warmly welcomed. All in all the establishment is awarded three golden spotlights and innumerable knives and forks, as the best theatrical digs north of the border.

The Ellen Terry 'menu' was prepared with equal love and care. I have before me a programme for 1951, in which we performed *A Marriage Has Been Arranged*, a curtain-raiser by Alfred Sutro. Also on the bill were Harcourt Williams as Master of Ceremonies, Nicholas Hannen, Athene Seyler and Margaret Rawlings in *The Dark Lady of the Sonnets*, Edith Evans reading two sonnets, Felix Aylmer as Disraeli, Norman Shelley as John Brown and Iné Cameron (Audrey's mother) as Victoria at Balmoral, Roger Livesey, Ursula Jeans, Robert Eddison and Paul Rogers in scenes from an Old Vic *Twelfth Night*, and an appreciation of Ellen by her great-nephew, John Gielgud.

This was a quite typical bill, and no one but Audrey could have cajoled such casts to give up a precious summer Sunday. The pattern of the day never varied. The sun always shone – or at least shines in memory. We would set off for the long hot drive swearing we would never do it again. And then ... there was Audrey, cheerfully getting the show on the road against the deadline, just prepared to listen politely to the worries with which eminent performers seek to protect themselves on these occasions, but equally prepared with crisp practical solutions. A splendid buffet was provided by Edy's friends, Mesdames Christopher St John (music critic and biographer of Ethel Smyth) and Clare Atwood (portrait painter) – Chris in her normal costume of trousers, thick white seaman's sweater and a scarlet woollen cap, which was replaced at tea-time by a wide-brimmed Ascot hat (her annual gesture to frailty), the rest of the costume remaining unchanged.

By the time we were making-up, the almost palpable love of Ellen in that place had had its effect. The audience might be small, the stage a postage-stamp, but we felt part of a great tradition – 'We few, we happy few ...' Tea on the lawn with the audience, who barely outnumbered us, followed the performance; and then we were being waved away down the lane by Chris, her pirate's cap back on her head. 'See you next year,' she roared.

Dulcie's continuing lack of work (apart from an unlikely revue on television which co-starred Fenella Fielding and Bernard Miles) was a worry to me as well as to her. All the more important then that I should succeed in establishing a firm foothold at Stratford for both of us.

Accordingly, I had been in touch with Glen, explaining that despite the financial problems the season had been for me 'the good life'. I had adored doing four plays in repertoire, and was relishing the country background of river and Cotswolds for my painting, the 'Bensonian' sporting activities, and life in a town where the theatre's importance was paramount. I longed for Dulcie to share these things as a participant and not a camp-follower. Glen was as usual courtesy and understanding personified. He and Tony were of course at this period operating in a buyer's market in their choice of actors; it was therefore no surprise when my request was rejected, but it was a terrible disappointment to us both, not made easier by the glowing praise for my 1955 contribution with which rejection was accompanied.

What was to be done? The answer was the play on which Dulcie had been working. It seemed to me to provide some excellent and varied parts which could mostly be cast from the company – who after eight months in doublet and hose, cloaks, togas, etc., would be thankful to get into modern dress. The original plan was a modest one – we would give a single performance without scenery to the rest of the company in the old theatre during the last week of the season. Suddenly there was an exciting development. We learned that Derek Salberg of the Alexandra Theatre Birmingham was looking for a play for the week between his repertory season and his pantomime – what is more, it was the week which immediately followed the

Stratford season. We sent him *Love Affair* and he accepted it.

Brian Oulton, Una Venning and Julie Somers were 'imported' to fill rôles for which there was no one available at Stratford, and as director I was proud of my company. Keith Michell and Maxine Audley played the ill-suited lovers admirably; and I made two important discoveries from among the Stratford spear-holders – James Grout and Ian Holm, the former as a stylish light comedian, the latter as an ebullient cockney artist's model. (I like to think the discovery may have been important for them too. Certainly when Glen came to see a performance at Birmingham he expressed delighted surprise at their skill and versatility; and Ian was to become a Stratford regular for many years, graduating to Romeo, Henry V, Richard III and other leading rôles before his wider successes in every medium.

Birmingham went well. John Trewin wrote a long constructive and encouraging notice in the *Birmingham Post*; John Barber's headline in the *Express* was 'Good! Try again, playwright Dulcie.' This brought Henry Sherek, that lovable gargantuan blood-hound of an impresario, hot-foot in pursuit. What's more, he liked it enough to buy it; but he made two stipulations for its future – both persuasive but equally fatal. Dulcie, ahead of her time as a playwright, had ended the play with a shock effect which left the future of the lovers uncertain. Henry required a happy ending (which could only be false). Secondly, he insisted that Dulcie and I should play the principal parts. Keith and Maxine were not available for the spring tour, so there was no embarrass-ment there. There was plenty elsewhere. We felt it was enough that one of us had written and the other directed the play; more seriously even, we did not regard ourselves as good casting. Professional integrity should therefore have required us to turn down Henry's offer. However, for Jimmy Grout, Ian Holm and Mary Law (one of the Stratford ladies-in-waiting, who was a most convincing débutante) there was the prospect of first chances in the West End, and for Brian Oulton a marvellous part as the French art-teacher. We couldn't deny them these oppor-tunities, and so, against our better judgment we decided to give it a whirl, in the spring.

Meanwhile there was a revival of *Alice* at the Chelsea Palace, with various cast changes – notably Dulcie (for Margaret Rutherford), triumphant as the White Queen, Juliet Mills making a most accomplished debut as Alice, and the great Leslie Henson making a no less accomplished farewell as the White King and the Frog Footman. They were neither of them good parts, but with his perfect theatrical manners there was no sign that he thought so. He just quietly set about making them better. As the Footman, he had to say: 'I've been sitting here for years and years and years – in fact ever since I was born.' This was modified to 'ever since I was spawn'; the audience loved it and it stayed in. Leslie had a slightly frog-like face and a throaty voice. 'I don't know what's the matter with me,' he croaked one evening; 'I think I've got a man in my throat.' That too was added to the text.

The survivors from the previous production were all most helpful to Dulcie in her difficult task of following Margaret Rutherford. Wally Crisham (who doubled Tiger Lily and Haigha) said to her thoughtfully one day, 'Margaret used to do something very funny on that line with her chins.' 'Thank you,' said Dulcie. 'I'm not yet so generously equipped in that direction. I'll have to get the laugh another way.'

It was not only Leslie's farewell, but the end of the Chelsea Palace. We were strongly tempted to collect a memento. Each dressing room had a framed NOTICE TO ARTISTES in boldly alternating scarlet and black. 'Keep your work clean. Be funny without being vulgar,' it commanded. 'Standing in wash basins is strictly prohibited. Very serious accidents have happened to artistes when trying to remove "wet white". The basins collapsed and THE GIRLS WERE TERRIBLY LACERATED.' One of these notices unaccountably found its way to our loo.

VIII
1956

Love Affair *on tour – in London – Tynan's notice and its effect – Dulcie's* Murder on the Stairs *accepted – Dulcie in Cape Town and Australia – Michael at Edinburgh and Berlin Festivals –* Village Wooing *with Brenda Bruce*

The dominant memory for us of 1956 will always be the fate of *Love Affair*, even though it was only one event in a world-wide range of activities. Why should this be so?

Failures are such a familiar experience in theatrical careers. But *Love Affair* was a very special failure, involving us each in double capacities, and it came when Dulcie was in urgent need of a success and I no less urgently wanted one for her. Stir in a measure of altruism (towards the rest of the cast) which helped to blind us to the effect of Henry Sherek's requested changes, and you have a recipe for disaster.

On the ten-week tour it seemed as if our misgivings might be groundless. Audiences were good both in numbers and response, and a study of the cuttings from twenty-four papers shows two bad reviews, three indifferent and nineteen good. The *Derby Evening Telegraph*, reporting the opening performance in Nottingham, went overboard. Under the headline, 'A tonic for the British theatre', the critic wrote: 'Dulcie Gray has given much to the theatre during her career as an actress. Now, and I say this with all respect, she has given it something much more necessary, something vital, something living'. He went on to praise every aspect of the play, the performances and the production, and to suggest it might be just 'the shot in the arm' the theatre needed.

London frankly did not agree. *Look Back in Anger* – a shot in the arm of a very different sort – had opened at the Royal Court a month earlier. New plays like ours which were trying to say something and also to entertain were to be judged for some years by critics whose palates had been pleasurably assaulted by the

66

abrasive strength and novelty of Château Osborne '56, and who for the moment found any other vintage insipid. (I will return later to the revolution sparked off by *Look Back in Anger* – a play which incidentally we both much enjoyed.)

Let me be clear about this. I am not complaining about the adverse London notices – painful though they were in the special circumstances. Criticism can and must be accepted, provided it is based – and is seen to be based – on an artistic judgment. I leave the reader to judge whether Ken Tynan's review of *Love Affair* comes within that proviso; but I only quote it because of its effect on Dulcie's life and therefore on mine. He wrote:

> *Love Affair* ... [is] a callow study of sex in a Pimlico art school written by Dulcie Gray, directed by Michael Denison, and starring Michael Denison and Dulcie Gray. This division of labour shatters at a stroke three cardinal rules: that actresses should not write plays, that playwrights should not act in their own work, and that directors should not appear in their own productions. It also suggests a fourth rule: that actors should not marry.

(How fortunate for us all that Tynan's 'cardinal rules' two and three were continually broken by Noël Coward.)

Terence Rattigan was so outraged that he took Dulcie off to the Society of Authors for an opinion on whether the 'review' was actionable. She was told that it almost certainly was, but was advised against litigation because of the difficulty of proving 'malice', and of quantifying 'damage' in the courts. No doubt she should have shrugged it off with the contempt it deserved; no doubt she would in similar circumstances today. But unfortunately hindsight does not confer its benefits when they are needed, and in 1956 she was shattered. So shattered that she declared she would never write another play – a promise that she has kept. So shattered that she felt an urgent need to get as far away as possible from the scene of her humiliation and from everything and everybody connected with it – which included me.

I understood this, and was glad for her when she was invited to Australia to appear in *Tea and Sympathy*, and when Brian Brooke suggested that en route she should play *South Sea Bubble* for him in Cape Town.

Although I was dreading the separation, I was thankful that it was to begin with Dulcie among friends in South Africa rather than in the unknown territory of Australia.

Before these journeys began, indeed just before the tour of *Love Affair*, there had been a significant development. Dulcie had completed the first half of a country-house murder story – in the Christie tradition – which I read and enjoyed. Her plan had been that the sweet old lady who owned the house should be the killer; but, to Dulcie's surprise, when Mrs Howard was creeping upstairs to do her worst, a pair of hands emerged from the shadows and strangled her. 'Why don't you finish it?' I asked. 'Because I don't know who did it,' she replied. I suggested she should send it to publisher Herbert van Thal (whom we had met at Lavinia Annaly's) and ask if it was worth finishing. The manuscript was returned when we were in Liverpool on the tour of *Love Affair*. 'I thought so. A rejection,' said Dulcie, showing me the envelope. But when I was packing on the Sunday morning for the journey to the next date, I found she had never opened it. It was no rejection. It contained a letter from Bertie saying that if she would finish it he would publish. It appeared in 1957 as *Murder on the Stairs*, and was to be followed at yearly intervals by sixteen more crime novels.

After the Cape Town season Dulcie flew via Mauritius and Cocos (then the longest hop on the world's scheduled services) to a press reception at Darwin, where, on the aircraft steps, she was insistently asked how she liked Australia.

To her surprise she found that she was regarded in some circles as almost a scarlet woman. Her character in *Tea and Sympathy* was a schoolmaster's wife who straightens out one of the pupils involved in a homosexual group. As far as the audience is concerned, the only evidence of her therapy is when, as the lights finally fade, she undoes the top button of her blouse; but this was enough to expose her to comment from Melbourne pulpits. In due course the production moved to Sydney where, although still plagued with insomnia (she had a remarkable session with a hypnotist which ended with him asleep and his patient wide awake), she enjoyed the sunshine and the swimming. Her own homesickness was as nothing compared with the sufferings of the rest of the company, a mere 450 miles from their Melbourne homes; and in cheering them up, particularly at Christmas, she cheered herself.

Her return journey included a blissful stop-over in Hawaii, and a chance meeting in San Francisco with Hermione Gingold. 'Why Dulcie Gray, what are you doing here?' asked Ging. 'On my way to Elizabeth Arden,' Dulcie replied, rather too literally.

Meanwhile, I had had the good fortune to be very busy. First there was a television production of *Rain on the Just*, which reminded me just how well written it was; next a part in *Who Goes Home?* (a dramatisation by Maurice Edelman of one of his political novels), in which Donald Wolfit appeared for the first time on the box. 'I don't understand the medium,' he murmured to me confidentially, as he moved unerringly up-stage.

Then came a real treat. Henry Sherek asked me to do a Shaw double-bill (*Fanny's First Play* and *Village Wooing*) for the Edinburgh and Berlin Festivals. It was my introduction to *Wooing*, and I have since been fortunate enough to play it in Hong Kong, Kuala Lumpur (without decor), Australia (on TV), a long provincial tour at home and a West End season. This first time was with our dear friend Brenda Bruce, the rest with Dulcie.

Brenda was the ideal leading lady for me at that moment. Devotedly married to Roy Rich (who had directed) she posed no more threat to my marriage than I to hers. It was an unclouded professional relationship – and the most enormous fun.

Among the hazards of the Edinburgh Festival for the visiting performer are the Lord Provost's late-night 'bun-fights', not because of any lack of friendliness but because a sausage roll and a glass of sherry are inadequate sustenance after a performance. At one of these functions Brenda and I were approached by a rubicund figure who introduced himself as General Sir Horatio Murray, GOC Scottish Command. 'I've seen your show,' he said. 'You ought to see mine.' (The tattoo.) We explained that we couldn't, because we were performing at the same time. 'Oh yes, you can. We have a special late show on Saturday. There'll be two seats for you in the Royal Box. Don't worry – no royalty present. Goodbye.'

We saw yet another starvation night in prospect; and we both had heavy colds. 'We will dress in wool from head to foot,' I said to Brenda, 'and I will bring a half-bottle of whisky and a mountain of sandwiches.' And so it was that two very scruffy-looking actors, one with suspiciously bulging pockets, presented themselves at the Royal Box where they were placed in the centre of the front row, surrounded by the General, his staff and their ladies in full rig, the majority of the men in the romantic glory of Highland Mess dress. What is more, in the General's quarters afterwards there was the most splendid buffet supper of salmon and sucking pig. I'm afraid we did little for the image of our profession.

I had not seen Berlin since a visit as a schoolboy in 1933, and of course the changes were dramatic. But films and television programmes have made the city so familiar that I will not weary the reader with yet another description. I will only say that before the advent of the Wall, when movement between West and East was that much easier, the contrast between the sectors was even sharper than now. With only a perfunctory identity check, one then moved directly from the bright lights, the traffic jams, the (perhaps slightly feverish) gaiety and activity of the West into the empty, grey and soulless desolation of the East. At the theatre I had a blonde Teutonic Goddess of a dresser. 'Call me Hermann,' she commanded.

On the way home we played a week of one-night stands in Holland – my third professional visit to that land of outstanding audiences. Indeed, at the end of a matinée for sixth-formers in The Hague I made a curtain speech telling them that they had been the most swiftly and genuinely responsive audience to which we had played at home or abroad. An added delight since my pre-war visits was my new appreciation of the Dutch Masters, in particular Rembrandt, Vermeer and Van Gogh.

I returned home to find that Henry Sherek had commissioned a TV play about the Edinburgh Festival entitled *Festival Fever* in which I was to appear with Stanley Baxter. There followed, from unobtrusive beginnings, the engagement which was to transform our professional lives.

IX
1957

Acting a barrister – Dulcie's brief return – tensions in live TV – filming with Laurence Harvey – Meet Me By Moonlight – reception of Murder on the Stairs – meeting the Crime Writers – the au pair and the press – Marjorie James and Rosie Headfort – the guest who became a host

Associated Rediffusion's original offer to me was to play the title rôle in their new weekly series, *Boyd QC*, for six half-hour episodes, with an option on their side for a further seven. However, by the time I finally hung up my wig, seven years later, there had been eighty episodes, of which the first forty were live.

Boyd was the world's first television barrister to command a series of his own; he narrowly preceded Perry Mason and was many years ahead of the inimitable Rumpole, who recently defended Dulcie and me on a charge of running a brothel. Having successfully defended myself for a year at the Haymarket, as a QC accused of murdering a judge (*Hostile Witness*, 1964), and having nevertheless been rapidly promoted to the judiciary in Granada TV's *Crown Court*, a brothel was a sad come-down; but as Boyd won seventy of his eighty cases, with no dinners eaten, no exams passed and a total ignorance of every aspect of the law, he was, I suppose, riding for a fall one day.

Boyd was written by Jack Roffey (a nom de plume for an Old Bailey official) with technical advice coming from the friendly if chillingly entitled 'Keeper' of the establishment, Mr Saunders; and from Mr Leslie Boyd, the learned Clerk of No. 1 Court, who also donated his surname. Its principal director was Michael Currer Briggs. All were outstandingly helpful.

Before taking 'artificial silk' (Lord Denning's felicitous description of me), I thought it advisable to pay a visit to the Bailey – my first in fact to any court of law. At that time my impressions of justice in action came either from American films, in which peripatetic counsel virtually climb into the box with

71

both witnesses and jury, or from a few English plays in which the judge was invariably a figure of fun and invariably addressed as 'M'lud'.

I think I expected a sort of Victorian melodrama in that noble pile on the slopes of Ludgate Hill. I expected silver-tongued advocates with tears in their eyes and tremors in their voices to be making impassioned pleas to sobbing jurors; I expected Dickensian witnesses, cheers and boos from the public gallery, judges banging their gavels like castanets in order to achieve silence for their next joke. I was astonished by what I found.

My first impression, a short-lived one, was that the reality was entirely undramatic. I was wrong. The drama was there all right, but it was on the most intimate scale – 'underplayed', as actors say. Voices were scarcely raised; the questioning was highly skilled, insistent, relentless, but it was the drip of water wearing away the stone rather than the battering ram crushing it to powder. I was struck by the meticulous patience, the dispassionate dignity with which the truth is sought; and by the contrasts – highly-trained, sophisticated minds clashing with the simple, the inarticulate, even the moronic, and not always having the better of the exchange. A true example:

Barrister: Mr Jones, is your full name John Jones and do you live at ...'Juste Intime', Clapham?
Witness: That's right, guvnor, but it's 'Just In Time'.

I was fascinated by the sudden changes of atmosphere – a judge sternly passing sentence for a serious crime, and a moment later becoming all sweetness and light when a pretty girl is unhesitatingly chosen by the next defendant for a dock brief from among rows of her far more learned friends.

As Boyd was to be transmitted live, I was surprised and thankful to see how much time in court barristers spent consulting their papers. I always learned my words, but I invented a form of notes in telegraphese so that if Boyd looked at his brief he would at least find something helpful. My most difficult problem was to suggest the 'meticulous patience' which had so struck me – in a programme time of precisely 24 minutes 30 seconds. Of this, my consultations lasted three to four minutes and my court appearances a maximum of fourteen; one pregnant pause too many, in the days when Boyd was live and editing impossible, and you ran the risk of disappearing into a detergent commercial before the pay-off.

The programme was immediately popular with the public and soon settled into a regular place in 'the top ten'. One result was that I was under considerable pressure to do up to thirty-nine programmes a year; but I firmly refused ever to do more than thirteen at a time. The dangers of over-identification with the character were grave enough even at that level – football games in Regent's Park used to stop when I walked past with the dog, and a taxi driver gave me his considered opinion that if Oscar Wilde had been defended by Boyd, 'e'd 'ave got orf.' Of course I was gratified by any evidence of the public's approval, and still more by that of the legal profession, but Boyd remained for me just another part – albeit a particularly rewarding one – which might lead, as the actor hopes of all parts, to bigger and better opportunities. I was not to be disappointed.

The first transmission was on Christmas Eve, the second on New Year's Eve; and on the morning of 3 January 1957 I welcomed Dulcie back at Heathrow. To my joy she was looking well and tanned from the sea and sun of Hawaii, but this I soon found was no more than skin-deep, and though she was as thankful to be home as I was for her return she was both nervy and exhausted. On top of this, our reunion was not made easier by the pressure under which I was working – 'weekly rep in an iron lung', it had been aptly christened. I left for rehearsal the moment I had got her home.

What is more, she wasn't even back for good. It had been agreed before she went to Cape Town that she would if possible play a season at the brand new Brooke Theatre in Johannesburg, after her Australian visit; so she was only home for nine weeks, in every one of which I had a *Boyd*, as the option had been taken up. The best thing that happened in an understandably tense and tiring period was that Dulcie appeared as a counsel in one of the episodes. My Old Bailey friends arranged for her to sit in on a trial one afternoon to get the atmosphere; she was put in the VIP seats in No. 1 Court, which are close to the judge. When His Lordship returned from lunch he gave Dulcie a long and suspicious look – she happened to be wearing a white feather hat and a scarlet dress, a colour scheme which exactly matched his own.

Soon Dulcie was off again, and *South Sea Bubble* in Johannesburg provoked markedly different reactions from those in Cape Town – or, I suspect, anywhere else in the civilised world. The best scene, it may be remembered, is between Sandra, the Governor's Lady of the British-owned Pacific island, and Hali Alani, the glamorous son of the native prime minister, in a remote moonlit beach hut, and the biggest laugh comes when she cracks him over the head with a bottle to stop his amorous advances. Dulcie and a youthful Joss Ackland were prepared for a growing tension in their Johannesburg audience as the scene proceeded, but not for their reaction to the climax. Instead of laughing, they stood up and cheered.

Meanwhile, as direct consequences of *Boyd*, I had been invited to play barristers in a film (*The Truth About Women*) and a musical (*Meet Me By Moonlight*).

The film presented a problem. It was to star Laurence Harvey. Back in 1948, when the success of *Jonathan* had made me 'head of the school' at Elstree, a brash and bouncy Laurence Harvey had arrived as a 'new boy'. I had little to do with him and he was certainly never rude or unpleasant, but I disapproved of his clothes, his green suede shoes (if memory is to be trusted) and his hair, which was brushed forwards and upwards from his brow like an overhanging cliff. By now he was a big star (which didn't worry me) and all my scenes would be with him (which did). I gave myself a severe talking to: my past feelings could not justify turning down a good job. So I accepted; and the night before shooting began, I went to see him in *The Country Wife* in the West End so that I could tell him how much I had enjoyed his performance. Unfortunately I didn't, and couldn't.

We met next morning at sunrise in a Surrey wood for a duelling sequence – though I was his second, not his opponent – and the warmth of his welcome winded me. He took me off to an expensive lunch, with far too much wine for a working day, and throughout the film was a joy to work with and be with. Success is supposed to spoil people; with Larry Harvey it had the opposite effect. A great bond between us was his love of the theatre, to which he returned with gusto from the studios throughout his all-too-short life. We never worked together again but I am glad that *The Truth About Women* gave me some insight into the truth about Larry.

The musical was a near miss. It was greeted ecstatically on the road, but the London critics had taken a dislike to two-piano mini-musicals and, although *Salad Days* had proved a durable success, they had recently gunned successfully for *Oh My Papa* and now gave *Meet Me By Moonlight* the treatment. Their disapproval was increased by two unlikely factors – the enthusiasm of the first-night audience, and a show-stopping duet sung by Jeremy Brett and Stephanie Voss. This requires some explanation.

The show had seen the light of day at the Salisbury Playhouse and had been bought for London presentation by the famous impresario, Binkie Beaumont, retaining many of the original cast who were great local favourites – notably Sonia Graham in the central rôle. Many Salisbury supporters came to the Aldwych to cheer on the 'home team', but they did it so vigorously that it was counter-productive. Harold Hobson in the *Sunday Times* expended more words on the audience than the performance. I wrote him a letter about it – the first of the very few I have written to critics – and he took it in such good part that he invited us to lunch at Pruniers, where a valued if, until his retirement, guarded friendship was established. It was of course the audience who tempted the musical director into signalling an encore to Jeremy and Stephanie; alas, as no encore had been expected or rehearsed, they embarked on the whole number again, instead of a shortened version. Dulcie, back from South Africa, assessed this as the moment that sank the show. It ran on through the autumn, however, giving a good deal of innocent pleasure to the cast as well as the public – but rather less to its backers.

The publication of Dulcie's *Murder on the Stairs* this year was attended by much friendly publicity and good reviews – which were a great relief to its author and her husband. She was already at work on *Murder in Melbourne*. Her 'method' in these early days of her literary career was to find a milieu and let her characters take charge. This was fine for the first two-thirds of a story (in my opinion, Dulcie's characters and their dialogue have always been her strongest suit), but when the time came to cut through the shoals of red-herrings and not only identify the killer but demonstrate that the clever reader could have identified him or her all the time, she was sometimes in serious trouble – having kept her options almost as open as her readers'. This problem gradually switched her interest from the who-dunnit to the why-dunnit – and in exploring the behaviour and motivation of psychopaths in *Baby Face, Murder in Mind, The Murder of Love* and *For Richer For Richer*, she wrote what are for me the most gripping of her crime stories. They all feature particularly nasty men, and until I became accustomed to this new facet of Dulcie's life I felt a little like Maugham's Colonel in *The Colonel's Lady*.

Were these monsters unsuspected aspects of me? If not, where had 'the little woman' learnt so much about them?

I was much comforted when I met the Crime Writers' Association at various gatherings. The dons, doctors, lawyers, intellectuals – of both sexes – and that distinguished former National Hunt jockey (Dick Francis), though intent on seeing that crime does pay, would all be at home in a civilised and stimulating Senior Common Room. They are much to be envied – in that they have found a socially acceptable and profitable way of sublimating their aggression!

CWA dinners are addressed by speakers of the calibre of Robert Mark, Compton Mackenzie and Norman Birkett, and 'Boyd QC' was fortunate enough to hear the latter tell a story which illustrates to perfection the surprises which can assail the ordered progress of the law.

Birkett was trying a little man who was not defended by counsel and had refused not only the offer of a dock brief and legal aid, but also to say anything in his own defence, except to plead 'Not guilty'. This greatly accelerated things. In no time the Clerk was enquiring whether the accused had anything to say before the predictable sentence was passed. 'Yes,' he said – which much surprised the court, which had grown accustomed to his silence.

> *Birkett*: Well what have you got to say?
> *Accused*: It couldn't have been me, my Lord.
> *Birkett*: What do you mean, it couldn't have been you?
> *Accused*: Well, it couldn't.
> *Birkett*: Why not?
> *Accused*: Because I was in prison at the time.
> *Birkett*: Well why didn't you say so?
> *Accused*: I thought it would prejudice my case.

Millie, our treasure, had developed a heart condition which was not helped by the stairs at Chester Terrace, but as she refused to retire, we engaged Claude from Avignon to ease the load on her. In those days any visit by either of us to Heathrow rated a press photograph. 'Meeting Dulcie?' I was asked. 'No. A French girl.' Ooh-la-la was the unspoken comment. 'Old friend?' 'No. Never seen her before.' They waited with me, mystified; and, when Claude appeared, dazzled her with flash bulbs. I explained to the startled girl that she was coming to a theatrical household. Back at Chester Terrace I introduced her to Dulcie and went out to fetch her luggage from the car. There I found a lurking reporter. 'I understand, Mr Denison, that you have just met an attractive young French girl at Heathrow.' 'Yes.' 'Does Dulcie know?' 'You'd better come in and ask her.' 'You mean she's here?' 'Yes.' 'Oh.' And he disappeared. (There's a happy postscript to that story. Some years later, Dulcie and I were invited to a reception for Ngaio Marsh where Agatha Christie was making her a presentation to mark some milestone in her career. A man I didn't recognise came up to me and said. 'Did you know you changed my life?' 'How was that?' I asked. 'I was the journalist who came to your house to ask about that French girl. I was so embarrassed by your reply that I went back to my paper and resigned. I now do PR work for a publisher and am much happier'.)

Claude left us after her allotted span, leaving but one other mark on our memories. She had learnt no English, but she did teach Titus French. To the end of his life he would lower his ample behind on the command 'Assis', and give a stately wave on hearing 'Donne ta patte.'

This period saw the deaths of two women who had enriched our lives over many years, Marjorie James and Rosie Headfort. Both set much store by good manners, and were blessed with humour. Both had been on the stage, but whereas Rosie had retired from the Gaiety in 1900 to marry her Marquess and live in a great Adam house in Ireland, Marjorie having retired for reasons which were never revealed, came to live as a spinster in a small flat on Harrow Hill where the inadequacies of her income were gallantly concealed. Each maintained a salon, with a flair and sparkle quite independent of their very different financial circumstances.

Rosie's we only saw in action when she returned to London as a widow after the war; in it she blended Society and the Arts as successfully, as a hostess, as she had in her own life. Marjorie's was undoubtedly the more unusual. Quite how it had started I don't know, but by the time I had my first invitation to tea in 1930, it was already a select Harrow institution. For twenty-five years or more there were always up to twenty boys who were on her list – in my day they included Jack Profumo, Dorian Williams and future generals, clerics, doctors and Civil Service mandarins. You had to be introduced by a regular, and if you passed muster, not only were there two or three tea parties a term to look forward to, but you were a 'member' for Marjorie's life. Parents, fianceés, wives and children were assured of a warm welcome too, together with a clear-eyed appraisal; and birthday and Christmas cards went regularly to all her ever-growing one-parent family. The talk – often, but not exclusively theatrical – was as good as the tea; above all, her home was an oasis of taste and civilisation among the rougher values of a school house.

During her last illness we were able to see Marjorie quite often. Although she had contributed so much to Harrow, with her productions as well as her salon, she had no official relationship with the school. 'Do you think,' she asked me, 'that they would fly the school flag at half-mast the day I die?' I promised to arrange it if I could and, thanks to Jack Profumo (he was then a Governor of the school), was able to tell Marjorie just before she died that her wish had been granted. I drove down to Harrow on the day and saw with emotion that the promise had been kept.

It was Dulcie who saw the most of Rosie towards the end, often having supper with her in her bedroom, when I was at the theatre. Rosie had fascinating stories to tell of how she had bridged that gap between leading lady at the Gaiety and châtelaine of Headfort in the high summer of the Edwardians. They talked too of John Osborne's theatrical revolution – Rosie's interest in the contemporary scene was undimmed – and one evening Dulcie happened to mention an affair of the heart which was much in the news. 'We never called it an affair, you know,' said Rosie nostalgically. 'We called it a "tuck-up"!'

Rosie was a Catholic, and after her death there was to be a Memorial Service at St James, Spanish Place – a very large church. Two of her children – Lord William Taylour, the archaeologist, and his sister, Molly – asked if I would be an usher, because they were concerned that Rosie's theatrical friends might get swamped by the big battalions of Society. I was happy with this mandate; and after a visit to Moss Bros I presented myself confidently at the church.

My confidence was short-lived. The only positive theatrical identification I made was Ernest Thesiger, who was already the wrong side of eighty. I installed him up at the front, and chose for his neighbours the most exhausted faces I could find in the hope that they too were of the theatre – though before my time. Then I returned to the west end of the church and encountered my fellow usher, who was disposing of Society with no such uncertainties. He was Brigadier Sir Norman Gwatkin of the Coldstream Guards and the Lord Chamberlain's office and was quite beautifully dressed. In my recollection he had searching pale-blue eyes (as quick to identify my Moss Bros outfit as they would a duchess); red curls fringing a noble cranium, and a matching moustache. He spoke without undue movement of the lips.

'You a Catholic?' he asked.

'No.'

'No. Neither am I. I think, don't you, it would be a good idea if you and I hang on at the back here. Then we shan't make fools of ourselves, when they ring the bell and so on.'

That struck me as sound tactics, so Sir Norman and I hung on at the back. By coincidence it was the day on which Pope Pius XII had died; and as well as Rosie's 'full house' Catholics came pouring in to say prayers, buy candles etc., watched with respectful Anglican curiosity by Sir Norman and myself. Among them there came a mother and her tiny little girl who, finding nowhere else to kneel, knelt down on the floor. I had seen them come in, then my attention returned to the service. However they had obviously come over to buy a candle from a little booth near where we were standing, for I felt an elbow in my side.

'I say,' said Sir Norman confidentially, 'that child has just eaten the candle – that can't be right can it?' How Rosie would have loved that!

We spent a relaxed winter holiday at St Paul. The Colombe was marvellous out of season – often crowded with celebrities at lunch time, it became a village inn at night, when the few residents would gather round a log fire after dinner and exchange anecdotes in 'franglais'. (In our early visits to France after the war, Dulcie had some linguistic forays of Churchillian splendour. The most notable was when she went in search of black cotton in Vence, and, brushing aside my offer of help, addressed the haberdasher with an authority that brooked no denial: 'Madame, je désire, s'il vous plâit, un fils noir.')

There was one regular in the bar in the evenings who engaged our interest and sympathy because he was always alone. He wore a yachting cap and had the bloodhound looks of Jean Gabin. Who was he, we enquired of Pierrot the barman. 'Monsieur Vilar,' he told us, and on no evidence at all we decided that he must be an impoverished relation of the great Jean Vilar – perhaps even an actor too. Why impoverished? Because he never stayed for dinner. We resolved to offer him a square meal.

We had heard from English friends of an excellent country restaurant near St Paul called 'L'Abbaye'. Driving near Opio in our diminutive hired Renault 'quatre chevaux', we had seen a sign marked 'Mas de l'Abbaye' pointing to a fine old Provençal farmhouse set high on a ridge, and thought we had found it. Monsieur Vilar was enchanted to visit an unknown restaurant in Opio, even at the cost of sitting sideways with his knees up to his chin on what passed for the back seat of the Renault. We turned up the precipitous track which led to the Mas and were disturbed to find it becoming progressively grassier – even more disturbed to find the windows shuttered and the door locked. There was however a bell, in answer to which appeared two shapeless creatures who squinted as us suspiciously. 'Leave this to me,' said Monsieur Vilar. 'Is it possible for us to have lunch?' he enquired politely. 'Ah no.' 'But you are a restaurant?' 'Ah no. Occasionally in summer we prepare an omelette for vegetarians passing-by.' Monsieur Vilar bowed – we all bowed – and he led the way back to the car. 'I have been so touched by your invitation,' he said. 'Permit me now to choose the restaurant and be your host. I insist. Please drive to Antibes.' Rejecting our protestations, he took us to an establishment in a back street which looked like the waiting room of a Swiss railway station, where his arrival was greeted with low bows and high excitement. 'I should perhaps have explained,' he said, as we began a memorable repast, 'that I am in fact Président de l'Association des Restaurateurs de la France.' He was also a millionaire industrialist with five houses in St Paul – one of which he lent us when the Colombe was full at New Year. Incidentally his name was Willard, which of course the French pronounce Vilar.

X
1958

The Importance *on TV – another American proposal rejected – the battle to kill live TV – Dulcie's Charles Ross year –* Love à la Carte – Epitaph for George Dillon – *Frank Hauser and* Candida *– delights of playing Shaw*

Before going to France we had been approached by the legendary Robert Atkins – the last survivor of a Shakespearean tradition stretching back a century or more – to do a tour for him of *Much Ado*. (The stories of Robert and his no-nonsense earthy approach to Shakespeare are legion. For my favourite, I am indebted to that splendid and courageous colleague, Esmond Knight, who, though almost blinded in action with the Navy in World War II, still continues to act – *and paint* – with resolution and skill. Robert was giving notes after a dress rehearsal of one of the histories at Stratford. The leading players were seated on chairs, the smaller speaking parts lounging on a flight of steps, and the 'spearholders' standing at the back as they had stood all evening. One of them was a languid youth draped on his spear, and it was to him that Robert gave the first note. 'I don't like your conception, old man. It's unsoldierly, inaccurate, and arouses the gravest suspicions.') Despite heroic efforts to raise the money – a problem with which he was only too familiar during his long unsubsidised tenure of the Open Air Theatre in Regent's Park – this time he failed, and so I was denied the experience which Dulcie had found so valuable at the outset of her London career.

Instead we toured *Double Cross*, a two-handed thriller, for Charles Ross, who had become a great friend while performing with Dulcie in the Watergate revue. He had now diversified his talents in many directions. He was in theatrical management; he was a restaurateur; he had opened London's first automatic car-wash; and he remained a highly talented performer, as well as a composer and lyric writer of charm and ingenuity, with a Coward-like capacity for putting over his own numbers better than anyone else.

81

Dulcie also played *Double Cross* in London in the summer – but with Terence Morgan, for by that time I was involved in the second series of *Boyd*.

Despite the great success of the first series, Rediffusion had been very slow in setting up the second. Negotiations with my agent had been laborious, in part because the company wanted to buy me body and soul, if they were to engage me at all, and I was determined to restrict my appearances as Boyd to three months a year. By the spring, agreement had been reached, and I was even invited to suggest a play for Dulcie and me to do for them before the series began. We chose *The Importance*, with Dulcie at last playing Gwendolen, myself moving to John Worthing, Tony Britton as Algy and Martita Hunt taking on the mantle of Lady Bracknell.

We rehearsed in a freezing boys' club in West Kensington – a squalid background for such elegant characters and dialogue. Martita had a characteristic solution to the problem. On the second day she arrived with a bamboo chaise-longue on which she reclined, wrapped apparently in sables; her lunch was a half-bottle of champagne and water biscuits; owing to a burst blood-vessel, one of the eyes through which she surveyed her surroundings was bright scarlet. We all eagerly awaited her delivery of 'A Handbag!!' She decided to whisper it. 'They can't say that I'm trying to copy Edith now, can they?' she said with a twinkle. It was undeniably different, but that doesn't mean it was right. In my view, Edith's was the only way to say it – a major chord in the orchestration of the scene; but then, I never saw Judi Dench's much-praised performance at the National in 1982.

The return of *Boyd* was widely welcomed by both press and public. Sometime in the summer I was invited to lunch at the Savoy by John McMillan, Rediffusion's head of programmes, to meet an American who, I understood, had the wish and the power to promote the showing of the programme in the States, 'provided the format could be suitably adapted'. I felt my hackles beginning to rise. 'What changes had you in mind?' I asked with stiff politeness. Middle Western viewers, I was given to understand, might be prepared to accept the archaic practices and costumes of the English courts provided my character developed a greater mobility, got out and about in ordinary clothes and ran criminals to earth. 'And then defended them in court?' I asked innocently. 'Sure, sure.' 'Or perhaps prosecuted them?' 'Yeah, that too.' I looked to John McMillan for support. His expression was inscrutable. (Why does this sort of thing always happen to me when American offers come along?) I embarked on a laborious and no doubt pompous defence of the existing format, explaining, as though to a child, the different rôles of police, solicitors and barristers in Britain, and the implausibility of combining them in one character, however dynamic. The atmosphere was now markedly chilly; my peroration made it worse. 'In any case,' I said grandly, 'the success of the programme here is because of its authenticity. Why should the British public be deprived of this quality for the sake of their American counterparts?'

Back home alone – Dulcie was on tour with *Double Cross* – I was reflecting on the consequences of what I had done (I had probably alienated John McMillan as well as the American) when the telephone rang. It was John, who swiftly cut short my apologies. 'I just wanted to thank you, Michael, ' he said, 'for saying so eloquently what I wanted to say myself.' Then why leave it to the wretched actor, I thought ...

All was not yet plain sailing, however, in my relations with Rediffusion. There were three hiccups in 1958 before things settled down to a sunlit calm broken only by the Equity 'strike' of 1961/62 in which I was one of the union's negotiators. The first hiccup occurred when I appeared as Frankie Howerd's counsel in a TV sketch in which I lost my trousers. The *Boyd* series was over; the character was not named as Boyd; press and public enjoyed it; I was happy to demonstrate that I didn't identify myself exclusively with Boyd. Only Rediffusion was not amused. Ruffled feathers were eventually smoothed down, but were swiftly ruffled again. The company had decided to transmit a weekly end-of-evening chat show to be called *Late Extra* and, having failed to persuade me to step up the number of Boyds per annum, invited me to present it. *Late Extra* was to be relaxed, glossy and sophisticated (attributes they wrongly thought I embodied) and they had got Shirley Bassey as star guest for the first one. I told them quite firmly that I was an actor – and no more an interviewer than a QC – but that I would do the Bassey interview as I was a great fan of hers and had never met her. I much enjoyed the meeting, but at the end of the show I said to the viewers, 'I hope you enjoyed the programme. Tune in again this time next week, and you won't see Uncle.'

'Did that mean you're not going to do it again?' they asked in disbelief. 'That's right.' 'But why?' I explained (as I had to Robert Clark in my film contract days) that when I wasn't acting on television I wanted to be acting in the theatre; I saw no danger to my theatrical ambitions from a moderate amount of Boyd – quite the reverse in fact – but with the accelerating expansion of television I didn't want people saying, in the West End or the Provinces, 'Oh, there's that chap who presents *Late Extra* appearing in a play by Shaw.' And so another potentially profitable sideline was rejected without regret, leaving the field clear for Parkinson, Harty and Wogan.

Throughout 1958 I had been endeavouring to persuade the company that any future series should be recorded, and not transmitted live. True, recording techniques were, by today's standards, rudimentary, but they were there. *Boyd* – even seen through a pale grey mist – was from the outset one of Australia's most popular programmes. (So much so that when four years later I went to Melbourne to appear in *My Fair Lady*, the headlines shouted 'Boyd Here to Play Higgins'. Denison was lost in the small print.) The main opposition to my plea came from the Royal Navy, in the person of Captain Brownrigg, who was a high executive of the company. He told me with enthusiasm that half the fun of television was seeing actors 'blow up', and that once they knew they could have another go they would never bother to learn their words. The gallant Captain was not to be argued with; but fortunately Peter Willes (head of drama and himself a well-known actor until war wounds ended his career) and John McMillan were more sympathetic.

And rightly. Just consider a typical transmission day. Up at 7.30 and away to Wembley at 8.15 in order to cope with rush-hour traffic and be ready dressed on the set at 10.00. There followed the 'stagger through' – to familiarise the camera crews and other technicians with the intricate movements demanded of them, to ensure they didn't photograph each other and that the many sliding panels in the court-set opened and shut as required. This process, with a break for lunch which I took anti-socially in a local pub, lasted till mid-afternoon. There were then usually two run-throughs, a break for supper which I didn't take at all, and then, with dry throat and racing pulse, a performance to millions of people. (Someone produced an apocryphal statistic that performers in live television had an adrenalin flow seven-and-a-half times above the normal. As we were without exception very tired, very hot and very frightened by the time of transmission, it certainly felt like it.) Afterwards there was a bout of hectic drinking; sad farewells were said – after all we had been through a lot together in four-and-a-half days; and then we were back on the North Circular – a danger to ourselves and others. The next morning dear Charles Leno (my Clerk) and I would meet the new cast, and the process was repeated. It was to remove this unrelenting strain on performers and technicians alike that I mounted my campaign for recordings. By 1960 the battle was won – even at the cost of Captain Brownrigg's amusement.

As soon as Boyd was finished I much enjoyed *The Inside Chance*, a play for BBC television in which I played a suburban bank manager who planned the robbery of his own branch – a fall from grace which, unlike the trousers, went unrebuked by Rediffusion.

As far as Dulcie was concerned, this was 'Charles Ross' year. All through the spring and early summer, while *Double Cross* was on its way to London, Charles had been writing the music and lyrics for Dulcie's adaptation of her first play, *Take Copernicus* (*Love Affair* was in fact her second). The result was a delightful musical, *Love à la Carte*, set in a small hotel in the Alpes Maritimes which bore a certain resemblance to the Colombe.

Dulcie resorted to a nom-de-plume, Alan Chester (after Chester Terrace) – a pity perhaps but understandable – and it was such a success at Richmond that Evelyn Laye came down and bought an option on it. Sadly, the changes that 'Boo' Laye asked for were beyond the skills of Charles and Dulcie to achieve to Boo's satisfaction, and high hopes were dashed.

Charles's resilience was, as always, remarkable. Dulcie just had time to fit in a highly sinister and successful TV performance in the title rôle of Patrick Hamilton's *The Governess* (directed by the inimitable Stephen Harrison) before Charles asked her if she would like to tour in *Epitaph for George Dillon* by John Osborne – an early and virtually unknown piece by the standard-bearer of the theatrical revolution. She read it and was immediately enthusiastic. In brief, it was the story of the effect on a humdrum household of the visit and eventual departure of an amoral and charming young man – a plot which, as Dulcie noted, had extra-ordinary parallels with Bernard Shaw's *Candida*.

One day when Dulcie was in rehearsal, I ran into Frank Hauser at Baker Street station. Frank was then in the third of the sixteen distinguished years in which he directed the fortunes of the Oxford Playhouse. 'The very person I wanted to meet,' he said. 'Can you and Dulcie come and do *Candida* for me at Oxford?' My heart leapt. *Candida* meant a great deal to me. I had been playing the Curate at the time of our marriage in 1939, and had given my last two performances on our wedding day. It had been my favourite play by Shaw ever since, and for twenty years, among other preoccupations, I had looked forward to the chance of playing Morrell – the Vicar.

Frank comes from a legal family in Cardiff, and I have no doubt that the success of *Boyd QC* was a factor in his invitation. It was certainly a factor in our ability to accept his £20 top salaries. Dulcie was worried on only one count. There had been two successful London productions during and immediately after the war; and in each, Candida had been portrayed as a matriarchal figure of around fifty. Was Dulcie not too young, she asked Frank? 'Just read Shaw's description of her – no one else seems to have done,' he said: 'A woman of thirty-three . . . now quite at her best, with the double charm of youth and motherhood . . . who has found that she can always manage people by engaging their affection and does so instinctively without the smallest scruple.'

And so began a blissful engagement. Rehearsals with Frank are so stimulating that there is a danger of performances being an anticlimax. For one thing, he is so marvellously articulate. It is a pity that his introductory talks to the countless casts he has directed have not been printed – or better still taped, for the manner is an integral part of the matter. There he sits with shining eyes, one leg crossed over the other and the 'free' foot quivering feverishly with excitement – or is it with frustration, that not even his own speed of speech can keep pace with the speed of his thought? In the early stages of rehearsal, when actors are laboriously feeling for their words – and their motivations – and speed is not in them, Frank is at his most constructive; but the foot shakes more convulsively than ever, as if to urge a sluggish orchestra up to tempo. There is another unique element, particularly noticeable at the beginning of his rehearsals: he treats everyone, whatever the size of their part, as respected friends of his with whose work he is familiar; and if members of a company have not met before, he manages to indicate how fortunate they are that this unaccountable lapse is now a thing of the past. Humour is his weapon – both in criticism and praise. He has a most infectious giggle and total artistic and intellectual integrity. Ask (among many others) Jeremy Brett, Judy Campbell, Judi Dench, Gordon Jackson, Barbara Jefford, Penelope Keith, Felicity Kendal, Ian McKellen, Leo McKern, Keith Michell, John Turner and Irene Worth. Dulcie and I are proud and fortunate to be of their company.

A director of wide range and versatility, Frank seems particularly at home with Shaw; and those three weeks working for him at Oxford were the prelude to many joys in the years ahead.

As is well known, Shaw expended much time, wit and malice trying to detach Ellen Terry from her long partnership with Irving. In Marchbanks, Candida and Morell, I believe he recreated in dramatic form this same triangle. I am not suggesting that Marchbanks was a self-portrait, but rather an illustration of Shaw's self-appointed function as gadfly and would-be disrupter of a relationship in which his adored Ellen-Candida was denied her freedom by a man who took her for granted as a subservient partner. As usual, GBS the playwright is fairer to the object of his dislike or ridicule than in real life GBS the critic was to Irving. Marchbanks attacks Morell with all the weapons in Shaw's power, but – and this is why actors love playing Shaw – Morell is given counter-arguments of compelling strength. To play Morell before lively undergraduate audiences, whose sympathies were entirely with Marchbanks, was as a consequence tremendously exciting.

Some two years earlier, just after the tour of *Village Wooing*, I had been invited to the Canonbury Tower to give a talk on 'Shaw and the Actor'. Although at the time I had only played one important Shavian rôle, I find to my surprise that there is little I would change today to explain my enduring love-affair with Shaw's writing – or indeed the general qualities I look for in any script I have been invited to perform:

I look for strong situations, whether in drama, comedy or farce; I want to be able to respect the playwright both for his ideas and craftsmanship, to feel that he is intellectually or technically my superior and that nevertheless a flesh-and-blood actor will not only be able but be needed to put across these ideas to a public of average intelligence. I require the ideas to be expressed in language which I can sell to the public as conversation but which will be bigger, brighter, and more coherent than it would be in real life. Finally I require the characters – and not least my own – to be sympathetic and theatrically interesting. By 'sympathetic' I mean either 'patently admirable' – in which case the actors' main problem will be not to make them crashing bores – or 'weak or wicked' in a way that the audience can condone or at least understand .

Shaw for me fulfils all these criteria. He also makes both actors and audiences work. Actors are happy to do so; audiences less so. His major achievement indeed was (and still is) to make people think for themselves. Agreement with his conclusions is of secondary importance.

His detractors accuse him of producing not people, but points of view designed to fuel his debates. There is some truth in this, but – a very big BUT – that is just where the director and actors come in, or should come in. The average actor spends 80 per cent of his career playing characters with neither flesh, blood nor a point of view. Give him the latter (with Shaw's peerless language to express it) and, if he's worth his salt, the flesh and blood and muscle will soon be developed.

Shaw was a great lover of women, his ardour being not noticeably affected by whether or not he was technically the Lover. He wrote wonderful parts for actresses – shining dynamic parts, serene compassionate parts, saints, prostitutes, suffragettes, man-eaters – but all feminine, if usually more articulate (which is not to be confused with being chatty) than most women.

May I remind you of the last words of his preface to the Ellen Terry correspondence:

> She became a legend in her old age; but of that I have nothing to say for we did not meet and except for a few broken letters did not write; and she was never old to me.
>
> Let those who may complain that it was all on paper remember that only on paper has humanity yet achieved glory, beauty, truth, knowledge, virtue and abiding love.

Those are not the words of a soulless propagandist, an irresponsible jack-in-the-box – and it's worth all the agonies of rehearsal for an actor to have a chance to bring the mind of such a man to an audience, and feel them kindle to his qualities and idiosyncracies and skill.

The year ended with a Christmas visit to Leila and Vivian Ward at Sudbury in Suffolk. Leila is the only daughter of Edward and Ivy Every – lifelong friends of mine who were so prodigal in their loan of pictures and furniture for Chester Terrace. Leila and her husband continue to this day her parents' tradition of hospitality towards us; but what I particularly remember of this visit was not the warmth of the Wards' welcome – that could be taken for granted – but the behaviour of some of the Suffolk gentry to whose parties they took us. At the first, a silence fell as we joined the festivities, swiftly and deliberately broken by the stentorian tones of a retired general. 'Television. Wouldn't give it house room!' At another I was given a drink by our hostess, but Dulcie got nothing. I naturally passed the glass to Dulcie, to the astonishment of the lady of the house, whose habit it was to give large glasses to men and smaller ones to female guests.

At yet another, a young man came up to Dulcie with shining eyes and asked her how he should set about going on the stage. Before she could reply, his mother bore down on them and said, in one of those peculiarly resonant county voices, 'I suppose he's been asking about the Stage. I've told him that if he wants to get on he'll have to sleep with everyone in sight. Isn't that right, Mrs Denison?'

I mention these trivial incidents because they illustrate some of the many variations of attitude to our profession which we meet in people who are inexperienced in dealing with actors. Broadly they range from red carpet (too kind) to tradesmen's entrance (too rude), but the majority fortunately come within these extremes; and given the ephemeral nature of most of our work, it is heartwarming how often we are reassured that it has given pleasure.

XI
1959

My last film – results of exhibition of actors' paintings – Let Them Eat Cake *– an experienced cast – King Juan the First of Redonda – our first Rolls – death of my father – Dulcie's* Baby Face *published – first meeting with Rebecca West – Dulcie a vampire*

1959 began for me with the third series of *Boyd*, followed by *Faces in the Dark* – quite the worst film with which I have been involved. It turned out to be my last and, although of course I didn't know that at the time, its shortcomings effectively cushioned the dismay I might otherwise have felt when the studio doors symbolically closed behind me. My character took advantage of the blinding of John Gregson to have an affair (off-screen) with his wife, Mai Zetterling. It ended very properly with him being drowned in a sinking car – I nearly shared his fate. This was my third picture with the adorable and talented Mai – how sad, particularly in view of her long and distinguished career in the cinema, that none of them should have had any distinction.

Also in the spring, there was a charity exhibition of actors' paintings for which five of my 'works' were accepted. How the charity benefited from my contribution I can't imagine, because I demonstrated my unshakeably amateur status by refusing to allow any of them to be sold – my reasoning being that, if they deserved to be hung, there was a good case for keeping them.

There were two unlikely consequences of this exhibition. I had long been an admirer of Edward Seago's lyrical cloud- and landscapes of East Anglia (an admiration much increased by my new appreciation of the problems he solved with such apparent ease). He was then secretary of the Artists' Benevolent Fund and sent me an appeal for a donation. 'PS,' he wrote, 'I so much liked your "Winter Landscape at St Paul de Vence".' That not only clinched the donation but was the starting point of a valued friendship which lasted until his untimely death.

The other consequence was professional. The private view

90

took place in the evening, to enable those working in the theatre to attend. Dulcie and I were 'resting' at the time, but we had been to some full-dress City dinner (white tie and tails for me and the 'family jewels' for Dulcie); impresario Emile Littler, who was looking for a Duke and Duchess of Hampshire for his forthcoming production of Frederick Lonsdale's *Let Them Eat Cake*, apparently felt that his search was over.

The history of the play was a strange one. It had gone into rehearsal in the late Thirties, with Laurence Olivier as the Duke – but without a final act. Lonsdale, it seems, like Sheridan, was reluctant to finish a play. (Was it because both were so devoted to the characters they had created, to the wit of their conversation and the clashes of their personalities, that to drop a final curtain on them seemed like an execution?) Anyway, the production was abandoned, either for want of a final act or because the one belatedly delivered was considered unsatisfactory. Cyril Raymond, that least dull of men, who in a long career was so often the neglected husband – notably, of course, Celia Johnson's in *Brief Encounter* – rehearsed the neglected husband in 1938 and played it with us in 1959. Even Stanislavsky would have regarded that as an unduly long preparation.

Emile had gathered an experienced cast. The six senior members aggregated two hundred and eighty-five years in the business between them. Austin Melford, soon to celebrate his diamond wedding to the adorable Jessie Winter (who had played my mother in *The Bad Samaritan*), was, at seventy-five, celebrating a career of seventy-five years – having appeared as a baby at two months. Phyllis Neilson Terry had first appeared in 1909, Harry Kendall and Cyril Raymond in 1914, Claude Hulbert in 1920, and Guy Middleton in 1928. Their parts were not large but, as members of a ducal house-party in 1913, they all had amusing things to say, and the eccentric splendour of their contributions will not be forgotten by those who were fortunate enough to be on stage with them, nor I hope by our audiences.

One day early in rehearsals, Harry Kendall, Dulcie, Wally Douglas (the director) and I were having a pub lunch.

'I'm very worried,' said Harry suddenly. 'I've counted my lines and there are only twenty-one. Do you think I can make a comeback with only twenty-one lines?'

'A come-back?' said Wally, looking affectionately at him with his very bright blue eyes. 'But Harry, have you been away?'

Harry was much encouraged; and somehow managed to

increase the impact of his part by saying each of his lines twice – without really appearing to.

Titus, our Labrador, made a correct if scarcely dynamic appearance as 'Hants' – the Hampshires' gun dog. For one of his temperament it was clearly a great strain, and my dresser had to take him to the pub afterwards 'and give him an arrowroot biscuit to calm him. He only made one mistake, however. Wendy Toye, who knew him well but was not expecting to see him on stage, suddenly said, 'It's Titus!' from the stalls. His duties forgotten, Titus looked searchingly into the auditorium, with a hopefully wagging tail. This got a big laugh, which embarrassed him dreadfully.

Quite early in the run there was a very strange occurrence. Dulcie answered the telephone to a caller who announced himself as the Home Secretary to Juan the First, King of Redonda. 'Who are you really?' she asked and the information was repeated, rather stiffly. She was told that His Majesty wished to create me a Duke of his island realm in the Caribbean and that our fellow peers were Dirk Bogarde, Diana Dors and J. B. Priestley. He had seen our play and considered that we measured up to his ideal of an intellectual aristocracy. If convenient, the investiture could be held that afternoon after the matinée. To everyone's astonishment, not least that of the press (who had been alerted in the interest of publicity for the show), it actually happened. I have my 'letters patent' before me as I write. It shows that I am Duke of Essexa-y-Stebbingo di Redonda (Stebbing was the name of the Essex village where we had our cottage).

But what of Redonda, and what *was* it all about? After a brief and hilarious 'investiture' on stage at the Cambridge Theatre, witnessed by our 'house party', His Majesty, who lived on a barge called 'Maudelayne' at Little Venice, invited us to 'take wine' with him at a pub nearby at our convenience. We could hardly wait.

His name was John Gawsworth and he was a poet and bibliographer. We have two copies of *Who's Who* (1951 and 1968) and he has a long entry in both. There is one significant difference, however. In the former he gives 'Creating Nobility' as a recreation; in the latter this has been deleted. Were we perhaps his last creations? (He was dead by 1974, because it was then we met his widowed Queen living in Stratford-on-Avon.)

This is the story he told. In the late nineteenth century, when the smaller Caribbean islands were being annexed in the name of Queen Victoria, two friends and drinking companions living on Antigua noticed that Redonda – an imposing lump of basalt, uninhabited except for sea-birds and looking a little like Ailsa Craig from the Ayrshire coast – had been left out. The friends were the Bishop of Antigua and an Irish writer, David Shiel. They decided it would be a good joke for the Bishop to crown Shiel on Redonda (if they could get ashore) and that is what they did, making Shiel a *de facto* King, which did not amuse Queen Victoria.

John Gawsworth's story then became even more extraordinary. He swore that Shiel was awarded a Civil List Pension, which on his death passed to his son, M.P. Shiel, who became the second King. The pension, we were told, continued into World War II, when Churchill, in search of economies, promptly discontinued it. The second Shiel, being childless, bequeathed his kingdom to John Gawsworth, who, when we met him, was still hoping to get the pension restored.

In 1984 we met the reigning monarch, King Juan II – alias Jon Wynne-Tyson, publisher, author and literary executor to both King Juan I and King Felipe. From him we learnt that there were a number of inaccuracies in John Gawsworth's story. For instance, the first Shiel was a trader not a writer. He merely 'annexed' Redonda in 1865 and may have called himself King. It was his son, M.P. Shiel, later to become well known as a writer of fantasy, who was crowned on the island by the Bishop on his fifteenth birthday in 1880. Nothing is known by King Juan II of the pension. His Majesty is making enquiries.

As a postscript to this strange tale I can record that we have seen our dukedom. We passed close to it in 1976 when flying low from Antigua to Nevis. It looked uninviting.

However, I shall always have a soft spot for its dynasty, which is uniquely civilised in having developed a tradition of literary succession.

During the run of *Let Them Eat Cake*, we acquired our first Rolls-Royce – a great moment, even though she dated from 1939. She had begun life as a Sedanca-de-Ville, that most elegant and snobbish of body styles, in which the owner was under cover and his chauffeur out in the open. By the time we bought her the front compartment had been roofed over, but it continued to betray its origins by leaking like a sieve. By present-day standards she was not expensive – around £800 if memory serves – but I decided to be prudent and have her inspected by the AA. The report was encouraging, except that 'moths were seen leaving the rear seat'; but even this had its value, for when I showed it to the salesman with proper indignation the price was reduced by £80. The car had an electric partition which could be operated by the driver or the rear-seat passengers. One day we heard it closing, and looking round saw that Titus, alone on the back seat, had pressed the switch with a fat Labrador paw. 'Bored with our conversation,' Dulcie suggested.

While on holiday at St Paul after the play closed, I learned of the death of my father – who had been our only surviving parent. (My mother had died within three weeks of my birth; Dulcie's father in an accident in Singapore in 1935; and her mother when trying to escape from the Japanese in 1942.)

My relationship with my father had been a strange one. When he returned from World War I he was thankful to see that I was happy with my mother's sister and her husband – in whose household I lived until 1938, by which time she had died and he was incapacitated by a stroke. My father remained in the shadows as far as I was concerned, with birthday and Christmas cards our only contact, until my posting overseas in 1943. He then suggested we should meet, on the reasonable grounds that it might be for the only time in my adult life, and we had a pub lunch somewhere in the City. We got on very well, but curiosity was the dominant feeling on both sides; after all, we had done without each other for twenty-eight years, and it would have been out of character for either of us to put on a show of emotion we did not feel. After the war – by which time he was a martyr to arthritis – we saw him and his wife regularly; he was, I think, proud of our successes (and he was devoted to Dulcie), but the theatre was an utterly foreign world to him and our relationship remained that of good friends of different generations rather than father and son. Filial feelings were reserved for the uncle who had given me a home throughout my childhood and adolescence.

For Dulcie, there now came a most welcome turning-point in her literary career. *Murder in Melbourne*, the fruit of her Australian tour, had been well reviewed; but with *Baby Face*, her story set in South Africa, her reputation took a remarkable leap forward.

Julian Symons, a master of the genre, described it in the *Daily Telegraph* as 'one of the most convincing portraits of a murderer in recent crime fiction' – an opinion echoed by other influential reviewers.

Baby Face had another happy and most unlikely consequence. At a party given by Margaret Rawlings for her daughter, Jane, Dulcie was introduced to Rebecca West. 'I read your book, *Baby Face*,' said Rebecca, 'and enjoyed it. I took it on a trip to South Africa, and it was such a relief. It must be the only book set in modern South Africa which has no political message whatever.' Rebecca was to become a great friend. How and why we were so blessed I cannot imagine, but blessed we were – in her company, her hospitality, her letters and her love.

The year ended with Dulcie touring (but, thanks to Noël Coward's insistence, not facing the London critics) as a six-hundred-year-old vampire, in a play wittily entitled *The Best Cellar*. I was in a television version of Dodie Smith's *Dear Octopus*, which (for reasons which are a mystery to me but may be clear to someone) was to be my last play on BBC television for twenty years. The notices tell me that it was a great success, and I had the joy of working with Gwen Frangçon Davies, Barbara Couper and Margaret Tyzack.

II The Sixties

The Sixties were for us a decade of intense, varied, and largely rewarding activity. We appeared together in the West End (and on tour) in every year but one; Dulcie wrote a further eight crime novels, and we collaborated in *The Actor and His World* – our young person's guide; I worked many anti-social hours for Equity, exposing myself professionally as one of the leaders of the so-called strike against the ITV companies, and personally by resigning from the Council over their change of policy about South Africa, and promptly being re-elected with an increased vote at the next election; we became founder members with Peter Donald (our first employer, in Aberdeen in 1939), Peter Bridge (then the West End's most dynamic young impresario), Brian Rix (of Whitehall farce fame) and Albert Finney in a production company, which began too successfully for its own good.

Darling old Millie Wooster of Lisson Grove, who had kept house for us since 1945, died, and was succeeded by Eileen Leahy of County Kerry, a no less devoted character, who happily for us, our friends and our dogs, still comes to us in any crisis, social or professional. We moved fifty yards from Chester Terrace to Cumberland Place, a smaller house but with an unrestricted view across its garden to Regent's Park; we sold the Essex cottage because of the threat posed by the development of Stansted Airport, and acquired a first toe-hold in our dream house in Buckinghamshire.

Above all we grew up professionally; and though we remain eternal students of the art and techniques of acting, we developed in the Sixties an attitude to our work, and to the place of the actor in the theatre and the theatre in society (a practical and not inflexible attitude I would like to think) which we share to this day, Dulcie instinctively and I more explicitly.

I
1960

The touring plan frustrated – meeting Miki Sekers – John Gale and Candida *in London – Christmas at La Garoupe*

I have already described some of our prior-to-London tours in the previous decade. At first we thought of these as something of a chore – and indeed until the relaxation of war-time austerities, many of which continued into the Fifties, travel and accommodation (and the manners that went with them) could be pretty grim. The public's response however more than made up for this; and gradually we came to realise, in the mid-twentieth century, what had been accepted as a matter of course by our great predecessors of a hundred years before – that the public in Leeds, Cardiff, Glasgow and anywhere else on the road deserved the same standards of performance and production as the metropolis. How far the touring scene had declined from this ideal was illustrated by the public excitement caused by an interview we gave on this theme to a sympathetic Manchester journalist.

We decided to put our convictions to the test. In Frank Hauser we had an enthusiastic ally; in the Oxford *Candida*, a production which could be so cheaply revived that, for a total outlay of £2000, we could add *The Importance* and play the two in repertoire. All that was needed was the £2000, and reasonable terms from the theatres we would be visiting. We went first to Joe Hodgkinson of the Arts Council Drama Department, who was enthusiastic; the proposal would need to be put up to the Council itself but their approval, we were assured, would be a formality.

Peter Donald, who as Chairman of Howard and Wyndham controlled major theatres in Scotland and the North of England, was happy to book us for the spring and summer (when the fourth series of *Boyd* had been recorded), so all seemed set fair. We gave an interview to *The Stage* outlining the scheme and declaring – perhaps a shade self-righteously – that this was to be a tour for touring's sake, and that the West End played no part in our plans. It was arranged that we would open with *Candida* at the Bath Festival in May, and add *The Importance* as soon as practicable.

Suddenly everything fell apart. The Arts Council refused to give us the money; they considered, we were told, that we had thought up a clever racket to provide ourselves with good parts, and that, thanks to our successes in films and television, the enterprise would be a cast-iron box-office success, and it was no part of the Arts Council's role to subsidise success. Bewildered by this reaction but clinging to the Council's prognostication of success, we returned to Peter Donald to ask him whether his company would back the productions as well as book them. For the only time in our dealings with him over more than thirty years (and an abiding friendship currently standing at forty-six), the innate caution of the Aberdonian came uppermost. 'I'm afraid I don't agree with the Arts Council,' he told us. 'A double bill of Shaw and Wilde could be a very dicey proposition. I would advise you to forget it.' This was a knock-out blow. Our summer-long crusade had been reduced to one (by now inescapable) week at Bath.

Meanwhile, during my *Boyd* series, Audrey Cameron had produced a radio version of Dulcie's *Murder on the Stairs* (the first of six adaptations for which she was responsible), and Dulcie had given a marvellous television account of the garrulous spinster in Maugham's *Winter Cruise* (she is the only passenger on a small cargo ship, it may be remembered, and has to be seduced in order to silence her). Among the ship's officers was a tall, fair and handsome young actor called John Gale, who was continuously and even excessively polite about Dulcie's performance. When they parted after the recording he astonished her by saying, 'Oh, by the way, Miss Gray, I'm just starting as a theatrical manager. If you or your husband should ever want a management please think of me.' Dulcie thanked him, told me, and we thought no more of it.

Before starting rehearsals for Bath, we flew the Rolls over to Cherbourg and spent a week driving round Brittany. We had chosen Brittany because I had become a passionate admirer of Christopher Wood, that tragically shortlived and deceptively naive recorder of Breton life and landscape, and I wanted to paint where he had painted. The weather was chilly; Brittany is not ready for tourists until 'after Pentecost', as innumerable notices informed us; but we enjoyed the break nevertheless. The Rolls caused a sensation, not least because our trip coincided with the wedding of Princess Margaret; the local feeling was that the rightful place for the owners of so venerable and magnificent a vehicle was at the Abbey, and that we must have been banished, until all was over, for some heinous social *bêtise*.

We returned to find that Frank had, as usual, assembled a splendid cast – old friends of his, who soon became new friends of ours. Ken Wynne was the new Burgess, as youthful and hilarious a father for Dulcie as Chris Hancock had been at Oxford; Jeremy Spenser took over from Jeremy Brett as Marchbanks, and Gillian Raine became a memorable Prossie. My old part – Lexy, the curate – of which I had given my last two performances on our wedding day, was in the hands of Greville Hallam – a young man of radiant friendliness and enthusiasm, qualities which he brought to the successful agency he ran after giving up acting, until, unbelievably, he was murdered by an intruder in his flat in 1982.

Despite the savage curtailment of the enterprise, Frank and GBS soon had us under their spells, and we moved down to Bath and into the ravishing Theatre Royal in high spirits. After the dress rehearsal we were introduced to Nicholas (Miki) Sekers, who had been invited by Frank to watch. The little Hungarian, his eyes bright with emotion, kissed Dulcie's hand and congratulated us in his fractured English. (His wife Agi told us later that he spoke six languages equally atrociously – including his native tongue.) And so began a friendship which was pure joy for us, until in his last years we suffered with him, when clouds of grief finally dimmed his hitherto undimmable zest.

Miki was born in Budapest and trained in the textile industry. By the middle Thirties, Hitler's anti-semitism was spreading its contagion into Eastern Europe, and Miki decided to seek his fortune in England. Whitehaven, on the Cumberland coast, had become an unemployment black spot, and a fellow Hungarian who had already started a tannery there advised Miki to apply for a grant to set up a textile mill. Miki, who could charm the largest bird from the tallest tree, persuaded the government to back him; and so began the dramatic success story of the West Cumberland Silk Mills and Sekers Silks. After switching to making parachutes during the war, the firm's fortunes advanced dramatically in the post-war years, thanks largely to Miki's contribution as designer, managing director and roving ambassador-salesman. He was now able to indulge his passion for music, opera and drama not only in the cultural centres of Europe but by creating at Whitehaven what came to be called the 'Glyndebourne of the North'. In the grounds of Rosehill (pronounced Rozz-heel), his pleasant eighteenth-century sandstone house above the town, Oliver Messel designed for him a delightful little theatre, and to it flocked the soloists, the ensembles, the companies of his choice. As the artists took their bows, the champagne corks were already popping back-stage; and then it was back to the house for marvellous Hungarian dishes provided by Agi – for the performers of course, but also for any members of the audience whom Miki, in the euphoria of the moment, felt impelled to add to the party. How Agi coped with the loaves and fishes was just part of the magic of Rosehill. We were lucky enough to perform there twice in the great days and once in the twilight that followed Miki's death. Our first appearance was with our *Candida*; but not until much had happened both to us and to the production.

The opening in Bath went well, and as we were going up to bed at our hotel we suddenly heard a voice describing the evening in measured but glowing terms. The unseen speaker was making a telephone call from a booth under the stairs, and as there was no one about we sat on the stairs above his head and eavesdropped. It was the only time in our lives that we have been aware of a critic's view before they appeared in his paper.

The paper, it turned out next morning, was *The Times*, the only 'national' to cover our opening; and the consequences of the anonymous criticism were to be far-reaching. A play currently at the Piccadilly Theatre in the West End opened and closed within the week; and on the Friday evening of our week in Bath (after a lavish country-house lunch party for the company at which our hostess, on learning that we would all be out of work the following day, clearly wondered whether she need have bothered), there came a visit from the manager of the Piccadilly after the performance, asking if we could open at his theatre the following week.

This was exciting, but presented problems. Frank's contract with the Oxford Playhouse did not permit him to use the theatre's funds to tour any of its productions – one of the reasons, incidentally, why we had required outside finance for our abortive scheme. A transfer to the West End needed, in addition, a member of the Society of West End Theatre Managers (best known to actors by its unfortunate acronym SWETM) to present it. Who could we get at such short notice? Dulcie suddenly remembered John Gale (of *The Winter Cruise*). 'I'd love to present you and Michael,' he said, 'but I'd have to see the play. I don't know it.' And so, on the bare stage of the Piccadilly, without costumes or props, we ran through it for John. At the end he came up on stage, as emotional in the Anglo-Saxon manner as Miki in the Hungarian. 'What a lovely play,' he said. 'Of course I'll do it.'

Nobody expected it to be anything but a stop-gap. For instance, John's press representative, on being given the choice of a lump sum for her services to the production or a percentage of the takings, unhesitatingly chose the former. She lived to regret it, for we were undeniably a success – so much so that after four weeks Sir Bronson Albery, that urbane father figure of London theatre owners, transferred us to Wyndham's, the ideal theatre in every way. It was a move which created quite a stir in theatre circles, for Shaw was currently considered box-office poison. Apart from *My Fair Lady* – a special case in every way – and Alec Clunes' labour of love with the short pieces at The Arts in the early Fifties, there had not been a successful Shaw revival in the West End since the John Clements/Kay Hammond *Man and Superman* of 1951. John Gale proudly sent the news to Frank (holidaying somewhere in the Aegean) in what was probably his first managerial cable, complete with pre-paid reply, presumably for any instructions from the director. The full exchange was, 'DENISONS TRANSFERRING WYNDHAM'S. GALE', and, in reply, 'CLEVER, CLEVER PUSSIES. FRANK.' We ran through the summer and on to the end of October, and, in the process, broke the long-running record for the play. Even more important, we were now at last considered theatre people by the theatre world.

When we opened in London we had to give another interview to *The Stage*, apologising for not being on the road, and promising to tour *Candida* when its London run was over.

Over the pantomime season there were no dates available for touring, so Dulcie did another Maugham (*The Letter*) for ITV. We learned in 1984 from our faithful friend Peter Willes that Somerset Maugham considered her the definitive Leslie Crosbie.

In 1978, the Christie family said the same of her Miss Marple. It was particularly poignant for Dulcie to play Leslie, as her parents had known the originals of the characters in Malaya.

We then went off to stay with friends in the South of France – and such friends. We have known Anne and Antony Norman now for more than thirty years. We were introduced to them by Stormont Mancroft, that brilliant and outstandingly witty former barrister, junior minister, business executive, contributor to *Punch*, and now hard-working member of the Upper House. He in turn had come into our lives through Rosie Headfort; and she, when I was for twenty-four hours a spy in Eire in the war (a story told in *Overture and Beginners*). Of such disparate material are forged the links of life-enriching friendships. The challenge of giving the flavour of such friendships without embarrassing the friend is, strangely enough, not dissimilar from the demands of a letter of condolence!

Anne's father was a highly successful Welsh ship-owner, and her mother an enthusiastic art collector with a happy predilection for Renoir. Antony's father was a very independent Liberal MP, an adventurous traveller through Russia and the Far East at the turn of the century, and a most vivid chronicler of his travels; he also wrote one excellent comedy (with a perceptive foreword by his friend Bernard Shaw) which he sent to Gladys Cooper, who sadly – and I believe unwisely – turned it down. Antony's mother, whom we met, was a daughter of Lord Aberconway – one of a family of inspired gardeners, creators of the famous gardens at Bodnant in Wales and later at La Garoupe on the Cap d'Antibes. There, Antony has worked knowledgeably and imaginatively to develop and embellish the staggering natural beauty of his inheritance into a work of art as remarkable as anything with which Anne has adorned their walls.

Antony is one of the fortunate few in whom an apparently effortless elegance goes beyond a wise choice of tailor and shirtmaker. He can be tough and dogmatic, and those who offend his values socially or politically are not suffered lightly. In Anne he met his match – not as a rival but a complement. Her elegance is on the same level as his, but, as befits a woman, more consciously contrived. She leads the way in her knowledge and love of painting, and books, and above all of good speaking in the theatre.

Individually and jointly they are intensely disciplined. But if that suggests a grim inflexibility, nothing could be further from the truth. A visit to their home is literally out of this world – a holiday from life, from which one returns refreshed in body, and also in spirit, for the house is full of interesting people and books and good talk. Despite appearances they are not in fact immune from the 'thousand natural shocks that flesh is heir to', but in facing them, their discipline once more comes to their aid, and their crises are never paraded.

On this particular visit we were to lunch with Antony's mother on Christmas Day, and Anne warned us that her mother-in-law could be difficult with strangers – particularly younger female strangers. Her strong personality, which had blossomed in the Nineties, had developed into eccentricity in old age. For instance, there was an Anglican chapel (built by her father on the estate), which had been long neglected. Antony decided to have it re-dedicated, and indicated that he expected his mother to attend. This she did reluctantly; but when the priest spoke the words, 'Thou didst not abhor the Virgin's womb,' she swept out, saying in ringing tones, 'I did not come here to listen to pornography.'

Lady Norman began her conversation with Dulcie pretty loftily:

Lady Norman: I understand from Anne, Mrs Denison, that you're an actress.
Dulcie: Yes, that's right.
Lady Norman: What have you been acting in recently?
Dulcie: *Candida*.
Lady Norman: *Candida*! Bernard Shaw's *Candida*?
Dulcie: Yes.
Lady Norman: And what part did you play in *Candida*?
Dulcie: Candida.
Lady Norman: And where did you play it?
Dulcie: At Wyndham's.
Lady Norman: In the West End?!
Dulcie: Yes. It was the longest ever run of the play.
Lady Norman: Ah. Congratulations. I knew Bernard Shaw you know. I used to go to his meetings. They were chaired by the most frightening woman I ever came across – Mrs Mandell Creighton, wife of the Bishop of London. She wore very long black boots which stuck out under the table.

Dulcie: She was my Aunt's mother. I often saw her as a child.

Even that tenuous relationship with Mrs Creighton was enough to produce vibrations in Lady Norman; and in the years ahead, when she had relinquished the château to Antony and moved into a smaller house on the estate, we were always invited to pay a courtesy call.

II
1961

The tour at last – Ionescu at Oxford – Boyd QC and the judiciary – rendezvous with the Lord Mayor – Heartbreak House – Michael Equity negotiator with ITV – 'The Strike' – 'The Strike' concluded

We enjoyed the tour of *Candida* as much as we had the London run, and were sad indeed to say goodbye to our colleagues, who had been with us for nearly a year. Incidentally, although our London record of 160 performances was recently surpassed by Deborah Kerr's *Candida*, if you add our ninety-odd in the provinces to our London total, our record is secure. (For some reason, the statistics of long runs both in Britain and America take no account of touring performances. This is manifestly unfair; I can think of some performances on the road which should count double.)

Frank wanted to follow up *Candida* with a revival of *Heartbreak House*, but owing to *Boyd* this had to be postponed until the autumn. There was just time before the series to do an Ionescu double bill of *The Bald Prima Donna* and *The Chairs* at Oxford and Cambridge, which kept some of the *Candida* cast together for a few weeks longer. The plays were directed by Harold Lang, a most perceptive young actor and director; and they are memorable to me for a remark he made while Dulcie and I were grappling with the intense technical and emotional problems of *The Chairs* – which include bringing thirty-six chairs on to the stage and filling them with people visible to the two aged characters in the play but not to the audience.

Harold made the point that, in everyday life, what the individual wants at any given moment is frequently at odds with what he is saying or doing under the pressures of the law, sex, economics, religion, social customs, etc.; and that therefore, in the theatre, it is important for actors not only to understand (and project) what they are saying, but also to know what their

109

characters *want*. A well-written play will provide the performers with ample clues for this hidden motivation; but often, in my experience, where the playwright has not done the job for us, it is both necessary and helpful for us to invent our 'wants'. These, if truly consistent with the character, may even be as interesting as what is said and done, and cannot fail to give greater depth of focus to a characterisation. What Harold was offering us, however, was a stimulating idea to help with the actor's unchanging duty to his public, to hold 'a mirror up to nature'; it was not an invitation to wallow in introspection as an end in itself. Harold died young, but I still try to act on his advice when studying and rehearsing a new part.

This year's penultimate series of *Boyd* marked the peak of its acceptance by the legal profession. One day I was sitting in on a trial at the Bailey listening to Maxwell Turner (who we knew as the husband of that splendid actress, Fabia Drake) cross-examining an expert witness for the Crown. It was an impressive performance, which inch by inch and with many pauses transformed a bland and assured Harley Street psychiatrist into a fallible mortal. While the unfortunate witness struggled with a particularly awkward question, Max Turner turned his back on him and saw me. He leant down, scribbled something on a piece of paper, folded it and handed it to his junior, indicating where I was sitting. The piece of paper made its way towards me by various hands, watched by the whole Court – or so I felt. It read: 'Dear Michael, most gratified. It is I who usually pick up tips from you! Max.'

Some years later, in response to an invitation from the Editor of *Verdict*, the Oxford University Law Society's Magazine, I attempted a summing-up of my happy relationship with lawyers arising out of *Boyd*:

That there is a link between the Law and what actors, with sublime effrontery, still call 'the Profession' is the hoariest of clichés – in other words, patently true. But what is it exactly? To the man in the street it means quite simply that barristers spend their whole time in court behaving like actors, which by his definition means dressing up, showing off and being grossly overpaid for putting forward arguments they don't believe in and exhibiting emotions they do not feel in language that is often unintelligible. This is hardly complimentary to either profession – though I must confess that as a spectator in the courts I have experienced moments of mystery as profound as any produced by the dramatists of the theatre of non-communication ... It may be true that among the legal ranks are a number of actors manqués or non-manqués – I wouldn't know – but it is certainly not the whole truth. No, the link is subtler than this and is, I believe, forged by both sides. If some of you have a sound working knowledge of the tricks of our trade, we are no strangers to the perils, delights and responsibilities of advocacy.

The actor is in fact a highly specialised advocate – the playwright's advocate – and appears only for the defence. Like the barrister he must cut elegant but not too flashy figures on the thick ice and skate swiftly and unobtrusively over the thin; like him again the actor must always be aware of the effect he is producing, not because he loves himself – he may do so of course, but this is not essential – but because only so can he be sure that his message is getting over. And this is his passionate purpose, however urbanely disguised.

If play or part is good the actor should be able to win his case – or in other words make the public co-operate in the creation of a work of art; if poor, he has the lawyer's duty of putting things in the most favourable light. In fact I think the actor's ethic of loyalty to a weak or lost cause is identical with what I understand to be the barrister's; and incidentally – and is this another parallel? – often produces performances which are the admiration of his colleagues, if not (for obvious reasons) of the public at large.

What else do we share? Even our styles and fashions of performance go hand in hand. In both professions there is at present a distaste for what one might call ham and ego, for the cult of the larger-than-life personality. Is it because of this change of taste that people ask us who we have today to compare with the giants of old – or are we lesser men? Are we in the lack-lustre grip of mediocrity or is the general level so much higher that the peaks hardly show? I will hazard an answer applicable to my profession, though whether to the Law I do not know. I believe that if Irving were alive today he would be at the head of the profession, as would Olivier have been eighty years ago; both, being great actors, would have instinctively adapted their genius to the style of the period; both would have transcended it. That said, I believe Irving would have found the going tougher in the 1960s than would Olivier in the 1880s. Part of the price that has had to be paid for material progress in 'the century of the common man' has been a growing, inhibiting suspicion of the uncommon man. To the extent that we allow ourselves to drift on this ungenerous tide we are not only lesser men ourselves but diminish the impact and opportunities for genius among our contemporaries.

A melancholy bond between our professions is that little or nothing survives us of the best of our performances in court or theatre except in the diminishing whisper of old law reports and faded press cuttings. What evidence there of a splendid voice, an eagle eye, the silence or laughter surrounding a riveting presence?

We both need clarity of mind and diction, self-discipline, good health, a sense of humour and a love of words. The links are legion.

Among the judges, my special hero was Carl Aarvold. I had admired him first in my schooldays when he was a regular member of the English three-quarter line for five seasons. He was now Common Sergeant (surely one of the most inappropriate titles for a high legal dignitary) and was soon to become Mr Recorder; and he seemed to me to combine, in apparently effortless balance, grave authority with humour, and the need for discipline with the quality of mercy.

Our first meeting with him was a memorable one. He came up to me in full Court dress at a Mansion House banquet and said, 'You won't know me. But I'm a fan of yours. My name is Judge Aarvold.' I could hardly tell a judge that I was a fan of his – though I was; but I could invite him down to the studios to see a programme being recorded, which he and his family seemed to enjoy. His counter-invitation was to the Royal Box at Wimbledon, where he still serves as President of the Lawn Tennis Association. There was no doubt about our enjoyment of that.

We had got to that particular banquet in a surprising manner. In 1924, at the age of eight, I had left a sheltered and comfortable home for the rigours of Wellesley House, a boarding school at Broadstairs. (I was a child of total innocence, which derived not from virtue but from a total ignorance, of which Lady Bracknell would surely have approved. For instance, though on clear days within sight of the French coast, I had no conception of a foreign race or land or language; and when set to learn the present tense of *avoir* I asked what it was.) The food at this establishment compared unfavourably with home cooking, except in one glorious respect. Every Thursday for breakfast we had the most delicious sausages.

One Thursday I was sitting next to a rather chubby little boy who refused his sausage. 'You must be out of your mind,' I said – or the 1924 eight-year-old equivalent. 'I'm not allowed to by my religion,' he replied gently. 'I'm a Jew.' I didn't understand that either at the time, but a wave of sympathy engulfed me for his sausageless future – a sympathy (which time has done nothing to diminish) eventually to be extended to his race. We became and remain friends, and when, as Sir Bernard Waley Cohen, my chubby friend became Lord Mayor of London, he invited us to the inaugural Midsummer Banquet which he had designed to bring together the learned and artistic professions. As we were leaving the glittering scene, Dulcie said to our host, 'I do hope we can return your hospitality one day.' 'Delighted,' said Bernard, 'but it'll have to be Sunday week. That's the last day I've got left in my calendar for the year.' 'Now, what have I done?' said Dulcie to me in the car. But thanks to our old friend John Stais of the White Tower, not only was a superb meal placed before our guests but a very smart volunteer force from the restaurant came to serve it on their night off.

Heartbreak House came successfully to Wyndham's in the autumn, with Roger Livesey (despite intermittent trouble with his voice) bringing his potent personal magic to Captain Shotover. I had wanted to play the part myself – I still do – but it was another marvellous consequence of *Boyd* that I was to some extent responsible for giving Roger, now and four years later as Lord Caversham in *An Ideal Husband*, two such splendid parts at the end of his career. He had been my first leading man when I emerged from the army, in Priestley's *Ever Since Paradise*, and there was a big debt of gratitude to repay. Dulcie and Judy Campbell were his vividly contrasted daughters (the latter coming closer than any other Hesione I have seen to having eyes 'like the fishpools of Heshbon') and Perlita Neilson, tiny, cool and bright as a button, was Ellie.

There was a macabre incident during rehearsals on the stage of the Lyric Hammersmith. As Hector Hushabye I had long periods of sitting around and I was glancing through a pile of yellowing newspapers which I had found back-stage. One was a *Daily Express* (I think) of 1938, and on its front page was a review of a play called *Death on the Table*, including a favourable mention for one of the actors – John D. Salew. On stage at that moment was John Salew rehearsing the part of Boss Mangan. At the end of the rehearsal I gave him the paper; he confirmed that it referred to him, and we all expressed astonishment at the coincidence. He died that night in the train on his way home.

(On a happier but no less bizarre note, some five or six years ago I was filming one of the early episodes of *The Professionals*. The final confrontation with Cowley – I was a baddie – took place in the attic of a derelict building, the floor of which was covered with newspapers. I had to come into the room and stop at a precise spot. Would I like a mark on the floor to help, I was asked. 'No,' I replied, 'I'll use one of these bits of paper.' While waiting for the lighting to be finalised, I looked down at the paper, and there staring up at me was a photograph of Jeremy Spenser, our Marchbanks, and an article by Harold Hobson praising Dulcie's Candida and looking forward to my Shotover.

In 1984, I played the Bishop of Lax in *See How They Run* at the Shaftesbury for Ray Cooney's Theatre of Comedy company. The action takes place in a country vicarage in 1944, and the period newspaper on the set contained on its front page the story of the attack by the Greek Communist guerillas on my unit in Athens in December of that year. A third remarkable coincidence. To paraphrase Noël Coward, 'Strange, how potent old newspapers are.')

Apart from two or three years in the Fifties when I had not stood for election because of absences from London (in South Africa and Stratford) and the early pressures of *Boyd*, I had been attending Council and Executive Committee meetings at Equity's Harley Street headquarters every Tuesday that I was in London since 1949. I was now once again Vice-President. Suddenly the tempo of meetings began to quicken alarmingly. Storm clouds of disagreement with the ITV companies, long visible on the horizon, were suddenly overhead, and I found myself in an even hotter seat than during the film campaign of the Fifties. Boyd had made me the blue-eyed boy of the ITV network; Equity asked me to be one of the small group of negotiators who would be battling out a vital matter of principle with employers who had in fact transformed my career for the better. It was an invitation I could not refuse, but I cannot pretend I looked forward to the prospect with any pleasure. I was however fortunate in my fellow negotiators – notably André Morell, Robert Flemyng, Ernest Clark and above all Equity's General Secretary, Gerald Croasdell, a man who in my opinion did more for the acting profession during his twenty-five years with the union than anyone before or since.

In order to understand the risks accepted, the hardships suffered and the discipline shown by my profession in the winter of 1961-62 – and in particular to understand why so unlikely a trade unionist as I was prepared once more to put my career at hazard – it is necessary to go back to the birth of ITV in 1954. Before that, the importance (and dangers) of television to performers and public were only discernible to far-sighted pioneers like Norman Collins. The BBC thought of it as no more than a junior branch of radio – one reason why Norman resigned from the Corporation to form ATV with his personal savings. But when in 1953 the government produced its proposals for ITV, Equity and the other entertainment unions woke up with a vengeance. It would be only too easy, they realised, for the new stations to import material which had already covered its cost of production abroad and could therefore be sold more cheaply than any comparable programme originating in Britain – in other words the old problem of the film industry in a new context.

But whereas, in the theatre and in films, Equity had been the prisoner of precedents and practices established either before it was formed or before its organisation was a force to be reckoned with, in television, for the first time, the union was there in strength before the medium had become big business, and indeed the major employer for its members. Hitherto, as we have seen, a 30 per cent quota (all too easily evaded) was the maximum government protection available to British films; the Television Act of 1954 provided that a proper proportion of programmes should be of British origin and performance. This pious hope (recently echoed in the proposals for cable television) was transformed by the far-sighted drive of Gordon Sandison into a 'gentleman's agreement' whereby a quota of 86 per cent was achieved and sustained. The BBC could hardly appear less patriotic than ITV and soon fell into line. This was the foundation on which British television has built its world-wide reputation.

It was a crucial victory. Just consider. A union founded when

80 per cent or more of performances were live, operates today in a world where 70 per cent are recorded.

Already, even by the end of the Fifties, new recording techniques and the use of cinema films on television, *without any payment to their casts*, were cutting in to the work available in the new medium. In addition, there was the growing impact of TV on cinema and theatre attendances (and therefore to an extent on performers' livelihoods) – calculated as a drop of 11 per cent in the first year, 42 per cent in the second and settling thereafter to an average of 30. As Gerald Croasdell put it in Equity's 1960 report:

> The time has long passed when a performance was an ephemeral thing ending with the fall of the curtain and needing the physical presence of the performer for any repetition. The performance can now be separated from the performer, transported all over the world and used to the profit of the employer and, unless most strictly controlled, to the detriment not only to the further employment of the original performer but ... also of his colleagues.

And so the principle of relating television fees to the size of the potential audience – a principle in some form inherent in all branches of entertainment – was seen by Equity to be something upon which a stand must be made. By the employers it was seen as a whittling down of their sovereign rights – which of course it was. Hence the embattled positions taken up by both sides.

In terms of financial strength, the opponents were ill-matched. Of Equity's then membership of 10,000, only 400 to 600 earned more than £2000 a year. The income of the dozen ITV companies, by contrast, was £78 million; and one of the leading companies made a profit of £$6\frac{1}{2}$ million out of a revenue of £$9\frac{1}{2}$ million.

In March 1961, Equity opened its campaign. It proposed first an increase of the 10 guinea minimum fee for a performance shown by one of the smaller companies (which could then for no further payment be broadcast on the network); and secondly that 'points' should be allocated to each of the ITV regions so that, for any showing outside the region of origin, performers would receive extra payment in accordance with the appropriate total of points. The system should, we suggested, be extended to regions overseas so as to rationalise and encourage the sale of programmes abroad.

These constructive proposals were in effect ignored by the employers and at the end of June the Council instructed the members to accept no engagements with the ITV companies after 1 November. In the absence of any significant movement by the employers, the instruction duly took effect.

I have described this action as a 'so-called strike' – and that is accurate. A strike involves a downing of tools, a breach of contracts, a walk-out. The Equity action involved not a single contract being broken. Its strength was that we were not walking out, but refusing to walk in – refusing jobs we had not got but which no one else could do; its weakness was that the working out of existing contracts took time, thereby prolonging the hardship of the members and delaying the full impact of the action until the New Year. The climax of our campaign was an inspiring meeting at Drury Lane in February 1962 – the largest gathering of Equity members to date. It was addressed by Felix Aylmer (then in the fourteenth of the twenty years in which he brought experience, statesmanship and humour to the Presidency of the union), by Gerald Croasdell (the key speech), and finally by myself. Felix and Gerald were quite a double act to follow, but I was proud to have been asked to do so. I give here two brief extracts from what I said:

For ten months the companies failed to spell out their objections to our original proposition. Was it, as we came to assume, because they thought it wouldn't work? No. At our last meeting with them the truth was out at last. Their objection was because it would work; it would strengthen performers' bargaining power at all levels; and they were frightened of it. Which put us in the ironical position of saying 'Oh, don't be too frightened. As rich and powerful employers, you would still have the edge in dealing with a profession that will always be chasing too few jobs.

Our principle is good in itself. Is it nevertheless inappropriate to our relations with ITV? No. It would give us what we want without jeopardising their prosperity. We have after all a (small) vested interest in that prosperity!

So. Do we stick to our principle or do we give in? The Council prefers the first alternative.

Is the membership's need for a quick solution so pressing that you ask us to resort to the gamble of arbitration?

On the level of fees, arbitration might produce an acceptable compromise; but on the principle, which could not be split, it would be all or nothing. We cannot risk it being nothing.

The meeting ended with such firm support for the Council that the companies had no alternative but to re-open negotiations; and soon a solution was achieved which gave Equity the essence of its demands. (On Christmas Day, some humorist at Rediffusion had put on *The Glass Mountain*, thereby turning the strike-leader into an involuntary – unpaid – strike-breaker.)

There was, at least for me, a fascinating postscript to all this. In 1971 the late Sir Frederick Leggett (who had a long and distinguished career in the Civil Service, much of it with the Ministry of Labour) wrote an account of his involvement in the 1935 dispute between Equity and the Managers, out of which, as his brain-child, was born the London Theatre Council, which orders negotiations, discipline and disputes in the West End to this day. In his document, Leggett quotes from a speech made by Lewis Casson to a members' meeting in 1935. Lewis said: 'We can only keep our power by means of the Equity "shop" ... If we called a strike tomorrow I am sure we could depend upon the loyalty of our members and that we would close every theatre in London. We are not going to do it; we are going to try a much harder task ... we are going to win this fight by the refusal of every single member of Equity to sign any contract which is not the Equity contract ...'

I don't know whether my fellow negotiators of 1961-62 knew of this speech. I certainly did not. But it was extraordinary to find that doughty old militant advocating so clearly, a quarter of a century earlier, the identical limited use of Equity's 'muscle' which had been our own policy.

Twenty years on, in 1983, there was an abortive attempt by the Council to call a strike in the provincial theatre. Besides quite properly instructing members to sign no new contracts, it instructed certain categories – improperly in my view – to break existing contracts. At the eleventh hour the strike call was cancelled. I like to think it was because most members felt as I do, and as Lewis Casson did, and that they will continue to do so in the future.

Meanwhile *Heartbreak House* had come to an end, and with no *Boyd* in prospect for the first time in six years the outlook was bleak.

III
1962

Michael to Australia to play Higgins in My Fair Lady – *Dulcie joins him* – Village Wooing *in Hong Kong – Greek holiday – Shakespeare in Berlin – opening the Ashcroft – Michael compère for Joan Sutherland – Oxford Law Society*

Into this vacuum came a cable from John McCallum in Australia asking me to do a three-month season as Higgins in *My Fair Lady* in Melbourne. (John, an Australian by birth, was at this time an executive of J. C. Williamson, the major producing and theatre-owning management in Australia and New Zealand. Googie Withers, his wife, in a heart-warming gesture of unselfishness, had turned her back on a highly successful career in England to emigrate with him; they and their children were now happily established in Melbourne, where Googie lost no time in becoming the theatrical queen of Australia. In the ensuing years she has made many successful forays to Britain and America, and seems, deservedly, to have had the best of both worlds.) John had in fact approached me to be the first Higgins in Australia three years before, but he had wanted me for eighteen months; not only was that too long a separation from Dulcie, but, in any case, *Boyd* made it impossible. Three months was much more like it, and I gratefully cabled acceptance.

I was offered the choice of going East-about or West-about. I had never been to America, and so it was arranged that I should spend two nights in New York and report on a couple of shows that John was interested in; this meant that I could also see the El Greco landscape of 'Toledo by Moonlight' (which did not disappoint), do some basic sightseeing, and get lost after a backstage visit to Zia Moyheddin, who was repeating his London performance in Frank Hauser's production of *A Passage to India*. From New York I flew westwards to Honolulu, where I spent a couple of hilarious sunny days surrounded by blue-rinse matrons who had unwisely taken to the local costume, and their menfolk

119

whose conversation appeared to be limited to travel arrangements. Then on to Sydney airport for a hurried press conference ('Boyd here to play Higgins') and off to Brisbane, where I was to rehearse with the company which was coming to the end of its Queensland season.

I had seen the show at Drury Lane on my last night in England; now I saw it just over a week later on my first night in Australia – and I was greatly impressed. The Australian company had been together now for a gruelling three years, yet the performance I saw was quite up to Drury Lane standard, with an excellent Eliza (Bunty Turner from Ulster) and Doolittle (Richard Walker) and an Australian chorus full of verve and in glorious voice.

I had a great welcome back-stage after the show, and the next morning started work in earnest – though mostly with the understudies, to save the principals' energies for the evenings. In charge was the company manager, a dear man built like a tank, who in the early stages 'played' Eliza for me. I shall never forget towing this monument of Australian manhood up Higgins' stairs, with him bawling 'Naow. I'm a good girl I am.'

I had learnt the lyrics of my numbers on the journey, but still had the considerable task of mastering the Professor's dialogue and fitting into the production in three weeks. Suddenly there came a bombshell. 'We're all tired out,' said Bunty to me early in my first week, 'and looking forward to our holiday.' 'What holiday?' I asked, mystified. 'Well, it takes them four or five days to get the scenery down to Melbourne and set up again. After all, it's nearly a thousand miles. So when we close here at the end of next week they're giving us a week's holiday.'

'And what happens to me?'

'Oh you get a holiday too.'

I was stunned. Not only were my three weeks reduced to two, but I would be doing nothing in the week before I opened in Melbourne. A recipe for disaster.

It was agreed, at my insistence, that I should give two of the last three performances in Brisbane – which involved a rehearsal period of only nine and a half working days. I may not have been the most distinguished Higgins but I was certainly the quickest. I suppose Boyd's experience of 'weekly rep in an iron lung' came to my assistance. It was traumatic nevertheless, and I was piloted through the show by Eliza and company on stage, and by my devoted 'rehearsal Eliza' behind the scenes where, what with the darkness and two revolving stages, an experienced guide was vital. The company – as well as the audience – applauded me at the end. Very unprofessional, but very touching. Had I been a Russian I would have applauded back.

In spite of the terror, I enjoyed Brisbane. I knew I was abroad. It was hot and humid; there was Surfer's Paradise on the doorstep, palm trees and a skyful of little green parrots arriving punctually for their afternoon snack. There was a pleasant drive up to Toowoomba for lunch in a splendid old Australian mansion with its splendid old Australian owner – Miss Lethbridge; and there was a concert, with Malcolm Sargent, his shirt-front and waistcoat just that degree whiter than anyone else's, conducting the National Anthem as though it was a newly discovered masterpiece.

By contrast, my week off in Melbourne was a vacuum of loneliness, homesickness and increasing trepidation as the opening approached. This was nobody's fault, least of all John McCallum's, who had done everything possible for my comfort. It was in part a natural reaction from the hectic experiences of the immediate past, which had filled my life to overflowing; now I had my first chance to realise that I was 'down under', nine thousand miles away from England, home and Dulcie. Also, in the Melbourne autumn climate I didn't feel abroad any more, though I knew I wasn't at home.

The feeling of being nowhere was accentuated by the Athenaeum Club, where I was staying. On my first evening I was informed that dinner was served at 6.20 pm. I duly arrived at 6.19 in the vast dining-room – which was already laid for next day's lunch. Acres of white linen and shining cutlery at round tables confronted me, but no sign of staff or members. Which table, which chair of three hundred should I choose? I made my choice and was studying a menu when I was suddenly aware that I was not alone. I looked up to see an old man, his complexion matching the table linen, who was quivering with emotion. 'You're in my chair,' he said. It was a moment to be recorded by H. M. Bateman. I made my apologies and moved; and we were soon joined by six other octogenarians, who made up the tally of residents. When they had got used to dining with an actor, and talking to an actor and listening to an actor (who at forty-seven must have seemed a mere boy), we became great friends. They all came to see the show and we eventually parted with real regret.

Higgins was my toughest professional assignment until *The*

Black Mikado burst upon me thirteen years later. Intellectually, physically and vocally it was a major test. I suppose I only did just over a hundred performances; and so my admiration for Rex Harrison, Robin Bailey (my predecessor in Australia), Brian Aherne (who did a National tour in the States), Tony Britton (who actually holds the record) and any other long-distance runners unknown to me is boundless. It was a comprehensive theatrical education in itself; I certainly felt I emerged from it a more complete performer, even though I lost a stone in the process.

This was due less to the rigours of the part than to the then licensing laws of the state of Victoria, which made it virtually impossible to get a meal and a drink after the show. As I soon found that dinner at 6.20 was a fatal preliminary to Higgins' six 'arias', I was reduced to sandwiches in my club bedroom afterwards, except when Bunty or her hospitable friends Bill and Margaret Gluth took pity on me. But even the Gluths were not regular nightbirds. In fact, Melbourne was a dead city when we came out of the theatre; what seems remarkable, looking back, was that anyone stayed up long enough to come to the show.

But come they certainly did. In fact I would wager that a higher percentage of the population saw *My Fair Lady* in Australia than anywhere else on earth – the reason no doubt being that Shaw's joke about Cockney and posh accents encapsulated the love-hate relationship between our two countries. Eliza was Australia's very own Cinderella, and Higgins the archetypal 'Pom'. Even the price that Eliza has to pay in terms of mastering un-Australian vowels is worth it for the humbling of Higgins – that Prince whose charm is his lack of it.

(My Eliza's career was an extraordinary one. Found, when quite unknown, by John McCallum at a London audition, Bunty became the toast of Australia for three years or so – deservedly. She was a good Eliza, luckily for me, and a dedicated professional who was still working at her performance and her voice when I joined the column. She then returned to England and the professional obscurity from which she had emerged; found the English winter a penance; was engaged to play Eliza in South Africa, married a lawyer in Cape Town and retired.)

Back at home, Dulcie was having a pretty frustrating time. Fortunately by now there was always a crime story to be written, an invaluable antidote to the crisis of confidence associated with 'resting'. (How strange is the terminology of the actors' world. 'Work' and 'play', instead of being opposites, are synonyms. 'Play' and 'resting', for us, are poles apart.) The book this time was *Murder in Mind*. Frank Hauser had given her the idea; but her own imaginative processes kept rejecting the 'foreign' tissue, and in the end Frank's idea only appeared – most effectively – in the book's closing pages.

(There have been three extraordinary coincidences connected with Dulcie's crime stories, of which *Murder in Mind* provided the first. The climax of the story revolves around the chance discovery by the central character of a dead body at High Beech, a well-known beauty spot in Epping Forest. During the writing of it, Dulcie asked me one day to enquire at our local police station in Albany Street whether the Woodford or Epping police would be in charge of enquiries. The answer, I think, was Epping. Imagine my feelings when the *Evening Standard*'s headline the following night was 'Murder at High Beech' ... Her 1967 offering was *The Murder of Love*, a particularly scarifying study – even by Dulcie's standards, which are not for the squeamish – of a psychopathic killer. The name she conjured out of the air for him was Manson – two years before that name reverberated round the world in connection with the bestial group-killings in California. Lastly, in 1981, Dulcie set *Dark Calypso* in a Caribbean island paradise which became the storm centre of East-West tension. She called her island Renata – two years before the American invasion of Grenada.)

During my stay in Melbourne Dulcie and I had some emotional telephone calls – at dawn for one of us and dusk for the other – but the miracle of communication only emphasised our separation, and the conversations were full of banalities as the golden minutes ticked away, like farewells at railway stations after the carriage doors are shut. I made up my mind to do something dynamic. Through contacts I had made at the Australian Broadcasting Corporation, I suggested that before I left Australia I should do a TV play for them. They were happy to cash in on the presence of 'Boyd' in Australia, and I was emboldened to suggest that the play should be *Village Wooing* and that Dulcie should play the other part. They jumped at the idea but couldn't afford her fare from England. However, we worked out that the joint performance fees would finance her round trip – tourist. I rang her again, but this time really with something to say. Was she still free? She was. Would she like to do *Village Wooing* with me in

Australia? She would. 'Then come as soon as you can, my darling.'

Dulcie's landing at Melbourne airport provided comedy as well as emotion. The press, there in force for my reunion with 'my fair lady', gathered round the first-class ladder; I, hugging to myself my shameful knowledge of Dulcie's economy status, positioned myself strategically under the wing. To my astonishment she emerged from the first-class door. The explanation was that, exhausted by the long haul from London to Sydney (thirty-six hours in those days), she had been befriended on the final short hop to Melbourne by a charming young air hostess, who had installed her in the virtually empty first-class compartment.

I had found us a totally impersonal flat in a grey mansion block called Cliveden, and there we went to pick up the threads of our life again – both of us exhausted, Dulcie by her journey and I by a most persistent Antipodean 'flu for which eight Higginses a week were scarcely what the doctor ordered. Within days, inevitably, Dulcie had caught it too. However, better days were just around the corner.

John and Googie had suggested that if they couldn't persuade me to extend my Australian season – and they couldn't – I should try to see whether the British Council, that sadly underfunded department of the Foreign Office, might not like to make use of us on our way home. I duly rang the Council's representative in Sydney, whose accent put my Higgins in the shade.

'Would you really do that for us?' he said. 'How frightfully kind. What? Just one moment, Mr Denison. What is it, Susan? Oh really? I say Mr Denison, may I ring you back. I've just heard the office is on fire!'

Clearly the spirit of Drake was not dead. When communication was resumed (the fire had been confined to the waste-paper basket), he promised to contact Hong Kong and Bangkok for us and offer them *Village Wooing*. Hong Kong was delighted; but from our man in Bangkok came a very haughty cable saying that *Village Wooing* wouldn't do at all but if we would present a Shakespeare programme with at least five changes of costume they could offer us a total of £37 for two performances. I must have spent most of the proposed fee on my cabled reply. I explained that we didn't in fact travel an expensive Elizabethan wardrobe with us and that to hire it in Australia and transport it to Bangkok and back would probably cost us £4-500; it would be cheaper for us to visit Thailand as tourists, which indeed we would do.

After recording *Wooing* in Australia (where it broke the existing appreciation figures for a play in Victoria), we flew off for my first sight of Singapore, a city with many memories of adolescence and family tragedies for Dulcie, who was seeing it again for the first time in twenty-six years. The architectural changes which were to transform Singapore, by our next visit, from a charming horizontal garden city into an oriental Manhatten were only just beginning, and so we found Orchard Road, where Dulcie's mother had had her last home, and the library which she had run so efficiently if eccentrically with the assistance of a crocodile and a python.

Then we were off to Hong Kong, the aerial approach to which is guaranteed to arouse the interest of even the most blasé inhabitant of 'Whicker's World'. Out of a blue impersonal sea appears a small conical island, then another and another at increasing tempo until, as the engines are throttled back, one is in the midst of an archipelago. Ahead is the high ridge of Hong Kong itself; we skirt it and head straight for a mountain on the mainland which is decorated with bold red and white chevrons indicating the urgent desirability of turning right (or left); this accomplished we appear to be about to ditch in the harbour; we are already lower than the blocks of flats in Kowloon when a runway materialises out of the water. A dramatic welcome indeed.

Nor did the social welcome disappoint. Clive Robinson and his wife Vera, the British Council representatives, looked after us as though we were old friends. They put us up in their flat on the beautiful south side of the island (the Council could not afford a hotel) and took infinite trouble with the practical problems of mounting and furnishing our performances; they ensured the necessary publicity but protected us from journalistic excesses; they guided us through the formalities of Government House, where happily the Governor, Sir Robert Black, was a friend of Dulcie's from Malaya; they took us swimming in Deep Water Bay, and on a day-long excursion through the New Territories and up to the border, where we picnicked overlooking China from a shady hill.

As we drove to their flat that first day through the August humidity, Clive explained that our visit had been made possible by a film distributor turned impresario, Harry Odell, who ha been a fan of ours since he had released *The Glass Mountain*.

There was also a delicate matter to be arranged. Hong Kong had two enthusiastic amateur dramatic societies, the Garrison Players and the Hong Kong Stage Club, who had each offered their services to us in the realms of set design, properties, lighting and stage management. The clubs were deadly rivals, and Clive proposed a judgment of Solomon which gave half the duties to each. We could only agree; and, enthusiastic and hard-working as they all were, it was like enlisting the Montagues and the Capulets in a joint enterprise on a particularly sultry afternoon in fair Verona. 'Will you *look* at that lighting?!' whispered Props to us scornfully. 'Have you *seen* the back-cloth?' hissed the Stage Manager. (It was indeed a bizarre account of the idyllic Wiltshire countryside, painted by a South African who had never been to England. Thatched cottages and willow trees were backed by a solid wall of sky-scrapers topped by television aerials. It needed a diplomatic approach to get these painted out in favour of blue sky and white clouds.) In the end all went well, and our helpers even sheathed their swords in the euphoria of the moment. We were in fact the first professionals to perform in what was then Hong Kong's new art centre.

Bangkok was our next port of call. We much enjoyed the Oriental Hotel overlooking the busy swift-flowing yellow river, the floating market, the temples and the royal barges; and we were entertained to lunch by the British Council representative who had received my cable from Australia. He was apologetic about the £37 but explained in extenuation that his budget for the autumn was already committed to one major 'manifestation'. A ballet company? No. A famous musician? No. Emlyn Williams? No. They were bringing out from England a distinguished professor to lecture – in a land abounding with creepy-crawlies – on English Wingless Beetles. On occasions like this it is easy to make fun of the British Council – easy but unfair. Much hard work and dedication are expended on its activities in circumstances which are unpropitious, often politically and almost always financially.

While we were in the Far East, our agency – which, as Linnit and Dunfee, had been absorbed some years previously by the oddly named Music Corporation of America (MCA) – ceased to exist overnight for some technical breach of the American anti-trust laws. Though fond of individuals in the set-up (notably Jack

Dunfee, and Kenneth Cleveland who had actually persuaded Rediffusion to use me for Boyd – a unique achievement on our behalf by MCA), we lost no sleep over its demise. Other agencies, keen to pick up its former clients, pursued us by cable on our homeward journey, but we decided to put them off until we got home.

We flew first to Athens. Ever since my war-time experiences in the liberation of Greece, I had longed to show Dulcie the land that had so fired my imagination after weary months of comfortable frustration in Egypt – and indeed to see more of it myself than the square mile of central Athens in which the liberators had been besieged by British-armed but ungrateful members of the Greek resistance.

So, after a week in the capital so hot that for the only time I can remember Dulcie could not even bring herself to window-shop, we hired a Volkswagen Beetle and set off for the romantic mountain country of the Peloponnese, exploring it first from the south shore of the Gulf of Corinth and then most happily from the port of Nauplion. There was an excursion to the famous theatre at Epidaurus, where the excitement of the local population persuaded Dulcie – in one of her more extravagant flights of fancy – that they were under attack by a swarm of bees. Actually it was an earthquake, which out of sheer inexperience we hadn't identified. We also visited Agamemnon's haunted hilltop at Mycenae, where our guide informed us that an English lord was engaged in an archaeological dig. It turned out to be Lord William Taylour, Rosie Headfort's younger son; and that evening we dined with him and his team in the garden of their taverna.

I was doing my stately breast stroke in the calm blue water below the hotel at Nauplion when Dulcie, whom I had left asleep, appeared excitedly on the beach. 'Darling, Laurie Evans has rung through from London to say that Rediffusion want to do another series of *Boyd* and can he be our agent?' My immediate reaction was that anyone who could locate me doing my breast stroke in Greek waters when en route from Bangkok to Heathrow deserved to be my agent.

A word about actors and agents – or more accurately about us and ours. In popular mythology, agents are credited with creating and directing the careers of their clients. In the ninety-odd years of our joint experience, that has rarely if ever been the case. Our work has been self-generated; our agents have argued terms, written awkward letters, come to see us perform, kept a record of our earnings for the Inland Revenue and themselves, and offered friendly advice and a shoulder to weep on. For the last twenty years or so, within the Evans organisation we have had the good fortune to be looked after by Ronnie Waters. A former actor who likes and understands actors and, crucially, is liked by our employers; tall, distinguished, with the last traces of a fine head of red hair; normally amused, occasionally panic-stricken, he is a fount of gossip (hardly ever malicious and, when it is, very funny) and a dear and trusted friend. For that alone he has earned his percentage – and our love. One day when discussing with him on the telephone what he should say in a letter to some management, I prefaced my suggestion with the words, 'I am just thinking aloud.' Ronnie appropriated the phrase and has used it ever since; but his version is 'I'm just talking aloud'!

It was marvellous to be home from our travels at the beginning of September and to see Eileen and Titus and the house. The Boyd deal was soon negotiated; we were invited (and accepted the offer) to open the Ashcroft Theatre in Croydon with a play about Henry VIII and his wives, of which more later; and then a mystery voice came on the telephone and said, 'What are you doing about your publicity in Berlin?' 'What we usually do,' I replied. 'And what is that?' 'Nothing.' 'Well, don't you think you'd better?' said the voice tetchily. 'You're giving a Shakespeare programme for the festival there in three weeks' time.'

It transpired that this had been arranged for us by MCA, whose collapse had prevented them getting word to us. We sent an SOS to Frank Hauser, who quite typically helped us choose the programme, and directed it. We were only away for a crowded forty-eight hours, during which I took our press conference in German (in the absence of an interpreter) and was miraculously granted fluency in a language I had barely spoken since interrogating my last German prisoner twenty years before. We gave our performance in the exquisite Oak Gallery of Charlottenburg Palace to resounding applause – one of the advantages of an oak gallery – lunched in blazing autumn sunshine at the Officers' Club by the lakeside at Wannsee and flew home.

Opening the Ashcroft was a great honour, but turned out a nightmare. The play (from the German) was intractable material. Having lost a stone playing Higgins, I was a sort of El Greco

Henry VIII, and not even the charm and talent of my wives, who included Dulcie, Gillian Raine and Polly Adams, nor the attendance of all South London's Mayors and their ladies, nor even the recitation by Dame Peggy of a specially commissioned poem by John Betjeman, could rescue the evening. Things were not improved by Croydon's inexperience at running a civic theatre; for instance, the box office closed for an hour in the early evening, just when one might have hoped for it to be besieged; and the stage doorkeeper, having been there all day, went home at five locking the dressing-room keys in his cubicle. Dulcie was unsuccessfully propositioned by an all-in wrestler who was operating in the adjacent concert hall; when he was equally unsuccessful with our very beautiful Anne Boleyn (Pamela Ann Davey), he felled her to the ground.

I must hasten to add that Croydon learned fast, and things have been better for a long time now; but my heart never warms to art complexes, which can so easily be more productive of complexes than art. Dressing-rooms at Croydon were frankly an afterthought, most of them only easily reachable by a lift, which cannot be used during a concert; and when, ten years later, we revived *Alice* there for Christmas, with a circus alongside in the Fairfield Hall, my dressing-room neighbour was the Boxing Kangaroo.

No sooner were we done with Croydon than I was approached to act as compère for Joan Sutherland in a television programme (to be recorded in Bristol) designed for her native Australia. Joan had severe back trouble at this time and was not allowed to make the long flight home, to the impatience of her compatriots who had not seen her since she had become a world star and were beginning to suspect – a not uncommon Australian suspicion – that she had risen above them. To fill the gap until she was able to return in person, she arranged to record six of her most famous arias. She would naturally have preferred an Australian compère but neither Robert Helpmann, Peter Finch nor Keith Michell was available so I was invited, on the basis of *My Fair Lady* and of *Boyd*.

It was a heavy day down at Bristol. I was fully engaged putting the arias into the context of those unlikely story-lines of grand opera, while Joan and Margarete Elkins (the Australian contralto) were busy performing them. I had no contact with either of them. We had a break at six and I made a rapid dash to where food and drink had been arranged. I was just about to raise a nut-brown whisky and soda to my lips when in came Miss Elkins – a golden-haired goddess in white lamé – whom I had only heard singing divinely in French and Italian. 'Do have this Miss Elkins,' I said, 'you've been working much harder than I have.' 'No thanks, too gassy,' rasped the goddess, in the tones of the unredeemed Eliza Doolittle.

My last memory of 1962 was speaking at the Oxford University Law Society dinner. On receiving the invitation I rang the secretary to explain that I was not a lawyer. 'Oh, we know that,' he said. 'Will anyone else be speaking?' 'Oh, yes.' 'Who?' 'No one you need worry about – Denning and Gardiner.' (The Master of the Rolls and a future Lord Chancellor . . .) Flattery on this scale was irresistible. The great men were charming, and it was Lord Denning who, having discovered that we had all been at Magdalen, said in his speech: 'What a remarkable coincidence that from the same college to speak at the same dinner there should come a judge, a silk and what I can only describe as an artificial silk.' In view of that splendid old car of ours waiting in the street, I might have replied that I too was Master of a Rolls. Unfortunately I didn't think of it until the small hours of the following morning – a striking illustration of the relative speeds of thought of Lord Denning and myself.

IV
1963

Overtures to Glen Byam Shaw – directors in the theatre – Binkie Beaumont's proposal – Where Angels Fear to Tread – *E.M. Forster*

Ever since my Stratford season in 1955 I had felt that on my own account, and still more on Dulcie's, there was unfinished business to be transacted between Glen Byam Shaw and ourselves. He (and Tony Quayle) had now handed over to Peter Hall at Stratford, and so Glen was back on the open market.

I have already described Dickie Bird's qualities as a director; Glen matches them in his attitude to the job, and surpasses them in the one respect that was vital to us at this moment. Whereas Dickie's *forte* was in light comedy, Glen's is in the classics – Shakespeare, Ibsen, Chekhov, Strindberg. After the hiatus in our joint career caused by my Australian excursion and what followed, there was an urgent need for us to return to the West End in a play which would erase memories of Croydon and revive those of *Candida* and *Heartbreak House*.

Would Glen be prepared to direct us in such a play? He would. He came to Regent's Park to discuss it. As evidence of the importance we attached to the meeting, Dulcie, who in those days smoked one cigarette a month, smoked ten in two hours.

I have known, respected and loved Glen since I was first directed by him when an Oxford undergraduate in a production of *Richard II* in 1936. In all that time the distinction of his appearance has remained unimpaired; the quiet voice and beautiful manners still cloak a will of steel. As a director he does not aspire to be a virtuoso, distorting the playwright's intentions to conform with a subjective vision which, however exciting, is almost certain to be self-indulgent. Glen is content to be an interpreter; but he brings to that rôle a level of research, taste, intuition and experience which, for my money, far outstrips the wilder excesses of the 'director's theatre'.

In my view, the theatre should never be dominated by writers, actors, directors or managements (let alone by critics). All the creative categories however have spheres in which their responsibilities are paramount, but the director is ultimately in command. Give me a playwright whose passionate commitment to his work is tempered by a readiness at least to listen to what the actors have to say – after all, when he is sitting impotently out front on the first night, it is they who occupy the firing line on his behalf.

The director's situation is not dissimilar, but is more complicated; for in addition to his more conventional duties he must keep the peace between players and playwrights (alive or dead), between both parties and himself, and between the whole production team and the management. Things are not only happier but usually more effective if he manages to pull off this many-sided technical and diplomatic feat. Usually, but not always. Happy companies may know failure; the less fortunate may achieve 'a strange heaven out of unbelievable hell'. But at least today it is no longer an axiom that theatrical pearls can *only* be the product of irritation; that unless a director has reduced junior members of a company to tears, and provoked one or more seniors to consider walking out he is not doing his job; nor (thanks to Equity) is it any longer an article of faith that a marathon dress rehearsal into the small hours is evidence of dedication (and even of deliberate policy to ensure that the company will face its critics too exhausted to suffer from first-night nerves) – when in fact it is only evidence of inefficiency.

A Month in the Country was our suggestion to Glen. He liked the idea and went away to re-read it – his only hesitation being whether our dates, which were dictated by the final series of *Boyd*, would clash with a commitment he had to Binkie Beaumont to do a new play for him.

The next development was an exciting surprise. Would we like to be in the new play for Binkie? For anyone of our theatrical generation the answer could only be yes; and when we learned that it was an adaptation of E.M. Forster's *Where Angels Fear to Tread*, and found that the parts of Caroline Abbotts and Philip Herriton were particularly rewarding, our joy knew no bounds.

Nor were we disappointed. The production was a considerable critical success, running in London and on tour for nine months or so. Keith Baxter – a Welshman – demonstrated a perfect theatrical affinity with the young Italian, to 'rescue' whose child the ill-fated expedition sets out from Tunbridge Wells; and Nan Munro as the angular spinster who precipitates the tragedy managed to be funny, awful and pitiable.

As an added bonus we saw quite a lot of Forster, who was enthusiastic about the adaptation by Elizabeth Hart (a tiny, short-sighted American blue-stocking) and was pleased with the performances – particularly Dulcie's and Keith's, the characters with which he was most in sympathy. (My character was a subtle and unflattering study of inhibited Anglo-Saxon attitudes, particularly that failure to 'connect' of which the author was so critical in himself. Just as Dulcie's Caroline reminded him of an abortive heterosexual romance, did my Philip perhaps put too clearly before him the reasons for its failure?) Dulcie was the recipient of a charming series of letters of diminishing formality: 'Dear Miss Gray – E.M. Forster' they began, and then 'Dear Dulcie Gray – E. Morgan Forster', finally reaching 'My Dear Dulcie – Morgan'.

It is said that everyone remembers what they were doing when they heard of Kennedy's assassination. In our case it was just before curtain-up at the St Martin's, so that, stunned by the news ourselves, we gave a performance to an audience which didn't know. It is an extraordinary fact that if you are performing a play of any weight when some earth-shattering event takes place, a line or passage of dialogue will suddenly acquire an intense topicality. So it was that night. One of us had a line about the ease with which the small and mean can destroy the great and generous. The significance of the words hung in the air between us – and for a moment we couldn't go on.

Every night Keith and I had a fight on stage, which culminated in his pulling my 'broken arm' away from its splint. Two minutes afterwards – as though by a stopwatch – members of the audience (usually male) would require the assistance of a specially reinforced detachment of the St John's Ambulance Brigade. (The same had happened in *Titus Andronicus* at Stratford when Tony Quayle so realistically cut off Larry Olivier's hand.)

As a preliminary to all this, and to put us in the mood, we had hired a car in Rome and driven north into Forster country, visiting Florence, Sienna, Urbino, San Gimignano and that haunted holy city of Assisi. We had to fly home on Easter Day but we spent the previous few days with old Stratford friends, John and Elizabeth Higgs, in their rented villa in the Alban hills.

On Easter Eve they dined with us in Rome and it was nearly midnight before we headed back to the villa. We stopped at San Clemente, a baroque church with an early Christian crypt where a dimly lit service was in progress. We were handed unlit candles, as we entered, by a smiling monk, and soon the church was in darkness apart from one candle on the altar. As midnight struck, other candles were lit from it until the church glowed with a slow crescendo of light – a most moving effect, but embarrassing for Dulcie who found that, alone of the congregation, she had been given two candles in the darkness.

V
1964

Silver Wedding – Shakespeare recital at home and abroad – the Queen's party for the profession – The Actor and His World – Hostile Witness *for Michael* – The Seagull *for Dulcie – Euphoria*

Almost our last date of the post-West End tour of *Angels* was in a wintry Blackpool. It was the first opportunity of *The Guardian*'s northern critic to see the show and, unlike his London colleague Philip Hope Wallace, he hated it. Forster must be turning in his grave at this travesty of a masterpiece – such was his general theme. It was with considerable relish that Binkie informed the paper not only of Forster's survival but of his enthusiasm.

Violet Farebrother, as my mother, dominated the one English scene in the play. We invited her for a drive to Blackpool's only accessible beauty spot, the Trough of Bowland. She was thrilled to climb up beside me on the front seat of the Rolls – it took her back, she said, to touring with Fred Terry who had been the love of her life. His wife Julia Neilson, we gathered, had been in the back seat – in every sense.

In April we celebrated our Silver Wedding. We had been married at St Saviour's Walton Street (just behind Harrods), and I thought – to Dulcie's initial embarrassment – that we should return there on the anniversary for a service of some kind. 'What a splendid idea,' said the new vicar. 'Nobody has suggested such a thing to me before.' And he promised to devise something for us, based on the marriage service.

On 29 April 1939 the church had been providentially filled with flowers for a smart wedding later that day; by a happy coincidence it was the same story on 29 April 1964. We sang 'Fight the good fight' – which gave Audrey Cameron the giggles – and the congregation, which included Ivy Every (widowed on the eve of her own Golden Wedding), Lewis and Sybil Casson and John and Lisel Gale seemed to enjoy it as much as we did. They all

135

came back to lunch at Regent's Park; and the next evening we had a drinks party for other friends. Among them was Jack Priestley who, having told us that he hated stand-up dos, was the first to arrive and was in scintillating form. Dulcie noticed however that he was beginning to flag, at just the moment that Stormont Mancroft arrived. 'Be a dear and go and entertain Mr Priestley,' she said to him. 'I think he's looking a little tired!' Stormont went over to Jack and addressed him with confident charm. 'Mr Priestley, my name is Stormont Mancroft. Dulcie has asked me to entertain you.' 'Then try,' said Jack.

1964 was the quatercentenary of Shakespeare's birth, and there were many performances and celebrations to commemorate it. Our contribution was a recital which we called 'Merely Players' (an expanded version of the Berlin performance) and we spent most of the summer taking it to Rome, Geneva, Montreux and a wide variety of English dates ranging from the Theatre Royal Bristol and the newly restored Regency Theatre in Bury St Edmunds, to the King's Lynn festival, Rhoda Birley's tithe barn in Sussex, and of course Rosehill.

We lunched with Miki Sekers in London first. (It is not easy to reproduce Miki's English on paper, but this anecdote requires the effort.) 'Michael, Dollcie,' he said over the inevitable glass of champagne, 'zees sing you do, do you read or do you aaact?' We explained that we came on with red folios which we placed on lecterns, but that we had in fact learnt the text, and therefore it was an acting performance. 'Sank God,' said Miki fervently. 'Why?' we asked. 'Well,' he said, 'some time ago zair came to Roz-heel Eedit (Edith Evans) to give a poetree recital. It voz very beauty full, bot, zeez old lady she kom on zee stage, put on her spectakolls and *raayed* – and byzikly I voz not vizit.'

The second half of our programme (at Frank Hauser's suggestion) consisted of the duologues between the Macbeths and various of their soliloquies, which we called 'The Plan – the Murder – the Consequences.' Glyndebourne were giving Verdi's *Macbetto* that summer – an opera which neither of us knew – so we went to see it with much curiosity. The first thing to strike us was the ludicrous effect – to English ears – of the o's added to familiar names. The murder of Duncano sounds less than tragic; and though Banquo's name needed no addition, Verdi (and/or Glyndebourne) provided him with a platoon of murderers who passed the time, while waiting for their quarry, singing a charming little Neapolitan boating song.

(Many thousands of satisfied customers have dined at Daphne's in Chelsea over the years. Not all perhaps have known that the proprietor and presiding genius is Daphne Rye – a large and friendly lady, who used to be in Binkie Beaumont's office. Lady Macbetto that evening was a monumental American diva who brought the curtain down after the banquet scene to tumultuous applause. Heading out into the garden for the interval we ran into John Gielgud. 'Isn't it jolly?' he said. We could only agree. 'And what about Lady Macbetto! Just like Daphne Rye opening a new restaurant!')

The climax of the Shakespeare celebrations, as far as the profession was concerned, was undoubtedly the afternoon party given by the Queen at Buckingham Palace. It was the most tremendous fun. The Queen appeared tireless and talked to everyone – a 'performance', if such it was, that filled her audience with affectionate admiration. The formal hour of departure passed unnoticed by Her Majesty's guests, by now put only too successfully at their ease. (I even negotiated my next West End engagement with Peter Saunders, whom I encountered in the Blue Drawing Room.) Eventually, as the summer dusk was falling, the company began drifting away, some of them to drive out of the inner courtyard in surely the most unlikely collection of vehicles ever to be permitted to park there.

Before I started on *Hostile Witness* (my play for Peter Saunders), there was a flurry of activity. We did a musical version of *East Lynne* for BBC2; the channel was new and the viewers were few, but we had the delight of working with Peter Graves for the first time. (Peter, now the eighth Baron Graves, wears his coronet lightly; he is a figure of grace and humour, much of it blue.) Edgar K. Bruce, the adaptor, was a most enchanting little actor of the old school, always exquisitely dressed with hat, gloves, cravat and silver-topped cane, and with a fund of matching anecdotes.

Next came our only literary collaboration, *The Actor and His World – A Young Person's Guide*, commissioned by Livia Gollancz and published to a friendly welcome, including generous comments from one very young person, Hayley Mills, and another, perennially young in heart, Sybil Thorndike. We took alternate chapters; and to me fell the task of writing a potted history of Equity and its well-intentioned but largely ineffectual predecessors – an exercise which taught the union's then Vice-President much that he should have known but didn't.

For the final chapter we persuaded Gerald Croasdell, John Macmillan (of Rediffusion), Richard Attenborough, Binkie Beaumont and Laurence Olivier (then creating the National Theatre from a sort of Nissen hut on the South Bank) to make assessments of the future in their various fields. These make interesting reading – for adults – today.

They all emphasise the importance of the live theatre to the health of the profession at large. As Gerald wrote:

> If actors are actors because they love acting, their pleasure and fulfilment only reach their peak in the presence of a live audience. But jobs in the theatre have been drastically cut by the advance of films and television; so Equity has a moral obligation to ensure that the rewards from these mechanical media are sufficient to permit actors to return for periodical refreshers to the theatre, because this will enrich their work not only on stage but in all other fields. In pressing film and television producers to pay this indirect subsidy, via the performers, to the theatre, we are asking them to support, not a rival, but the unique and vital source of the talents they so urgently need – and say they need.

'After all,' wrote Dickie Attenborough, 'if you haven't learnt to play to an audience that is in front of you, how can you expect to play effectively to one that isn't?'

Ironically, it was Larry who was most cautious about the future of live theatre: 'It is like the elder partner in a firm who feels his position shaky, definitely shaky. He must either retire or firm up and say, "I'm the head of this family and I'm not retiring." If the National Theatre can become a focal point which the profession has lacked since the time of Henry Irving, then that focus can spread and grow.'

Looking back I find little to disagree with in the prophecies of our experts.

I had hesitated to accept *Hostile Witness* for two reasons: first, my part was a QC, and after eighty *Boyds* on the box my actor's instinct was to get away from the law. (Peter Saunders' equally valid managerial instinct was to keep me within its clutches.) Secondly, there was no part for Dulcie; and though we have always been scrupulous in not saying to managements, 'It must be both or neither' (indeed, of our London plays we have been together in only just over half), nevertheless we do prefer joint engagements. For the moment there was nothing in view, so that cleared the way for Peter to persuade me that my fears of being typecast were groundless. True, the play was by Jack Roffey, who had written *Boyd*; but though the character was a QC and most of the action was in court, I would not be wearing wig and gown, because I would be in the dock accused of murdering a judge – a most un-Boyd-like set of circumstances. (My part had first been offered – I was told – to Margaret Lockwood, but she had turned it down because she would *not* be wearing wig and gown.)

Anyway, *Hostile Witness* installed me for nearly a year at the Haymarket in that unique No. 1 dressing-room with its two tall windows, its charming dilapidated period furniture, its open fire and, above all, the spine-tingling atmosphere of famous men and women of the theatre to whom it has been a haven before and during triumphs and disasters for most of this century. (Before 1910, the Star dressing-room was in what is now the manager's office.)

The part was long and arduous – the character being under strain throughout – and ended with thirty-five minutes standing in the dock, from which I was conducting my own defence. As the run went on I began to develop a phobia about those thirty-five minutes, and with it came unpleasant symptoms of faintness, varying pulse rates, etc., which in turn fed the phobia. Oliver Plowright, our friend and doctor for many years, finding nothing wrong, suggested another opinion. Dr Bayliss (now Sir Richard and the Queen's physician) gave me an electrocardiogram. 'Have you any life insurance?' he asked after studying the readings. It seemed an ominous question. 'Yes,' I said. 'Then you should get them to reduce your premium,' he said with a smile. His opinion, in a nutshell, was that I had become frightened of being frightened. And with that opinion the symptoms subsided.

Meanwhile, Dulcie played Arkadina in *The Seagull* for the Birmingham Repertory – a wonderful part in a wonderful play, but an unhappy experience. Being on her own – not just without me, but as the only outsider in a resident company – she was in need of a warm welcome. But, particularly in the Swinging Sixties, visiting stars were sometimes objects of suspicion and Dulcie's natural friendliness fell on stony ground. (By a coincidence her current thriller was *No Quarter for a Star*.) Fortunately, Tony

Britton was in Birmingham with *My Fair Lady* and, to Dulcie's and my abiding gratitude, became the friendliest of escorts in their free time.

During the run of *Hostile Witness* we modernised our motoring. Our 1939 Rolls (christened Nancy after Dulcie's Duchess in *Let Them Eat Cake*) was replaced by a very beautiful and rare 1951 Hooper-bodied Silver Wraith (Euphoria – Effie for short) – the last model, I believe, before those enormous headlamps were absorbed into the wings in the interest of streamlining, thereby marking the end of the great era of specialist coach-builders and starting the process which has produced, in the Camargue, the ugliest, most expensive and least identifiable Rolls in history. (What use is all the electronic wizardry in the world, the most comfortable seats, the thickest carpets – without beauty of line to go with them?)

VI
1965

*Peter Donald, Peter Bridge and the birth of Allied Theatre Pro-
ductions – farewell to Essex – Peter Bridge's extraordinary decade –*
An Ideal Husband *– Oscar Wilde and Fingal O'Flahertie*

In June 1965, *Beautiful For Ever*, a true story of a fraudulent
Victorian 'beautician' who retailed Jordan water from the tap
and even arranged phoney assignations for her clients, provided
meaty television parts for Ellen Pollock, and for Dulcie as her
pathetic dupe. Dulcie's notices were superb. Here was further
evidence of her versatility (a dangerous commodity), to set beside
The Letter, *The Winter Cruise* and *The Governess*; but it was to be
her last major part in the medium for some time.

This was nevertheless a year bursting with activity for us
both. As if *Hostile Witness* were not enough for me, the Equity
Council was beginning to agonise anew over South Africa, and I
soon found myself at odds with the majority of my colleagues
and, for the first and only time in the quarter-century of our work
together, with my special hero, Gerald Croasdell. (The controversy smouldered on, bursting occasionally into flame, until the
summer of 1966; for the sake of continuity, it has the next
chapter to itself.)

But first to happier matters. Peter Bridge, already with a string
of West End successes to his credit, had been a friend for some
time but we had not yet worked for him. He now came to us with
a plan for multi-star revivals which would tour the major cities
and then come to town for limited seasons. He felt that a
guaranteed London run and a firm stop-date would be enough to
neutralise any antipathy his distinguished casts might feel against
touring – an antipathy which he knew we didn't share. John
Trewin, the critic, had drawn up a list of plays worthy of revival,
and Nigel Patrick, another close friend of Peter's, had suggested
that the enterprise should be called 'The London Theatre of
Comedy'. At much the same time, Peter Donald, who had had a

141

change of heart about touring the classics since the success of our *Candida* and was desperately in need of product for his theatres (they each needed around forty shows a year, excluding the pantomime), had decided that he must produce his own, and approached us for any ideas. The first and most obvious idea was to put him in touch with Peter Bridge.

The two Peters could not have been more different but they were united in a love of the theatre. In 1939, Peter Donald had stood out against his three brothers in Aberdeen, where the family owned most of the places of entertainment, and obtained their grudging agreement to try live entertainment instead of films for six weeks in their beautiful theatre. Dulcie and I – on our honeymoon, and junior members of the company – were part of this experiment, which was extended 'by popular demand' to sixteen weeks. (His Majesty's is now one of the showplaces of the Scottish theatre circuit and recently had a £3 million facelift at the public expense.) After war service with the Gordon Highlanders, Peter was invited to join the Howard and Wyndham organisation, which owned the principal theatres in Glasgow, Edinburgh, Manchester, Liverpool, Newcastle and Leeds and had a booking organisation with links to a score of other dates. In due course he became Managing Director of this considerable empire – a position he held when Peter Bridge came into his life.

Every human being is unique, but some are more unique than others. Among them was Peter Bridge – unique in his extrovert passion for the theatre, unique in his knowledge and love of our profession, and in his admiration for playwrights, directors, lighting experts, unique in his round-the-clock devotion to the telephone, unique for the output he managed to squeeze into this, the most active period of his life. Between 1958 and 1970 he put on sixty productions, of which a dozen were considerable box-office successes and another dozen were artistically distinguished. Among the latter were three major productions of lesser-known plays by Shaw, Hugh Leonard's *Stephen D*, Giles Cooper's *Happy Family* (in which Dulcie and I had the best notices and shortest run of our careers), and a number of esoteric offerings found in the Edinburgh fringe or student drama festivals, and transported to London by Peter's enthusiasm, to the anxiety of his backers. He discovered Alan Ayckbourn in Scarborough, introduced him to London audiences in *Mr Whatnot* and was responsible for presenting the first two of our most prolific playwright's great successes, *Relatively Speaking* in 1967, and *How the Other Half Loves* in 1970.

Peter was just forty in 1965 but looked much younger. Married to his devoted Roslyn, and now with three young sons, he had spent most of the Fifties in a variety of front-of-house jobs in the West End; and for three years had been in charge of sport for Associated Rediffusion.

To our great delight, 'the Peters' rapidly discovered an identity of aim; and during the spring and early summer there was a series of meetings in our house where the programme and objects of Allied Theatre Productions (as the company came to be called) were exhaustively discussed.

As well as the Peters and ourselves the team represented a wide variety of theatrical strands. Albert Finney, the bright new star of both classical and modern theatre, was ably represented by his partner, Michael Medwin; Brian Rix brought his own brand of down-to-earth experience and undiminished zest; John Stevens was a West End manager (and partner of our old friend, Murray Mcdonald) and a useful ally for Peter Donald whenever the rest of us got too excited; so, last but by no means least, was 'Rocky' Stone, a financial wizard whose advice was often required.

It was agreed that, although 'all-star revivals' ('presented by Peter Bridge in association with Howard and Wyndham') should be our bread and butter, 'Allied' should concentrate on new writers, subsidising out of our mainstream activities those whose work seemed promising, to enable them to write full-time for two or three years. In this we frankly did not have great success, though John Spurling was a writer of quality whose *Macrune's Guevara* (a fascinating if uneven piece) was performed by the National in 1969 and later in at least eight foreign countries including Germany, France, Australia and the USA. He has written ten other plays, all produced, and has recently completed a three-part epic, *The British Empire*, of which the first part has already been staged at the Birmingham 'Rep', and the complete work has now been recorded for the BBC radio. For myself, I much enjoyed being a sort of theatrical 'tutor' to him for a couple of years and look forward to the real breakthrough he deserves.

Meanwhile, as *Hostile Witness* ran on through the summer, Dulcie went off filming with James Garner and Melina Mercouri in Portugal and Rome. It was a run-of-the-mill thriller called

A Man Could Get Killed, and Dulcie's part involved the minimum of professional skill; but, fortunately, among the British on the picture were Roland Culver and his wife Nan (who had been with us in Aberdeen in 1939) and the three of them enjoyed a profitable summer holiday.

Also that summer, we reluctantly sold the Essex cottage which had given us so much joy since 1947. It seemed very likely then, as it does again now, that the plans to make Stansted into London Airport No. 3 would go ahead; we would have been on the flight path to and from one of the major runways – no location for a peaceful haven.

Our eighteen years at Stebbing had changed me profoundly; a townsman at the beginning, I was by now a countryman working in towns, and the happier and healthier for it.

But to return to our enterprise 'of great pith and moment'. What should be Allied's first production? It was vital that it should succeed both on the road and for its short London season; and that it should be lavish, and have a fist-full of good parts. After many alternatives had been considered, Dulcie came up with the inspired suggestion of Wilde's *An Ideal Husband* – inspired for the enterprise, if not for us personally.

We agreed to sacrifice ourselves for the common good by playing Sir Robert and Lady Chiltern – the ideal husband of the title and his lady. To those unfamiliar with the play, to speak of playing two such central rôles as a sacrifice requires explanation. Wilde's full names were Oscar Fingal O'Flahertie Wills and it was once said that only his most successful characters were the work of Oscar Wilde, the rest were entrusted to Fingal O'Flahertie. The Chilterns are O'Flahertie to their fingertips; they are just possible to play when they are together, but confront them with Mrs Chevely, Lords Caversham and Goring, and even their daughter Mabel, and they melt like ice in the sun.

With the Chilterns disposed of, Peter was free to indulge in star-struck casting. Of all the elements of his hectic managerial career I suspect that casting gave him the most joyous excitement, and for a reason which further emphasises his uniqueness: it gave him the chance of saying a practical thank-you – and gratitude came easily to Peter – to scores of men and women whose work had given him pleasure. They ranged from the stars of his boyhood like Jack Hulbert and Cicely Courtneidge, and Celia Johnson, through the whole spectrum of theatre to the youthful cast of some unlikely performance in an unlikely location seen the night before and earmarked for 'promotion'.

This time there were to be no gimmicks. Maggie Lockwood was offered what the press inevitably called 'the wicked lady' part of Mrs Chevely, and (because she doesn't appear in the final scene) needed to be reassured by Dulcie that the part was a good one! Richard Todd was persuaded to quit the film studios after more than fifteen years to play the plum part of Lord Goring; Perlita Neilson – such a success in *Heartbreak House* – was an enchanting Mabel; and there was a perfect part for Roger Livesey – his last on the West End stage – as Lord Caversham. His wife, the irrepressible Ursula Jeans, was less well served but it was a joy to us and to Peter to have them both with us.

The plan was that the stars of the production were all to receive a basic salary (£60) and good percentages of the box-office takings. The play of course was in the public domain, so there were no author's royalties, and the basic running costs were low. This was just as well, for the sets and costumes had cost a fortune. From the opening in Manchester onwards we had the most tremendous success with the public, broke records everywhere and within five weeks were in profit. Such speed of recoupment was almost unheard-of. The advance booking at the Strand, where we opened in December, was extremely healthy – which was just as well, for the press were nearly as scornful as they were for Anna Neagle's *Charlie Girl*, which opened the night before and was to play for over 2000 performances. This mass exhumation of former film stars – British at that – was regarded by the critics as turning the Strand and Adelphi into a disaster area. The public happily thought otherwise.

Vyvyan Holland, Oscar Wilde's son, was invited to the play (with his wife Thelma and son Merlin) and expressed his warm approval. It seemed harsh to me that his father's work should be making money for everyone but the family. P.B. agreed. The problem was that Vyvyan, though a shy and gentle man, would not have taken kindly to charity. Eventually, with Thelma's connivance, he received for his birthday new curtains for his study and a pair of binoculars for bird-watching in The Boltons.

VII
Equity Interlude

To ban or not to ban – letter from Derek Nimmo – disagreement with Gerald Croasdell –a narrow defeat – The Charles Farrell Declaration – resignation – my reasons – re-election and speech to AGM – a counsel's opinion – an encouraging letter – the situation in 1984

At its best, the world of the theatre has much to teach society at large. The common professional tensions between the sexes are notable for their absence; the generation gap is meaningless, it being normal for all generations to be involved in a production, and not abnormal for the juniors to be top of the bill. As the theatre is a meritocracy in which the only criterion is talent – and talent comes in many guises – it follows that race prejudice has happily no place either within its ranks.

The 'agonising' to which I referred over Equity's policy towards South Africa was not therefore a conflict between opponents of apartheid and those who supported or were indifferent to it. All opposed it. The battle was between those who wanted the union to ban its members from working 'within the context of apartheid', because it was evil and unclean; and those who felt that by working in South Africa and giving performances to the Black majority, our members might plant a seed of theatrical enjoyment in virgin soil from which a forest might grow – even one day a mixed forest.

The decade from 1954 marked a gradual development and hardening of Equity's attitude. It began with a simple general motion passed unanimously at that year's AGM supporting the Council 'in total opposition to race prejudice'.

1956 was a watershed. It was agreed that contracts for South Africa must in future contain a clause that a definite proportion of performances, to be decided by Equity, should be open to all non-Europeans and if possible to persons of any colour, race or

146

creed. This was carried, and by 1957 had become an 'Instruction', binding on all members.

In 1960 a complete ban was called for, and defeated. In 1961 an important proviso was added to the Instruction, namely, that the performances to non-Europeans must be given in the same theatres as those to white audiences.

In 1962 a resolution calling for a total ban was passed by 88-57 (Equity's membership was then 11,000). The Council decided not to implement this, and was soon able to announce the first ever performances to non-Europeans in some of South Africa's major theatres.

In August 1964 the South African premier, Dr Verwoerd, spelled out his dislike of multi-racial audiences; and at the end of the year two of our members, Dusty Springfield and Adam Faith, who in separate engagements had been promised access to multi-racial audiences, left South Africa abruptly when these promises were not fulfilled.

This then was the background against which, in a series of emotional and exhausting special Sunday meetings in the early months of 1965, the Equity Council sought to come to terms with what some (of whom Gerald Croasdell was as ever an eloquent spokesman) saw as a fundamental change in South African attitudes, requiring a fundamental change in ours, while others (including Felix Aylmer, André Morell and myself), who found nothing surprising in Verwoerd's speech, argued for an empirical approach which would enlist the support of South Africa's theatre managers to step up the number of performances to non-Whites.

Before the first of these meetings Derek Nimmo wrote a most important letter to the Equity office from Johannesburg. Among his points were the following:

Nothing could give the Nationalists (*Afrikaners*) greater joy and liberal South Africans greater sorrow than for us to impose a ban.

It is the Nationalists' deliberate policy to decrease English influence, of which the theatre here has always been a strong-hold. It is ironic that the very playwrights whose work should be performed here are those who have withheld permission . . . This country desperately needs plays of anger, of truth, of ideas. It also needs people of tolerance coming into the country . . .

I have sounded a number of left-wing people who are still at liberty ... and they have all pleaded with me to write asking you not to enforce this ban.

I am afraid we are not in a position to enforce multi-racial audiences but it is most important that we should continue to provide entertainment for non-White audiences ... If it were not for our pressure these shows would not be held.

This is a matter of conscience ... not something to be decided by a craft union. If you impose a ban I would disregard it and take the consequences. Our feelings about apartheid are, I am sure, identical but my way of trying to combat it is I think a positive approach and yours I am afraid is desperately negative.

The opposite point of view was put in a letter from Leon Gluckman, a South-African-born theatre manager who had left his native country largely because he found that 'the whole humiliating and unrealistic policy of separate performances had become unpalatable.' There was just a chance, he felt, that a ban might induce the South African managers to lobby the authorities in favour of some relaxation.

So the battle lines were drawn. I cannot speak for the other principal protagonists but I know that I approached the conflict fearing – with every justification as it turned out – that decisions would be based on emotion rather than on the art of the possible.

At the first meeting, André Morell and Marius Goring argued (by letter) in favour of maintaining the Instruction. So did I, in person. I also introduced what was to be my *leit-motiv* throughout the controversy:

We are all united in hatred of apartheid. But that is the negative side. The positive side is freedom for all in their theatre-going in South Africa. It is this alone which matters to Equity. I suggest that we must examine our consciences very carefully to see whether, if we decide on a ban, we are serving our cause in a practical manner or whether we are merely taking up that Anglo-Saxon attitude familiar to the world, of salving our consciences at the expense of others – and thereby joining the writers in a gesture which is political rather than professional.

I would suggest the continuance of the Instruction, and that we tell the press that our goal remains unchanged, and that, although a non-political body, we contain individuals of passionate and varied political convictions whose individual actions and reactions in a political context must remain their own.

I don't believe such a policy would be a defeat. To hold the line after a long and laborious advance is not only an essential phase in preparing a further advance, it is also more honourable and more effective than to abandon the field, proclaiming high-mindedly that we don't like the enemy's methods.

The next speaker was Charles Farrell, one of Equity's founder members and the union's honorary treasurer from 1949-75 – a stalwart and warmhearted figure with whom I rarely disagreed. This was one of the occasions. Although he would not impose a ban, he favoured the withdrawal of the Instruction and a declaration, to be signed by members individually, that they would not work in South Africa unless its government relaxed its policy.

That admirable actor-barrister, Peter Copley (who, like Gerald, makes his effects in argument by speaking more quietly than anyone else – something, incidentally, which I both admire and envy but have never managed to achieve myself), made a characteristic contribution which boiled down to a subtle variation of the Instruction, the effect of which would have been a ban.

There were other speakers of course, but their contributions were broadly in agreement with either Charles, Peter or myself. So the stage was now cleared for Gerald.

He dismissed my argument about 'holding the line', on the grounds that, as the Instruction referred to the possibility of multi-racial performances and these were now impossible, to maintain the Instruction would be hypocritical. 'The increasing opposition of Africans to segregated performances is apparent,' he stated, though with a most untypical paucity of evidence. However, he accepted that my views could be sincerely held. He then moved on to the possibility – or rather the desirability – of a ban. The enormous doubt, he said, was whether we should instruct members on a moral issue; and whether, if issued, such an Instruction could be enforced, without damage to the union's primary tasks. He did not believe so. He therefore proposed the publication of a pledge as suggested by Charles.

No vote was taken, but it was agreed that Councillors who

wished to propose resolutions should do so in writing, in time for a further meeting.

Charles, Peter Copley, Andrew Faulds and Roger Snowdon produced resolutions closely connected with their speeches at the first meeting, and all in favour of the withdrawal of the Instruction. I at least produced something new. I argued that if the South African managers wanted us (and if they didn't, the whole debate was academic), they should be pressurised to co-operate with us in interpreting the Instruction as follows:

that *they* should increase the number of performances to non-Whites, and reduce seat prices for them; and

that *we* should authorise and encourage our members, under proper safeguards, to give such performances free.

I also said that I could never sign Charles's proposed pledge, because the publication of its signatories' names would suggest that absentees from it were in favour of or, at best, complacent about apartheid. It would be unjust for me and for others – whether few or many – to be stigmatised for disagreeing with the signatories about the tactics needed to achieve an aim we shared with them.

At the crucial meeting, I nearly made it. My resolution was lost by 8-11; but I had two absent supporters (William Devlin and Noel Howlett) whose letters, alas, did not count as votes. Their presence might have persuaded one other Councillor to vote on my side.

The Council agreed on an amalgamation of Charles Farrell's and Peter Copley's resolutions which would be debated at yet another meeting. I was of course bitterly disappointed; but worse was to come.

At the subsequent meeting, a new contestant entered the lists – Marius Goring. He had begun as a supporter of the Instruction, but had now somewhat gingerly crossed the floor picking up scraps of ideas en route and, under the noble banner of compromise, produced what I hope he would now agree was a veritable dog's dinner of a resolution.

He was in favour of the Farrell pledge, agreed with me on the lack of evidence of a Black boycott, thought that the Instruction should be maintained in case anyone still went to South Africa; however, as multi-racial audiences were now forbidden, it followed that the Instruction should be withdrawn. He said that I had stressed the need for a positive policy but (unlike himself?)

had not offered one, dismissing my proposal of free performances as patronising.

He believed that this farrago represented the views of the majority of the Council – and by God he was right. The only small mercy was that the Instruction escaped summary execution, though it remained in 'death row'.

The victors now turned their attention to the form of the personal pledge; and there was unanimous agreement in Council (I was absent on this occassion) that the names should be published. This drew from me a letter in which I said that, while leading members of the profession could look after themselves, the majority were not in that situation. It was not unrealistic to suggest that politically committed managers or casting directors might allow the presence or absence of an artist's name to influence their casting. If the Council had intended publication this should have been stated on the declaration.

The Council rejected the argument but postponed publication of the names; they rejected also – most irresponsibly in my view – important approaches from South African managers who were eager both to employ our members and to continue non-White performances.

Some 2400 signed the declaration, out of a membership which had risen to 13,500. Not exactly a democratic landslide, but given the normal apathy of Equity members to the doings of their union – the ITV 'strike' being a notable exception (surely because it was seen to be of crucial professional importance) – it was a respectable total. And there the matter rested, with the names unpublished, until January 1966.

I cannot believe that anyone was happy with this situation. I certainly was not. True, the Instruction had not been withdrawn, but its effect had been emasculated; true, the names had not been published, but the list was ready for the printers. Things had already gone too far for my peace of mind; for Gerald they had not gone far enough.

Gerald comes of Quaker stock. He was up at Cambridge (President of the Union – the youngest ever – and a member of the Apostles) during the political ferment of the Thirties; and, like many of his most idealistic contemporaries, finding the Tories totally unacceptable, the Liberals a spent force and Labour rudderless since MacDonald's participation in the National Government, turned to Communism as the only effective answer to Hitler and Mussolini, first in Spain and later on a wider stage. He remained, throughout, an active supporter of the League of Nations Union and of collective security, but espoused simultaneously every congenial cause of the Far Left. He volunteered for the army in September 1939; but when the Communist Party decided that the war was imperialist and therefore 'unjust', he successfully led the anti-war case as Chairman of the University Labour Federation. By 1940, however, the invasion of Scandinavia and the resignation of Chamberlain turned 'the "phoney" war of inaction and suspect motives into a just and necessary war in defence of humanity' (Gerald's words) and from his service as an army Air Liaison Officer on carriers he emerged with a mention in despatches and an OBE.

He came to Equity as Legal Officer for a year, and stayed for twenty-five, during most of which I was a councillor. Politics have always meant much more to Gerald than to me; and such politics as I profess are far removed from Gerald's. And yet, within the Equity context, we were able to work in total harmony — with the one exception of this South African matter.

As this is my book and not his, I will say that this was the only occasion in those twenty-five years when he allowed his emotions to dictate a course of action that was not in the union's best interest. He was so devoted to the concept of Equity making a self-denying gesture of revulsion from apartheid, that, even if he didn't block, he certainly did nothing to encourage the attempts by South African managers to make common cause with us — which in my view would have been a surer, if less spectacular, path to the goal we both desired and still desire.

In January 1966 Gerald decided to return to the attack; and so did I — by letter, as I was broadcasting. I remained faithful to my idea of free performances, and to the Instruction.

Even from the minutes, that least atmospheric medium, it is clear that Gerald made a powerful speech.

> The performances to non-Whites were so few and so ill-attended that they amounted to no more than a minor tax paid by South African managers to secure the services of our members.
>
> We should no longer operate within the context of apartheid by negotiating separate performances.
>
> So ... the Instruction should be withdrawn, and this should

be accompanied by the publication of the names of those who had signed the Declaration.

This was agreed and even strengthened. The union would no longer 'offer support or protection' in connection with theatrical engagements in South Africa. This was passed with twenty-three in favour and two abstentions.

My immediate reaction was that I could no longer work 'within the context' of this Council. However, I decided first to write for advice to Felix, who had clearly been unhappy with the decision but had deliberately not chosen to sacrifice his authority against so strongly flowing a tide. As he done most effectively during the birth pangs of Equity, he believed in being there to exert his influence when the tide was on the turn. He counselled me against resignation:

> Democratic organisations survive on the understanding that minorities abide by a majority decision ... The present attitude to South Africa is an example of mob mentality ... Convince a group that something is morally wrong, and 90 per cent, having their emotions involved, are willing to suspend their normal judgement.
>
> Nonetheless, there are of course occasions when resignation is both necessary and effective; and don't think that I underrate the importance of the present situation.

I was not equipped temperamentally to play Felix's waiting game. Whether effective or not, resignation was necessary to me. I based my decision on the following grounds:

1. I question our right to withdraw support from any member who is in benefit and who is not in breach of any rule or instruction. If we *have* the right I question the propriety of exercising it. The principle once established, why stop at South Africa? Why not withdraw support from members working in any country whose policies do not find favour with a majority of the Equity Council?

2. Multi-racial audiences – as anything but an exception – are inconceivable in South Africa as long as the present party is in power. This is not a new development; they were equally inconceivable when the Instruction was framed and yet good came of it. Indeed the only important change in the theatrical scene in the last ten years or so – and as far as I know the only

relaxation of apartheid – has been 'the opening of major theatres to non-Whites'. This has been an intrinsically good thing, a very remarkable achievement on Equity's part and is now to be cast away. Multi-racial *audiences* may not have resulted from the Instruction, but multi-racial *occasions* (White performers and non-European audiences) did – practically the only such, apart from church services, in contemporary South Africa. To throw this away when under no pressure to do so (except from within our own ranks) is in my view a shameful and unmitigated self-defeat.

3. The last straw, as far as I am concerned, is of course the decision to go ahead with the publication of names of signatories to the Declaration ... the only effect of which will be to emphasise dissensions in the ranks of Equity, not to assist in the remotest degree the victims of apartheid.

My resignation was acknowledged 'with regret' by Gerald, but he made no attempt to answer my argument – perhaps because he realised that nothing he could say would be acceptable.

I then set about organising my nomination in the hope of re-election – a hope that was to be handsomely fulfilled. That achieved, I decided to challenge from the floor at the AGM – I was not a councillor again until after the meeting – the paragraph of the annual report referring to South Africa.

My speech overran the allotted time-limit, but I had arranged with Dulcie to pick it up from wherever I had got to. My announcement of this, when the buzzer went, got a big laugh – a welcome moment of relief on a tense occasion – and I was given the meeting's permission to continue myself.

Much of what I said was, naturally, a re-working of my contributions to Council debates and of my letter of resignation; but there was a new element of public accusation of the Council's shortcomings. For instance, I expressed satisfaction that I had helped to keep the Instruction in force until January 1966. It had resulted in twenty performances by our members to non-Whites which would not otherwise have taken place:

But they were not multi-racial performances, they did not provide evidence of dramatic strides towards a multi-racial society, and so, with the kind of logic I have learned to dread and will always fight, the Council decided that if there couldn't be multi-racial audiences NOW, it was better for the souls of the non-Europeans and of our members, that the non-

Europeans should have no performances from our members at all . . .

The Council still pays lip-service . . . to the right of members to work in South Africa, but they have crippled them by cancelling the Instruction; and – worse – in withdrawing support and protection from them they have, I believe, gone far beyond the proper powers of a trade union over its members.

I told the meeting that, having still had no answer to the substance of my resignation letter, I had rung up a good friend of mine, Sir Peter Rawlinson QC (now Lord Rawlinson) – a former Solicitor General and future Attorney General – and asked him: 'Is a trade union entitled to withdraw support from a member who is in benefit and not in breach of any rule or instruction?' His answer was 'No.'

'The Council,' I concluded, 'has therefore taken a decision which is outside its powers and which penalises those members who in this matter of conscience prefer action to mere protest. I ask you to help me reverse it . . .'

I asked in vain, as far as the AGM were concerned. But my campaign was not without its successes. The members' names on the list remain unpublished; and I went with Gerald to a consultation with counsel (Mr Peter Pain QC).

There I learned that the relationship between a union and its members is one of contract. (It was ironical, as I later said in Council, that the contract with his union was the worst an Equity member then had: I was to spend many long hours over the next few years trying to improve it.) I got a 'good notice' from the QC for my resignation letter and my speech at the meeting, which he described as 'succinct and pithy' – but he said it was 'no part of (*his*) function to say which side was right'. He had to confine himself to advising whether the Council's withdrawal of protection was lawful. 'Trade union law,' he wrote, 'is an intricate subject unrewardingly barren of justice or logic. Its approach to the emotive subject of apartheid will probably seem horrifyingly stilted and unreal to those who read this opinion.' It did to this reader.

What emerged was that, as the Equity rule book contained neither a definition of 'protection' nor a rule defining the rights of the members (!), the Council could withdraw with impunity what it had no obligation to provide. The propriety of doing so was another matter; but not one on which the law could pronounce. It must however continue to give legal advice on contracts, legal assistance and assistance in the event of stranding. So there were some crumbs of practical comfort, amid the general inadequacy of the rule book.

In 1968 there came to Equity a letter which was balm to my soul, in that it rounded off this episode on a note of practical common sense and of hope, not least for the evidence of co-operation which the writers (Andrew Ray, John Fraser and Olive McFarland) had received on a three-month tour of South Africa. The letter told how, deprived by the loss of the Instruction of the *right* to give non-White performances, they had set about organising them nevertheless – with no admission charges.

In the coloured township of Athlone near Cape Town, with the help of the state-supported Afrikaans Theatre Company, they played to a capacity audience. In Johannesburg, thanks to the gallant and unique Helen Suzman (aunt of Janet), contact was made with the Government's Non-European Affairs department, who helped organise a show in Soweto which had a rapturous reception.

'Most liberally minded people,' our trio continued, 'are keen for overseas artists to come to South Africa ... as they feel some exchange of ideas is better than none.' They quoted not only white Liberals such as Helen Suzman and Athol Fugard as agreeing but also prominent non-European writers, actors and musicians.

In fact they were pleading – in vain of course – for the reinstatement of the Instruction and for Equity authority for free shows – in other words for my original plan.

What is the situation today? Since the mid-Seventies, thanks to the pressure of South African managements supported by SAFTU (the South African 'Equity', which has members of all races) – but shamefully without our help – all major theatres in the country now accept multi-racial audiences. Of course this does not mean the end of apartheid, nor does it mean theatres suddenly filled with audiences as predominantly black as the population – White theatre will probably never be more than a minority interest; after all, it is no more than that here. What it does mean is that in the context which matters (or should matter) most to Equity, an important victory has been won.

Was the news greeted with delight at our union's HQ? Not for a moment. The 1976 Council organised a referendum which reaffirmed the status quo, and there was yet another in 1983. In neither was any mention made of 'the victory' I have referred to; so the majorities won by the two Councils were based on an incomplete picture.

We now have the ironical situation that there has been movement towards our goal from South Africa, answered by ineffectual inflexibility here. (From these strictures I except Equity's new President Derek Bond, who had the good sense – though the timing was admittedly provocative – to accept an engagement to play to multi-racial audiences in South Africa on the morrow of his election.)

The heroes of this seemingly interminable tragedy are not the absentee idealists, whatever the colour of their skins; they are the men and women in South Africa, whatever the colour of theirs, who, at a personal risk unknown to the absentees, are chipping away at this monstrous doctrine, not for personal glory but for the sake of its victims.

And that applies, not to South Africa alone, but wherever civilisation has given way to man's inhumanity to man.

VIII
1966

Obstinate success of Ideal Husband – *the Plan in danger* – On Approval – *a bargain in Buckinghamshire – an unusual opening in Glasgow – tampering with a masterpiece – galvanising Norwich –* Happy Family *and tragedy – an enquiry from Prince Charles*

The Equity pressures apart, 1966 moved along smoothly for us. It soon became apparent that ten to twelve weeks would be quite inadequate to accommodate the crowds who wanted to see *Ideal Husband*. This created a problem. Part of the master-plan had been that, when Production A had reached London, Production B should go into rehearsal and then tour. Meanwhile Production C, using as many of the Production A company as possible, would be rehearsing, ready to follow B around the circuit and eventually replace it in town – and so on.

I had never forgotten the delights of doing four plays in repertoire at Stratford and assumed that our colleagues at the Strand – of whom Roger and Ursula had built their reputations in repertoire at the Old Vic – would be equally enthusiastic. I had discovered with excitement that Shaw's *Getting Married* and Priestley's *When We Are Married* would 'cross-cast' very effectively, with splendid opportunities for many of the present company.

However, back in their homes, earning by now good money in a copper-bottomed success in the West End (a situation rare enough for any actor to wish to savour), our colleagues seemed to have lost the pioneering spirit in which we had set off around the country at £60 a week. They expressed polite interest in other plays in which they might be involved – but only in a hypothetical future, after *Ideal Husband* had had its full commercial run. For them 'the Plan' was forgotten, and any move to implement it was rocking the boat.

They were frankly incredulous that Dulcie and I were determined to leave the show, overlooking the fact that while they were playing Wilde we were saddled with O'Flahertie. Peter

158

Bridge (PB) and Peter Donald (PD) were firmly on our side in this, in spite of the general dislocation and expense involved in cast changes; they had been, after all, architects of the Plan and were loth to see it abandoned because of a great success. Its appeal to PB was as an outlet for his inexhaustible managerial energy. (Incidentally, he did mount both *Getting Married* and *When We Are Married* within the next three years, but as separate productions.) For PD there was the clamorous hunger for product of his provincial theatres – stimulated but not appeased by our one production.

It was decided that we should do Frederick Lonsdale's famous comedy, *On Approval*. It was a play in which Dulcie had appeared (without me) in Aberdeen; and I (very much without her) in a unit production which I had directed in Cairo during the war. Dulcie would now have the marvellous bitchy part of Mrs Wislack, I would again have the Duke of Bristol in my care, and the quartet would be completed by the lovely Susan Hampshire and one of our greatest friends (with whom however we had never worked before) – Robert Flemyng. Direction by Murray Mac-donald, costumes by Worth, and splendid sets by Pamela Ingram of the Yvonne Arnaud Theatre at Guildford (where we opened) gave an appropriate gloss, to offset the smallness of the cast in the large provincial theatres.

We left *Ideal Husband* on a Saturday in July, started rehearsing *On Approval* the following Monday and celebrated our brief nocturnal freedom by going to see Noël Coward in *Song at Twilight* (his last West End play) and receiving his usual heart-warming welcome back-stage afterwards.

Our play went well from the start of its preliminary canter at Guildford, but we were dismayed when Susan said she would have to leave us at the end of the three weeks there. BBC television wanted her for something which she thought she ought to do. She didn't specify; but, looking back, I think she was right. It was *The Forsyte Saga*.

We then went to the Normans in France for a much needed holiday, where Murray rang to say that Polly Adams, whom we had suggested to replace Susan, would love to do it. We enjoyed ourselves the more for those tidings.

While all this had occupied the foreground of our lives, there had been a development on the home front of which the consequences are with us still.

One cloudless February Sunday, which in earlier years would have found us at the cottage, we took the Rolls down to the White Hart at Nettlebed, high in the Chilterns between Henley and Oxford. It was a pub I had known and loved since I was up at Oxford in the Thirties, and which had been run for all that time by the earth-motherly figure of Clemmie (Mrs Clements), who had a particularly soft spot for her 'boys' of all ages – from Oxford before and after the war, and from RAF Benson during it. We explained to Clemmie that now that the cottage was sold we should probably be seeing more of her. 'Good,' she said, with the scorn of the hill-dweller for the lowlands, 'I could never understand what you saw in Essex.' Over lunch we congratulated ourselves on no longer having the obligation to go in one direction every weekend. A misty look came into Dulcie's eye. 'Do you remember that house we saw on the way back from Stratford in 1955?' she asked. 'Yes. Vaguely,' I said. 'Are we near it now?' 'Not far.' 'Could we have another look at it on our way back to London?' 'Of course.'

And so we drove over hill and dale until we came to the gates of the house, which stand half a mile below it in the valley. Beside them was a notice: 'Flats, Maisonettes and Houses to Let'. 'Well,' I said, 'that gives us a chance to have a closer look. Not that we want anything of course.' 'Of course not,' said Dulcie hastily.

The drive climbs steadily in a gentle curve, the panorama of lake and woods and fields widening all the way. At the top you come first to the severely classical mansion, which appears to be on just two floors, tall graceful windows lighting the lower with smaller square ones above; beyond is a long low range of buildings, which include the stables, of which vestigial traces remain. The view is breathtaking.

Beside the house was a Rolls-Royce, the exact twin of ours – a coincidence indeed, as we were later told that only twelve had been made by Hoopers.

We surveyed the whole place in wonder.

'You know,' I said, 'if one was ever to live here it would have to be on the ground floor of the main house. However pleasant the other apartments were, I would always have the feeling that life must be better behind those great windows.'

'Let's see what's going,' said Dulcie. 'Just for curiosity.'

The caretaker, Mr Fountain, recognised us, and remarked on the coincidence of the two cars. The other belonged to

'My Lady', as he called her – the Hon. Mrs Elspeth Hoare.

He told us that there were three flats going, of which we would like two but not the other.

'Why not?' Dulcie asked.

'Nobody does, madam.'

'Where is it?'

'In the mansion.'

'Which floor?' This was my question.

'The ground floor.'

Our pulses, I am sure, were now racing in unison.

'Then I suppose it's the most expensive?'

'No, sir. It's the cheapest.'

'Ah. Well, may we see it? We're only interested in the cheapest.'

A moment later we were in one of the most beautiful rooms Dulcie and I had ever seen. It was completely empty. Eighteen foot high and more than thirty long, with exquisite early Adam mouldings and marble chimney piece, its blue walls were entirely covered by white tendrils, swags, sphinxes, acanthus and other motifs – the whole, despite the exuberant detail, miraculously conveying an atmosphere of unity and calm. Three tall windows looked out across the lake, by now in shadow, to the still sunlit fields and woods beyond.

'How much?' one of us managed to say.

'Ten pounds a week.'

'We'll think about it,' I said hoarsely.

That at least was true. We thought of little else until a five-year lease was ours.

Back from France at the end of September we had ten days of intensive rehearsal with Polly. It was good to see what a marvellous comedienne she had become since our first meeting in that dreadful opening of the Ashcroft. Then we were off to Glasgow.

There was more than usual press interest in the follow-up to *Ideal Husband* (as it was correctly considered) and there were many friendly references to our return to the road while the Wilde comedy was still running in town.

The first act went well. But at the interval, the safety curtain was lowered; and never rose again. The public were reimbursed, and an alcoholic press reception (critics and all) was held in Dulcie's dressing-room; the story was in the national as well as the local papers next day. The press all came back for the

Tuesday night, and one way and another we did a bumper week.

Bobby Flemyng is immensely strong, and only the most solid of sets, properties and furniture are safe with him. In the Scottish set of *On Approval*, we had some tall-backed reproduction Jacobean chairs. By the time we got to Liverpool (Bobbie's home town incidentally, where his playing was particularly vigorous), these were already a mass of metal brackets and other anti-Flemyng defences. Not enough. Dulcie leant back during the tea-party scene and the whole chair disintegrated. She turned a slow backward somersault, and dislodged her wig. Bobby and I formed a defensive screen between her and the audience – as though she were a rugger player who had lost his shorts – and she emerged a moment later bewigged (fortunately not back to front) and only slightly hysterical. (Provided an audience has seen a comic disaster, they love it, and become one with the performers in happy hysteria; what are unforgivable are private jokes among members of a cast resulting in one or more of them losing control. Many distinguished performers – not least Gielgud and Olivier – were compulsive gigglers in their early days and had to learn the hard way that, in the theatre, laugh and you laugh alone.) Two young sailors asked to see Dulcie after the show and were most enthusiastic. Predictably, what they had enjoyed most was 'the disaster'. 'But can you explain one thing, Miss Gray? When you fell over we both thought we saw a small furry animal on the stage. But it had gone by the time you were back on your feet. What could it have been?' Dulcie offered no explanation.

On Approval is, I believe, as much a masterpiece of its genre as *Private Lives*, but it has – or rather had – one serious flaw in the final scene. The selfish Duke plans, with the collusion of the equally selfish Mrs Wislack, to win back the love of his fiancée by pretending to be seriously ill in the servantless shooting lodge in which they are all marooned.

As both characters are bad 'actors' they make a complete hash of it; but, unbelievably for a playwright of Lonsdale's comedic instinct, the scene takes place off-stage and is only reported to the audience. I mentioned my frustration at this to Murray, who agreed. 'So what can we do about it?' I asked. 'You can write it,' he said. So I did. Murray approved; so did Frances Donaldson, Lonsdale's daughter and literary executor; and so did the public. It is now incorporated – without acknowledgment or fee! – in French's Acting Edition of the play; and subsequent Dukes of Bristol and Maria Wislacks (including Edward Woodward,

Boyd QC (1956-63)

top   *Candida*, 1958 (with Jeremy Brett)
above   Dulcie with Keith Baxter in *Where Angels Fear to Tread*, 1963

With Robert Flemyng and Gillian Raine in *Happy Family* (*top*)
and *On Approval*, 1966 (*above*)

right Rebecca West
below At Chalet Coward,
September 1966

Kenneth More and Jeremy Brett, Geraldine McEwan, Patricia Routledge and Penelope Keith) have played and others presumably will play a page and a half of Denison without knowing it – and hopefully getting some satisfactory laughs.

One of our last dates of the tour was at the Theatre Royal, Norwich. It was then a decayed cinema. Now, within the same walls, it is one of the most attractive and successful theatres in the country. The transformation has been effected by the enthusiasm of the city fathers, and especially – I am sure they would agree – by the dynamism and expertise of Dick Condon, the theatre's manager. But this was very much in the future in 1966; and as I considered the squalor in which we were working and our audience was sitting, in contrast to the splendour of Norwich and the size of the potential theatrical catchment area in the wide spaces of East Anglia, I felt constrained to make a curtain speech every night of the week warning the local citizens that the demon Bingo might soon deprive them of live theatre in their city, unless they showed unmistakably that they wanted it. They certainly did and do. I hoped we played some part in the recovery, however small.

Although happy with the way *On Approval* was going, the two Peters and we were concerned that 'Allied' should not appear to be interested only in revivals. So the search was on for another play – ideally one suiting the *On Approval* quartet – which we could rehearse and put into repertoire with it when we got to town.

PB had seen Giles Cooper's *Happy Family* at Hampstead and sent us scripts in great excitement. There were fascinating offbeat parts for Dulcie, Bobbie and myself, but it was felt – may she forgive us – that Polly was not quite right for the key figure of Deborah. Dulcie and I then pleaded the case of Gillian Raine, who, though she had had a small part with us in *Ideal Husband* and had appeared once or twice in *Boyd*, had had nothing worthy of her skills since her great success as Prossie in our *Candida*.

As for Giles, we had not seen him since Dulcie, he and I had all been drama students together just before the war. We remembered him as a sort of Aguecheek figure – with flaxen hair, sleepy blue eyes and pink cheeks frequently scarlet with embarrassment at the strange demands made on a very shy young man by his strangely chosen profession. After war service, there emerged not indeed an actor but a playwright of great individuality. He came up to see us in Newcastle and we had a marvellous supper after the show – part nostalgia for the Webber-Douglas, part eager planning and discussion of our joint project, the thought of which gave us all intense pleasure. Within a month, Giles had fallen to his death from a train.

With his widow's consent we decided to go ahead with *Happy Family* – always provided *On Approval* established itself successfully in town as a launching pad. This it did. *The Times* gave it a rave, Harold Hobson went completely overboard, and John Trewin paid us the greatest compliment of all by saying: 'A very young playgoer (*in 1927*), I have never forgotten the original quartet. It is the warmest praise to say that the present revival is fully as good, and that in future Michael Denison's Duke will march with Ronald Squire's.'

There were of course conflicting points of view, one of which by playwright Frank Marcus in the magazine *Plays and Players* had dismissed the production and our playing of Lonsdale's masterpiece for its lack of social significance. This prompted Peter Bridge and me into a reply which I wrote and he signed:

His mouth waters at the prospect of a hypothetical National Theatre production which would reveal that *On Approval* is a moral tract ... But would it? I have too much respect for those in charge in the Waterloo Road to believe it. (*The National was still at the Old Vic.*) I discerned no overtones in their production of *Hay Fever* – though of course that was directed by its author, who may not have realised the social significance of what he had written ...

Does Mr Marcus remember, I wonder, what *On Approval* was called by its author when first produced in 1927? *A Farce*. And it appeared under the management of, and directed by, that well-known master of the moral tract, Tom Walls.

One last point. He dismisses our plan of adding ... *Happy Family* ... as being without artistic interest, on the curious grounds that neither (*play*) is typical of its period. I suggest the only thing untypical is that both are considerably above the average of their contemporaries in entertainment value and style ... This is why we are going ahead, instead of resting content with the success of *On Approval*, and this I think is a not unworthy artistic motive.

I only hope that the public will agree.

As we shall see, they didn't.

*   *   *

Prince Charles was now at Gordonstoun, but earlier had been at Cheam with Charles Donald, Peter's son. To our great delight, the Prince, then eighteen, accepted an invitation to come to the play and sup afterwards at the Donalds' flat, where we were invited to join the party.

He was at that time very keen on acting and had, he told us, just appeared in *Macbeth* at school. He was very complimentary about *On Approval* but clearly had some problem on his mind. He called me 'Sir' – out of respect, I presume, for my age; I called him 'Sir' for obvious reasons. There ensued one of those conversations which I had not indulged in since, as an officer cadet, I had been confronted by CSM Tankard of the Grenadiers at Bulford in 1941. It went something like this:

HRH: That was an awfully good wig you were wearing, sir.
MD: I'm glad you liked it, sir.
HRH: Yes I did, sir. Tell me, sir, how did you stick it on?
MD: With spirit gum, sir.
HRH: Spirit gum, sir? What's that?
MD: Well, sir, it's what you use, sir.
HRH: I see, sir. Because the master in charge of make-up at Gordonstoun told me to use Copydex. And when I came to remove my whiskers I removed half my face.
MD: Well, sir, I suggest you tell him about spirit gum.
HRH: (with a laugh) I will, sir.

This ended the 'Sirs' – on his part anyway – and the evening continued in relaxed informality. I longed to know more about 'the master in charge of make-up' – such an unlikely assignment for that particular establishment. Clearly he knew little of the subject. Was he a junior member of staff who had just been ordered to get on with it; and has Copydex now been discarded from Gordonstoun's make-up box?

IX
1967

Perils of West End repertoire – death of Vivien Leigh – Norman and Sarah Collins – The Murder of Love *– meeting Edward Heath – Harmar Nicholls disappointed – 'Theatre under the Tories' – Olivier, the National and touring –* No. 10 *in Canada, and London – a trauma*

We began to rehearse *Happy Family* at the end of January, but as three of us had long parts in *On Approval* we did not open until early March. Donald McWhinnie, a close friend of Giles, directed; and his method was as far removed from Murray's as Giles's was from Lonsdale's – further, in fact, for the two playwrights shared a fastidious and calculated use of words. But whereas Murray came to the first rehearsal with a detailed plan of moves and business, Donald came – apparently – with nothing.

Appearances were deceptive. He came in fact steeped in the atmosphere of the play, but seemingly so confident of our interpretations and our sense of theatre that it was very difficult to get comments or criticism out of him. I was reduced to the expedient of criticising myself and then asking Donald if he agreed. As he usually said 'Yes' but didn't elaborate, this hardly constituted progress. And yet progress there was, as was proved by the astonishing response of the first-night audience and of the press the next day. (By this time, without understanding Donald's technique, we were more than happy with it, and when the next year we had another problem play for John Neville at Nottingham, we unhesitatingly asked for Donald to direct it.)

In spite of the praise, it soon became apparent that 'our' public had little desire to see us in Giles's grown-up nursery world of meccano and pedometers and ignorance of the facts of life. What is more, the unease they felt about it began to infect the audiences for *On Approval*. Why had we put on the second play? Was it because the first was not such a success after all? We had thought the public would enjoy comparing a four-hander of 1927 with one

166

of 1967. We were wrong. Above all we were wrong in thinking that the public would accept repertoire in the commercial West End. We were not alone in making this mistake.

Even Brian Rix, who between 1950 and 1964 had had two four-year runs and two of three years – and might have been thought to know what the public wanted – had to withdraw relatively quickly two of the three farces he presented in repertoire at the Garrick that same spring.

(A more recent example was Duncan Weldon's and Louis Michaels' gallant repertoire season at the Haymarket in 1982 – sadly Louis, a great benefactor of the theatre, did not live to see it in action – which brought to the West End three plays of quality with well-known players, most of whom were in two of the three. This was not the success that was hoped for a number of reasons. The public became confused as to what would be on offer on a particular night; 'cross-casting' severely limited, if it did not prohibit, touring; the necessity to pre-judge the number of performances of each individual production made the programme too inflexible for the vagaries of public reaction; and, finally, the normal heavy expenses of set-changing in repertoire were made worse by lack of storage space at the Haymarket and the necessity to move elaborate productions into and out of the theatre at every change of programme.

Duncan was characteristically quick to learn his lesson – fortunately for us all – and since then his Haymarket productions have all been independently cast, and therefore able to tour as well.)

Back in 1967 'the Peters' likewise realised that the failure of *Happy Family* had put paid to the cherished plan, and that henceforward the needs of PD's big theatres must be met by productions individually mounted. But at least we had shown that touring could be profitable; and soon a trend was established which gave many of the country's large playhouses a security then undreamt of. Fortunately too, PB's enthusiasm was still undimmed; with fourteen productions, 1967 marked the peak of his output.

'The Peters' already had autumn plans for us, but first *On Approval* continued at the St Martin's until the middle of May (never quite regaining its original momentum) and then went on a lively and encouraging tour for a further six weeks; so that by the end, the four of us had spent nearly a year with that demanding but intensely satisfying comedy. A happy time.

One of our last dates was Manchester, where in those days we always stayed at the Grand Hotel. Among the restaurant staff was Trevor, who was a fan of ours, but for whom the sun rose and set on Vivien Leigh. He longed for a photograph of his idol, but was too nervous to write himself. Dulcie wrote for him, and before the end of the week there came a most affectionate card to us from Vivien – in very shaky writing – promising that Trevor should have his photograph.

Within a fortnight she was dead. She was only fifty-three. What extremes of triumph and disaster, joy and grief, radiant beauty and ill health, love and loneliness (despite the loyalty of friends) she had known within the short span of her career.

Dulcie's current book, *The Murder of Love*, had caused her problems, particularly in its early stages; and she had asked Norman Collins for advice. I don't remember now how or when Norman and Sarah Collins became friends of ours. It could have been through ITV, of which Norman was the founding father and *Boyd* was one of the earliest and most durable successes. (If so, the friendship was happily unaffected by staring at each other across the barricades during the 'strike'.) Or was it through Jack Priestley – a mutual friend? It does not matter. What matters is the friendship, which lasted till his death and which endures with his children and with Sarah – his loved and loving wife for more than fifty years.

Norman brought many blessings to many people, including Dulcie and myself.

Just consider. His interests and activities over a working life of nearly sixty years included: journalism (editorial staff of the *News Chronicle*); publishing (Gollancz); authorship (fifteen novels); television (from Controller BBC to Deputy Chairman ATV); board membership of Sadler's Wells and the Royal Court theatres; wide-ranging charitable work for National Playing Fields, Displaced Persons and Age Concern; a stint as a Commissioner of Inland Revenue; membership of the Loch Ness Investigation Bureau, and of the Carlton Club. Despite this record, he received no recognition from the State. Surely it can only have been because he was one of nature's cross-benchers – how was the Establishment to reconcile the Royal Court with the Carlton, or the Inland Revenue with Loch Ness? Add Norman's humour, so mischievously in contrast with his sober-suited establishment appearance and no slavish respecter of persons or parties – and perhaps it seemed safer to neglect him. A pity. He would have made a good Lord.

He made his mark – his many marks – with humanity and with style. Style in his writing, in his invaluable pioneering work for television, in his stimulating hospitality, his crisply timed anecdotes – above all in that marvellous marriage.

(One example only of Norman's stories. One weekend in the Thirties, he and Sarah were guests of Jack Priestley's in the Isle of Wight. Fellow guests were a well-known poet and his small son. Jack did not take kindly to the child, who was dressed – no fault of his – in the manner of Little Lord Fauntleroy.

At some point in the visit there was an excursion to a neighbouring farm, whose owner was extremely explicit about the prowess of his prize bull.

'Oh please, please,' said the poet going very pale. 'Not in front of the child. He doesn't know the facts of life.'

'Then don't tell him,' said Jack. 'They're too good for him.')

Norman had always shown an encouraging interest in Dulcie's writing. As a man of many careers himself, he did not share the view, widely held (if not widely confessed), that for Dulcie to have two professions was one too many. Not surprisingly Norman's attitude commended itself strongly to Dulcie.

The Murder of Love was the story of Connie Jennings, a research student at Oxford, who is writing a thesis on 'The practice of the Courts' – in the days before abolition of the death penalty – and is advised by her supervisor, Bob Rennalds, with whom she is a little in love, to attend a murder trial then taking place in Oxford, because the accused (named Manson) is an interesting type. Connie indeed finds Manson of such obsessive interest that after his execution she visits his mother, his wife and his mistresses in order to build up a picture of the man and understand if possible what drove him to kill. This, to Connie's surprise, much distresses Bob Rennalds, who, it emerges, had once been a psychiatric patient. An interesting beginning, but with as yet no ending in sight.

Norman was quickly on to the fact that Connie was involved with two abnormal men – one living and one dead – and suggested that Rennalds should find Manson interesting because he recognised in him some of his own psychopathic tendencies; and that he should become disturbed when Connie sets out on her relentless search for clues to Manson's character, in case it should lead to an exposure of his own.

Dulcie now gratefully saw her way through the wood. She would run Connie's twin obsessions in double harness until they merged into nightmare. In so doing, she wrote one of her most effective crime stories.

The *On Approval* run in the West End had enabled us to enjoy a busy social life. At a reception at the French Embassy one evening, Dulcie found herself next to the French actor, Jean Louis Barrault. She told him one of our favourite stories, which she had first heard in the early Thirties from her uncle, Cyril Bailey, a famous classical don at Balliol. It went like this:

A friend of Uncle Cyril's had had, at the age of sixteen or so, a profound mystical experience which had changed his life. It was naturally of great importance to the boy, and of interest to his family, but unknown to the world at large. In due course, however, when the boy had become an Oxford professor of international renown, his experience aroused a corresponding curiosity; and he was invited by the Sorbonne to tell them about it.

Highly gratified, he gave his Oxford friends the news, adding, 'I think, don't you, the very least I can do is to open my remarks in French.' His friends, who knew what his French was like, tried to dissuade him on the grounds that he was to address a learned society who would probably find his English easier to understand.

'That is to miss the point,' he said grandly. 'I am going in a quasi-ambassadorial rôle, and I must show courtesy to my hosts.'

'Well, it's your invitation and your experience,' said his friends. 'You must do it your own way.'

So over to Paris he went to talk about his past, and addressed the astonished Sorbonne as follows:

'Messieurs, mesdames, quand je regarde mon derrière, je vois qu'il est divisé en deux parts.'

Quite recently we heard the story being told by a South American diplomat in London – with an important difference. Gone was the professor to whom it really happened, and in his place was that most celebrated of linguists, Winston Churchill, who had more diplomatic star appeal.

(The story dated from long before Churchill's linguistic reputation, so the authenticity of Uncle Cyril's version is unimpeachable.)

Also this summer, we had our first meeting with Edward Heath.

Sir (now Lord) Harmar Nicholls had persuaded him that the Tory party's image vis-à-vis the Arts needed a good deal of attention if Jennie Lee's great success as Minister for the Arts was not going to convince the electorate that Labour was the natural party of subsidy, and the Tories by contrast were mean and even philistine. Heath asked him to bring forward some members of our profession.

The son of a Tory coal-miner, Harmar had won his political spurs in Churchill's final administration by convincing the great man in the run-up to the election that the Tories could safely out-bid Labour's housing target – and being proved right. He had met Dulcie on a TV panel game, and an immediate and lasting friendship began for us with him and all his family, including his enchanting actress-daughter, Sue. We had made no secret to him of our basic Tory sympathies, and Harmar I suppose thought that we would help demonstrate to his leader that there was 'an acceptable face' of theatre in contrast with that of the much-publicised militant left.

Ted Heath is one of those people – as Jack Priestley was – who is more at ease as a host than a guest; and when at our first meeting Dulcie expressed admiration for his newly decorated chambers in Albany, he left his other guests and happily showed her all over the apartment. Harmar determined to build on this foundation, and used his considerable powers of persuasion to induce us to come out as strongly for Conservative policies as some of our professional colleagues did for Labour.

It was a seductive argument. Why should the only audible voice from the theatre be a socialist or Trotskyist one? It was not as if this represented the majority of performers, who probably voted Tory – if they bothered to vote at all. As an ardent politician, Harmar thought apathy even more dangerous than outright opposition. We could help alert our apathetic colleagues and demonstrate to the world at large that the 'trendy-lefty' image of theatre folk was by no means the whole picture.

I fear I disappointed Harmar – and other Tories over the years – by rejecting, and persuading Dulcie to reject, these and similar overtures. I believed, and still believe, that members of our profession have a positive duty not to parade their political convictions. The reason is a purely practical one. If a performer's politics are known – let alone notorious – and are in conflict with the part being played, this is a disservice to the playwright, and to the audience, who are constantly comparing the character's views with those of the performer. And even if the political performer and his character are in sympathy this is no better, for a work of art may seem to degenerate into no more than a propaganda vehicle.

Peter Donald, as a theatre owner and impresario, had no such scruples; and nor had I in writing this year, at his request, a paper entitled 'Theatre under the Tories'. This was less inconsistent of me than it may seem at first sight.

It was my first enunciation of a theme which remains constant in my theatrical philosophy, and which under my signature was to appear in Arts Council articles, theatre programmes and, perhaps surprisingly, in the house magazine of the AUEW, over the next decade – as well as, anonymously, as part of the Equity submissions to Sir William Emrys Williams' far-reaching theatre enquiry.

Bearing in mind that this first 'edition' was addressed to a political party in opposition, in a theatrical climate where the avant garde were looking forward in anger to the final destruction of the Establishment, the clarion call with which I began was less of a cliché then than it appears today.

'The theatre should have no politics,' I wrote, '— that is to say it must not be the plaything of politicians, or have any party allegiance; though it must of course be free to treat political themes, uncensored by the attitude of the government of the day.'

I then remounted my hobby horse about the importance of the provincial theatre, and the danger – which then appeared terminal – that the country might lose its remaining major regional play-houses and with them any prospect of large-scale touring.

I commended Howard and Wyndham's 'Tory solution' in Glasgow, where they had sold the King's Theatre to the Corporation, who then appointed H and W to run it on their behalf. Glasgow thus acquired a civic theatre overnight, at a fraction of the cost of new construction and without the Corporation being flung into the deep waters of theatrical management, where councillors are not normally at home. I compared the potential benefits of this arrangement with the demise of John Neville's brilliant artistic success at the Nottingham Playhouse, brought about in large measure by the theatre becoming a pawn in local authority party conflicts.

I argued that, though admirable, the Glasgow decision was

only a beginning. 'A theatre is only as important as what goes on inside it' and if potential playgoers were to be wooed into becoming regular playgoers there must be a regular pulse-beat of high-quality productions circulating throughout the country. One essential prerequisite of this was that local authorities who had acquired their theatres must be prepared to guarantee against loss the productions they had invited to come their way. And why not?

The theatre was surely 'no less an amenity than an art gallery, a museum, a library, a park or playing field'. Yet these things, which, unlike the theatre, had no potential for profit, were accepted by ratepayers – many of whom never used them – as proper objects of subsidy.

The actors too must not be forgotten. (There was then no touring allowance or other reflection that the actor on the road had still to maintain his London base where four-fifths of his employment opportunities were concentrated.) Bobby Flemyng, during the *On Approval* tour, found from breakfast conversations in more than one seedy commercial hotel that he was the only 'resident' responsible for paying his bill out of salary.

I ended as follows:

> Given the talent available the theatre should be able to play an increasing part in enriching people's lives. And further, the recording of successful productions in colour for television will not only reach the millions who were unable to see them live but add to their profitability. Sold to the hungry world television market they could earn valuable foreign exchange.

I am not suggesting that what I wrote on this theme had any effect; but I can report that today the position of the most important provincial theatres is more secure under civic than it could have been under private ownership; and that, thanks to Equity, the lot of the touring actor – though no bed of roses – has immeasurably improved. Also, the importance to the public, to performers, to the theatre's profitability and potentially to the national balance of payments of recordings of noteworthy stage productions is at last being recognised.

There is still – and always will be – much to be done. For instance, when I chaired an Arts Council working party on touring in 1976 we found that, in the period we considered (1973-75), one commercial company, unsubsidised except for local guarantees against loss (Triumph Productions) had produced 600 weeks of touring compared with the National's fourteen. The National's touring record has since improved; in the period 1975-84 it has averaged nearly eleven weeks a year, but considering that its touring is subsidised separately from its main operation, and is guaranteed against loss by the Arts Council, in my view the company still falls short of being national in coverage as well as name.

When I went to see Larry Olivier in 1963 in connection with his contribution to our little book, *The Actor and His World*, I asked him specifically about his touring plans for the National. He indicated quite candidly that they had a low priority in his thinking. He had himself done much touring at the outset of his career, and hated it. And so one of the sweetest fruits of success when it came to him was that he need tour no more. He did of course – but comparatively rarely and in special circumstances. There was the triumphal progress with Vivien to the Antipodes in the early Fifties, a European tour of *Titus* in 1957, a visit to Canada ten years later; but the British provinces saw little of the greatest actor of our day once that mantle was deservedly his.

His justification to me for this attitude (which dies hard on the South Bank) was that he would not risk the distortion of productions by having them play in 'unsuitable' theatres, with inadequate facilities away from base. If the provinces were to see National productions they must be *exactly* as they were at the Vic and later in the new building. This was, in my view, perfectionism run mad.

'My' Arts Council working party was told by a spokesman for the National that productions designed for the Olivier stage were untourable, because no other British theatre had the same dimensions. Our comment was: 'The concept that any production at a National Theatre should be designed ... as immobile does not commend itself to us.' And we concluded that 'the Arts Council must now make a touring obligation a condition of the National Theatre's grant in aid, as it once was.' Though my report was accepted by the Arts Council, this recommendation has never been implemented.

In 1984, *Amadeus* – one of the National's greatest successes – went on a protracted tour – but presented by Triumph Productions not the National, and assuredly not in the National's original set. One final illustration. The two sets for 'our' *Heartbreak House* – so well received at Wyndham's in 1962 – were carried around the country on our prior-to-London tour in one pantechnicon. During the prior-to-London tour of *The Black Mikado* in 1975, the little cobbled lane beside the Grand Theatre Leeds was filled from the Tuesday of our second week there with *six* large pantechnicons bearing the symbol NT. For what? *Heartbreak House.*

I am aware that I am using a domestic hammer to crack Stonehenge. But my point is a serious one. The vital ingredients of theatre are play, players and public. Given the funds and artistic skills available to the National, there is no reason why provincial tax-payers, who have contributed as much per capita to those funds as people living in or near the metropolis, should not see more of 'their' company. Indeed there is every reason why they should – even if, due to the vast maintenance costs of the London building, it should be in 'one-pantechnicon' form.

Any lover of Constable or Turner knows that the preliminary sketch may often have more life and movement than the finished masterpiece. So can it be – with plays not dependent on elaborate scenic effects – in the theatre. I am certain that, until the National gives touring its proper weight (and its designers the appropriate instructions), provincial playgoers would prefer to see the company regularly with reduced decor than rarely with the full works. The RSC has recently begun to follow in the footsteps of the pathfinder – Toby Robertson's lamented Prospect Company. May the National too get the message.

The final months of the year and the beginnings of 1968 were taken up with *No. 10*, Ronald Millar's adaptation of a political novel by William Clark (then Vice-President of the World Bank) about a political crisis in 'Zimbadia'. Alastair Sim played a wily Wilsonian premier, Dulcie his wife (the only woman in the cast), John Gregson an idealist liberal Foreign Secretary and myself an idealist right-wing Minister of Defence. What I was doing in Alastair's Cabinet was not explained – nor explicable, except on the good theatrical grounds that without a maverick there would be no play.

We had an enormously successful tour, thanks to Alastair's assured place in the hearts of the Scots public; then flew to Canada for 'English Fortnight' in Toronto – the male ASM in charge of wigs and toupées being arrested when we changed planes at Montreal for attempting to enter Canada with eight disguises, one of them female!

It was for Dulcie and me a first opportunity to sample living and working across the Atlantic, and we loved it – not least the marvellous room service so inappropriately called 'European Style'.

We played the 3500-seater O'Keefe Centre for the Performing Arts – a luxurious and impressive building, ill-suited to the presentation of straight plays. The amplification system is at its best at the back, but from there no change of facial expression is detectable on performers' faces; come closer until you can see features, and the acoustics perversely deteriorate.

Perhaps things are better now, but when, for my sins, I returned in 1977 as old father Barrett (of Wimpole Street) – in the musical version – it was as daunting as ever to tread that stage. On this second occasion however, I was able to see Nureyev with the Canadian Ballet Company – a personality and a medium which could at last in every sense fill that theatre.

In spite of these problems, *No. 10* went well – graced one night by the sparkle of Princess Alexandra and Angus Ogilvy – and with Hugh and Shirley Walker, the Merrys and the Cunninghams we made very special friendships. Hugh ran the O'Keefe with professionalism and charm – the shortcomings of the theatre were not his fault. Of Scottish descent, he is a transatlantic version of Peter Donald (as indeed Shirley Walker is of Peter's Cleone), and they share passions for the theatre, the golf course and for entertaining their friends. So we were made to feel most happily at home.

We lingered a couple of days in Montreal to see 'Expo', and to spend a day with Pam Harley, one of Dulcie's oldest friends, who took us up into the Laurentian hills where the fall colourings were at their peak.

Back home, we played a week at Golders Green and opened at the Strand to pretty indifferent reviews. We were an experienced cast and, with one exception, took them philosophically – the more so perhaps because they were directed at the play rather than our performances.

The exception was Alastair, who appeared deeply wounded. Our sympathy evaporated however, when – to our astonishment – he began to take his disappointment out on the company, on stage. Particularly on me. Eventually, for the first and I hope the only time in my career, I began to retaliate in character. I was helped in this shameful proceeding by our rôles being at daggers drawn. Was this, I wonder, why I was chosen as his principal target?

I was not the only one. Poor John Gregson got the treatment too; and when, for the fourth or fifth time, Alastair, in spite of her remonstrances, failed to give Dulcie a 'clean' cue for her first entrance, she was moved to roll up *The Times* and bring it down on his head saying, 'You silly old fool' – getting a bigger laugh than his own cherished business with some Alka-Seltzer. Her cue was clean thereafter.

Alastair was a comedian of genius; and it is no part of my purpose in this book to go hunting for feet of clay. The story is nevertheless admissible for its effect on us. It is certainly the only occasion on which Dulcie has made an unrehearsed assault on a fellow performer; and for me it was the first of only two occasions – the other still many years ahead – when I actually dreaded going to the theatre each evening. For one who loves his work as much as I do, it was a trauma not to be forgotten.

X
1968

Meeting 'the Auk' – Dulcie and the yashmak – Peter Willes, Eileen and Funeral Games *– Nottingham expedition – The Bakers' Arms – Out of the Question – Gladys Cooper – distinguished gathering – Lewis and Sybil – a revolution and a heresy discussed – Sybil and* Village Wooing *– 'Envoi' by an old friend – Noël comes to lunch – Fleur Cowles and Tom Meyer*

After these events a holiday was badly needed, and at the beginning of March we flew to Tenerife, which disappointed us apart from the bonus of meeting Sid and Val James for the first of many times; we then went on to Marrakesh which we adored, in spite of a bad beginning.

We stayed at the historic Mamounia Hotel – historic for us because of Churchill's recuperative visits during the war – and had specified a room with a view over the famous garden towards the Atlas Mountains. We arrived after dark and were taken *downwards* to our room; our bathroom had a self-flushing WC which operated throughout the night at two-minute intervals despite appeals for a plumber. Eventually thanks to double doses of Mogadon we fell asleep, only to be woken in an excessively jolly manner at six am in the mistaken belief that we were part of a package tour with an early flight.

In the circumstances my interview with the manager was very restrained. He apologised profusely and explained that the King of Morocco had suddenly reserved a hundred rooms for diplomats – which had not been required. He could now therefore move us to our proper room – adding as an afterthought that it was Churchill's. True or false, it was perfection, and I painted and Dulcie wrote happily on its balcony.

The Mamounia's garden is bounded on one side by the ancient crenellated red-ochre mud wall of the city. Over it we could see a dusty flat expanse which was seething with activity. Row upon row of Bedouin tents, some furnished with rich carpets and silver

178

lamps, others with cheap imported equivalents; a wonderful variety of tribal costumes, dominated by the brilliant clashing colours of the Touaregs; horses everywhere elaborately caparisoned, their riders armed with swords and rifles. In the middle of the tents was an empty space, apparently a sort of parade ground. Upon this the tribesmen came galloping in line abreast twenty or thirty at a time; pulled their horses savagely back on their haunches, simultaneously firing their rifles one-handed into the air. It was a dramatic spectacle, and was known as a fantasia. One morning they had gone. The area might have been hoovered; there was not a scrap of paper, not a bottle or tin can – nothing to show that hundreds of men (and horses) had been encamped there to honour their King.

(Walking Titus in Regent's Park I used to commiserate on summer Mondays with the staff whose job was to clear the weekend's litter. If the weather had been fine it would take them the whole week to clear things up – in preparation for the next load of British rubbish. Why have we become so thoughtless and filthy in our habits?)

Ted Seago had given us a letter of introduction to 'the Auk' – Field Marshal Sir Claud Auchinleck – who was living in retirement in Marrakesh. He was away visiting his sister in Spain and we did not meet him until our last day.

We came upon the great man in his very poky little flat (where he lived alone with an Arab servant) listening to an Australian test-match commentary on his radio.

'Ted told me you were coming. How lovely to meet you. How long are you staying?'

'We have to go tomorrow.'

'Dammit. I've just got a new car. And I thought I might drive you over the Atlas and into the Sahara. It's worth doing you know.'

We shall always regret that we couldn't accept that invitation. Then eighty-four, he was such a keen-eyed, courteous, craggily beautiful old man. His room was a miniature museum of the Indian Army – in which he served from 2nd Lieutenant (1903) to his retirement as Commander-in-Chief (1947).

'Which were the best years?' I asked him.

'When I commanded my battalion, the 1st Punjabis,' he replied without hesitation. 'As a high-up you lose touch with the men.'

We much admired his sharp-focus little landscapes – like Lord

Alexander he was a pupil of Ted Seago's. How many old soldiers are talented painters; the tradition I suppose going back before photography, but lingering on in the training of young officers of the Auk's vintage to give them an eye for country – spurs, re-entrants, covered lines of advance, dead ground, etc.

Emotionally (we felt), his heart was still in India. We left him at sunset, a whisky and soda in his hand, gazing at the distant Atlas – his surrogate Himalayas.

Dulcie's book this year was *Died in the Red*, the story of a nasty little murder in a nasty little suburban hairdresser's. As part of the publicity campaign, she was to address the Men and Women of Today Club in the Derry and Toms' roof-garden restaurant. On the way up in the lift Dulcie recognised the principal speaker at the luncheon, whom we had met; but he either didn't recognise her or decided, as author of a serious work, to rise above a mere crime-writer.

The Men and Women of Today looked to Dulcie like the men and women of the day before yesterday, and as she was speaking first she decided to cheer them up with a mildly risqué story. So she told them the wartime chestnut about the American in the Middle East, who at some official gathering found himself sitting next to a figure swathed in veil and yashmak, but with the most lustrous and appealing eyes. After showing her pictures of the wife and kids back home – an opening gambit to which Dulcie herself in the war had often been exposed – he put his hand on her knee and watched for a reaction. The beautiful eyes widened, which he took for encouragement. He moved his hand higher and the eyes still looked searchingly into his face. Higher still and the tension was becoming electric, when from behind the yashmak came a hoarse whisper. 'Dinna jump when you get to the crutch. I'm MacGregor of British Intelligence.'

The Men and Women of Today were enchanted. Not so the principal speaker, who – quite unknown to Dulcie – had written a work of scholarship about the emancipation of women in the last days of the Ottoman Empire. His address involved numerous references to the casting off of the yashmak – each of which brought the house down.

Before our next joint enterprise I was approached by Peter Willes (now in the early stages of a most distinguished contribution to television, as Head of Drama for Yorkshire TV), to appear with

Vivien Merchant, Bill Fraser and Ian MacShane in Joe Orton's *Funeral Games* – his last television play. I was to play a phoney priest, head of an esoteric sect of his own invention; and Peter felt constrained to explain to me at length that the play was not against religion but against religious charlatans – like Molière's *Tartuffe*. Thus reassured, I agreed to do it and we all had a marvellous time, with Orton's black humour and Wildean rhythms.

Before it was shown I thought it best to make to our housekeeper, Eileen (a devout Catholic), the same speech that Peter had made to me. I need not have bothered. 'Mother's laughter was heard all over Camden Town,' her daughter reported next day.

The hierarchy in Monaco, however, was too sophisticated to share the simplicity of Eileen's faith, and *Funeral Games* was banned from the local TV festival.

Eileen Theresa Leahy has now (1985) been part of our lives for more than a quarter of a century. Born in Dingle, Co. Kerry, seventy-three years ago, she has four attractive children, whom she resolutely brought up through the war years, with her soldier husband more often than not away. She came to us when newly widowed in 1958. There are now six grandchildren and two great-grandchildren to swell the clan.

Eileen's standards of work and behaviour and faith have never wavered in a wavering age. Yet she is tolerant of those many who do not share her certainties; a tireless good neighbour to young and old; a lover of dogs and birds; no stranger to grief and hardship, yet full of laughter. So slight now that a puff of wind would blow her away, were it not that she is as tough as old boots.

Her conversation can only be described as a stream of consciousness, which is best left to flow past the listener unchecked. The general theme will then become apparent, though only God and Eileen will have understood it all.

When we moved out of London in the Seventies we made a home for her within our country flat. She has occupied it periodically, but never for long; the pull of Camden Town, with its unending demands on her apparently inexhaustible sympathies, is still too strong.

She has picked up from us the theatrical habit of calling everyone 'darling' – from 'Madam, darling' to 'Lord Carrington, darling'. I hope we never have to be without her.

*　　*　　*

Maisie Mosco was one of the few young playwrights who submitted to us at 'Allied' a script which we felt was virtually ready to go into production. It was called *Vacant Possession* and was a highly original study of three old people (two men and one woman) so terrified of the outside world and its infections that they never opened a window and regarded the young couple who were quite prepared to wait for vacant possession of their house as sinister space invaders. John Neville, who had finally decided to throw in his hand at Nottingham, was equally enthusiastic about the piece, and suggested we should do it for him together with a rather unwieldy modern Russian play called *Confessions at Night*, by Arbuzov, author of *The Promise*. Neither seemed likely to set the Trent, let alone the Thames, on fire, but our parts in *Vacant Possession* were worth going a long way to play, and so we agreed.

It was an awkward time at Nottingham. John, who has among his many gifts the capacity to inspire intense personal devotion both in the public and among colleagues, had virtually gone by the time we got there, leaving the company in a sort of Götterdämmerung, wondering whether if they accepted contracts with John's successor it would seem a betrayal of John.

Fortunately for us, we were not involved in this crisis of loyalty, though acutely and sympathetically aware of the atmosphere it generated.

Fortunately too, we had very special 'digs', with Bernard and Valerie Baker in their graceful late-Georgian house in the shadow of the Minster at Southwell. Valerie is a cousin of Kitty Black, a very old friend of ours from the days when, in a position of influence with Binkie Beaumont, she had successfully pushed Dulcie's candidacy for her first West End part in *The Little Foxes*.

Valerie herself, deflected by marriage and the demands of three small children from her chosen career in the theatre, was locally famous as a Notts County Champion at golf, and as the director of the most professional amateur theatre in the country – at Averham (pronounced Air'm) on the outskirts of Newark. Her theatre – a large converted barn at the bottom of a vicarage garden – was famous itself as the birthplace of Donald Wolfit's career; busts of Sir Donald and Valerie still adorn its foyer.

As hostess, informed theatre enthusiast and critic, dog lover, steadying influence on the golf course and stalwart friend, her hospitality has meant much over the years to Dulcie and me, and we count ourselves much blessed whenever a provincial engagement brings us within range of 'The Bakers' Arms' – for the moment located in her native Sussex.

Bernard, her husband, was a quiet man, and by the time we met him already a martyr to bronchitis which later turned to emphysema. But if at first he seemed to melt into the crowd, the crowd individually and collectively were to him of intense interest, as would be shown when they had gone, by his comments – shrewd but rarely unkind. A brilliant scholar at Harrow and Cambridge, he felt it his duty to turn aside from the academic world to help his father run the family steel business in Sheffield. He was a professional Old Harrovian – the *Harrow Record* the most consulted volume on his bookshelves – and though in this context I am a rank amateur, I was welcomed with particular warmth for having been to the right school. Although apparently so self-effacing he was undeniably the head of the household, and like Valerie a generous and devoted parent – in joy, in tragedy, and in all that lies between.

For one of John Neville's lost army we were able to offer a temporary solution. Annie Teeton (now Rowan) was quite the prettiest stage manager in Dulcie's and my experience; more important, she was also the most efficient. Dark, petite and with rosy cheeks she looked like a young sixth-former, but had that effortless command of cast and staff with which age has nothing to do.

We recommended her to John Roberts, our next West End employer, who though alarmed by her youth and charm – qualities which though agreeable anywhere are viewed with some suspicion in a stage manager – agreed to engage her and never regretted it.

John, a friend of ours since our South African tour in 1954, came up to Nottingham with an American play, *Absence of a 'Cello* by Ira Wallach, which he was going to present with Gladys Cooper and directed by Nigel Patrick, and had rechristened *Out of the Question*. Would we play the leading parts?

John explained that it had already been anglicised by the author. Not enough, it seemed to us. For instance, his egg-head professor (my part) was housed 'in a duplex apartment on the King's Road' instead of a conversion in Bloomsbury or the approaches to Hampstead; and Dulcie's part was far too cosy for an English blue-stocking. Nigel felt as we did and, together, with John's approval (and I'm afraid the author's disapproval), we two experienced play-doctors got to work to haul a most entertaining comic idea across the Atlantic.

The play was about the pressurising of an impecunious academic to join a monster commercial organisation which kept its labour force of all grades in a sort of Olympic Village and fed them on evangelistic slogans promising health, happiness and the pursuit of profit. It had not been a great success in New York, perhaps because professor and firm were of the same nation. But make him English or French (Pierre Dux had a great success with it in Paris) and have him being brain-drained to America, and the comedy was much sharper. I was particularly pleased with a short quarrel scene I wrote for Dulcie and me, which not only made her part far more astringent but earned her a round of applause every night.

Anyway, although Ira Wallach – a gentle creature – was so miserable that he never saw it in London, he was at least able to cry for eleven months on his way to the bank.

They were eleven particularly happy months for us – back at the St Martin's for the third time in the decade (an experience now and for the foreseeable future only available to casts of *The Mousetrap*), and above all working with Gladys Cooper for the first time and falling inevitably under her spell.

She was nearly eighty when we met, and was slim and lithe and vital. True, the face which had been a pin-up for sixty years was very lined, but they were lines of humour and experience, etched even deeper by her worship of the Californian sun. The blue eyes sparkled with fun and occasionally outrage – particularly when decrepit old ladies struggled up to her room after matinees, confessed to having been fans of hers since their schooldays and then expected her to help them down the stairs.

She had always loved driving, especially driving home to Henley after the show, and was very angry indeed when her family (daughter Joan and son-in-law Robert Morley) applied a veto. 'I don't know what they're fussing about,' she said to us. 'I'm perfectly safe. I just get into the fast lane of the M4 and keep up a steady 60 mph.' (We understood the family's anxieties.) A week later she said, straight-faced, 'Well I've agreed. Come and see my hire car.' Outside the theatre was a Lotus Elan, so low and streamlined that it barely showed above the kerb. Towering above it was its driver, a handsome bearded young man. Gladys lowered herself almost horizontally into the passenger seat. 'It does 120,' she said gleefully. 'That'll teach Robert.'

Robert, who loved her dearly, had his 'revenge' on her eightieth birthday, in a manner which made theatre history. He and John Roberts 'bought out the house' (i.e. offered their money back, or seats for another performance, to those members of the public who had booked that night) and installed eighty of Gladys's friends – as the sole audience – in the front half-dozen rows of the stalls. The secret was successfully kept from Gladys; even the company was only told ten minutes before curtain up.

The performance began normally. Gladys's first entrance was greeted with hysterical applause by the gallant eighty, trying – and failing – to sound like a full house on a Dame's eightieth birthday. Gladys, who had been in management herself long ago, was puzzled. 'What's the matter with the house?' she whispered to Dulcie. 'I thought we were a success.' The door bell rang on the set and Gladys said to Lucy Fleming (Celia Johnson's daughter, who was playing ours), 'That's my grandson. Let him in will you darling?'

But instead of the grandson came a beaming Robert Morley with a tray of champagne. Astonishment, affection, gratification, outrage, and resignation, as she apologetically toasted the audience, were successively to be seen on Gladys's face.

'Very nice dear, thank you,' she said to Robert. 'Now off you go – we have a performance to give.'

'That's where you're wrong,' he said. 'We're giving you a very special present – a night off and supper at the Ivy. House lights, please.'

And the lights came up on our 'very special' audience which included the family, of course, Sybil Thorndike and Lewis Casson, Zena Dare, the Culvers, Ambrosine Philpotts, Tim Nugent and many many more – all standing and applauding like mad.

At supper, Dulcie found herself next to Lewis – a little deaf, a little blind, but now, with all political passions spent, a most congenial companion and devoted to Dulcie. (What a year this was for theatrical anniversaries. Some time before – within a week – we had attended two theatrical diamond weddings: Lewis and Sybil, and Austin Melford and Jessie Winter.)

The old man suddenly said to her, 'Dulcie, I have recently become very preoccupied with the question of eternity. Do you think, if Sybil and Michael don't mind, you would have lunch with me one day so that we can discuss it?' Alas, Lewis died before the lunch could be arranged.

*   *   *

I had been a long time winning my spurs with Lewis (Sybil, by comparison, was a push-over) because, I think, as one of the new Equity councillors in 1949, when the membership rejected him so abruptly (significantly not Sybil, who served for another ten years or so), I was associated in his mind with a bitter humiliation.

We had one memorable meeting in 1965 which was such fun that, if any ice remained, it must have broken. It was a splendid party at the Savoy to mark the opening of *Three Sisters* by Lee Strasberg's Studio Company of New York, as part of Peter Daubeny's World Theatre Season. It was to be savaged by the critics; but fortunately the same company also presented *Blues for Mr Charlie* by the young black writer, James Baldwin, which provoked the National Front but was otherwise admired.

There were no formal seating arrangements at the party, so theatre guests just made up tables as they came. Ours consisted of Lewis and Sybil, Frankie Howerd, David Warner and James Baldwin (who declared himself a great fan of Dulcie's from her late-night films on American TV). The buffet was superb. 'Better than our cocoa and biscuits, Lewis darling,' boomed Sybil as we all tucked in.

The careers, backgrounds and ages of our table could not have been more diverse, but the result was an enthralling free-for-all that kept us up into the small hours. There was inevitably discussion of the notorious Strasberg 'method' as well as of the related revolution sparked off by John Osborne; and, to my surprise, there was broad agreement that, among much that had been of high quality in the previous decade, there had been one besetting sin – arrogance. Though perhaps an essential attribute of all revolutionaries, it had had a particularly unfortunate effect in the theatre. New playwrights, having dismissed the well-made play, had wrapped themselves up in introspection – often obscure, gloomy, shapeless and hard to share. Actors had had to develop a style of acting to match – we are as much at the mercy of the playwright as the public is – and all too easily fell for the heresy that 'it doesn't matter what you do, it's what you are that counts.' Arrogance again, with inaudibility as a by-product. Some critics had claimed that only socially significant themes had any place in contemporary theatre. This, we agreed, was the greatest nonsense of all; the revolution had been necessary because the cult of the 'French window' was moribund, but it was no answer in the long run to substitute as a panacea the cult of the 'kitchen sink'. Each is a useful invention but they are not alternatives. Well-equipped houses need both – and much besides. So does the theatre.

Lewis's Memorial Service, in June 1969, was at the Abbey, and the family asked me to be an usher, together with Paul Scofield, Emlyn Williams and Dickie Attenborough. Honesty compels me to reveal that Emlyn and Dickie did nothing except engage in animated conversation in the nave. Paul and I were the work-horses, each accompanied by one of the Abbey's professional ushers. Mine was very complimentary about my contribution. 'I suppose, Mr Denison,' he added, 'you wouldn't consider taking it up?' 'One day, perhaps,' I said.

He insisted on seating me in the front row opposite Sybil – ethereal in white – who was surrounded by all the Casson clan. Next to me was John Gielgud who was to give a reading, and was clearly both nervous and emotional. I decided to put him at his ease. I should have known better.

'How glorious the Abbey looks now it's been cleaned,' I murmured.

'Much better when it was dirty,' he flashed.

I had forgotten that he was an old boy of Westminster school, to whom the cleaning must have seemed the work of vandals.

We saw Sybil whenever we could in the nine years that were left to her – years of increasing disability and often agonising pain from arthritis, which however could never quench her capacity for enthusiasm, for loving and for faith, so movingly described in John Casson's *Lewis and Sybil*.

One illustration. In 1970, in a triple bill of one-act comedies by Shaw, we included our much-loved two-character *Village Wooing*. The female character had been written for Sybil and created by her in the early Thirties. So we invited her to a perform-ance, followed by supper at home. Pat (John's wife, and a most devoted daughter-in-law) was her escort; and at the end of the show I went down to the stage door from the dressing-rooms to suggest to Pat that she should take Sybil straight on to Regent's Park to save her climbing two long flights of stairs to Dulcie's room. Sybil would have nothing of the plan. 'Oh no, Michael darling, Dulcie was so wonderful and I want to tell her right away.' As she climbed the stairs on my arm, she began to sing. 'Forgive me,' she said, 'but it helps. And it's better than screaming when the pain is very bad.'

On her memorial in the Abbey are the following words:

Dame Sybil Thorndike CH
wife of
Sir Lewis Casson

St Joan or Hecuba, great actress of your age,
All womanhood your part, the world your stage,
To each good cause you lent your vigorous tongue,
Swept through the years, the champion of the young.
But now the scripts lie fading on the shelf,
We celebrate your finest rôle, your self.
The calls, the lights grow dim but not this part –
The Christian spirit, the great generous heart.

There is no indication of the author. It was in fact Jack Priestley.

On 29 October, Noël Coward came to lunch at Cumberland Place (and declared that the little house had once been occupied by Gertie Lawrence). Having been two or three times to his Swiss home, a return of hospitality was long overdue.

(On one particularly busy day in Noël's life – his only ballet had been damned with faint praise, and his only novel (*Pomp and Circumstance*) had fared little better – he was meeting the press, of whom by then he had had a basinful, at an evening reception to launch the 'Night of 100 Stars' in aid of the combined theatrical charities. We were talking to him when a smooth and unattractive journalist interrupted us. 'Mr Coward,' he said, 'for what do you suppose you will be remembered when you are dead?' 'Charm,' said Noël – with none at all.)

His charm will certainly be one of the attributes that we remember with gratitude and joy. For it was compounded of good manners and his unique talent to amuse – himself as well as others – and would flower wherever the circumstances were propitious. They certainly seemed to be that day at lunch.

To make up the party – we could only seat four with any comfort at Cumberland Place – we had invited Fleur Cowles. Fleur and her husband, Tom Montague Meyer, were then comparatively new friends of ours – but she still seemed perfect 'casting' for this particular occasion. There cannot be anybody, I would swear, now living in London, who knows more interesting people – royalty, presidents, diplomats, statesmen, lawyers, artists, writers, musicians, singers, dancers, actors. What is more, she and Tom know them not as social 'scalps' but as friends. Of course, as hosts, they enjoy the celebrities that gather under their roof – but not more than the celebrities (major or minor) do themselves. I was privileged to be talking to Harold Macmillan at Fleur's on the day he had become the Earl of Stockton. 'In my young days,' he said 'there were many hostesses in London giving these sort of civilised parties – now Fleur's the only one.'

Fleur is American. Her first husband, 'Mike' Cowles, was owner of *Look* magazine. In the nine years of her marriage to him, her influence helped quadruple its circulation (with a matching increase in advertising revenue) by turning it from 'men only' into a publication for all the family. Four years into the marriage, Cowles gave her his 'most exciting and expensive gift' – the wherewithal to create and edit *Flair*, which in only thirteen monthly issues set new standards of presentation and content in the magazine world. Alas 'no magazine was ever sold by more mistaken methods' – Fleur's own words. It sold 365,000 copies a month, but it was priced at less than a third of its production costs and, because of unique features of its format – the famous hole in the cover, etc. – failed to attract the big advertisers.

Prior to all this, service as a budding teenage speech writer for the War Production Board had led to her first White House assignment by President Truman with the Post-war Famine Emergency Committee. The White House, once entered, became almost a second home. President Eisenhower sent her as Ambassador to the Queen's Coronation in 1953, then to Greece and England as a 'Presidential agent' on the Cyprus issue; also to Egypt, Brazil and Iran.

By 1955 her marriage to Mike Cowles was over, and she set up home in London as Mrs Tom Montague Meyer. Almost immediately she began to paint, with growing and eventually phenomenal success; within four years she had her first one-man exhibition – my fellow feminists must forgive me, it is what she calls it herself. Since then she has had thirty-five – nineteen in the USA, seven in the UK, two each in Holland, Germany and Brazil, and one each in Italy, France and Spain.

(For one who began painting a year earlier, I cannot claim a similar success. I must rest my reputation on one unlikely event.

In 1970, Elspeth Hoare, owner of the next-door flat in our Buckinghamshire home, decided to move to Bath. Her rooms were a treasure-house – furniture, pictures, books, porcelain of exquisite quality. She had become a great friend; but what to give her as a leaving present? I decided to paint her a little 'loo' picture of the house for her new home.

A few weeks later she rang me from Bath, sounding flustered.

'Michael dear, I thought you ought to know. My new central heating caught fire the other day – and I'm afraid, among other things, your little picture got damaged.'

'Darling, I'm so sorry about the fire – but don't worry about my picture. I'll do you another.'

'Oh no – thank you – that won't be necessary. I just wanted to tell you that it has gone with the Canaletto to the best man in Bristol to be restored.'

To be restored in one's lifetime should be a source of pride. Alas for mine: the 'best man in Bristol' improved my canvas no end.)

To return to Fleur's painting. She specialises in flowers and lions and tigers – in fact all the 'big cats' – in butterflies, and in strange little boats afloat on seas without horizons, abandoned by humanity but filled instead with flowers or lions or tigers. Every detail is painted with great precision and with a palette the brightness of which would have won Winston Churchill's approval (and probably did). Her 'trick' is to juxtapose her favourite subjects in a surreal dream world, and to vary their scale. For instance, in the picture which she gave us, a small but dignified tiger rests on the leaf of a giant parrot tulip (floating in space), and is watched over by a butterfly and a moth of Fleur's imagining which are almost as large as he. Not surprisingly, Dali is a hero of hers, and she has written authoritatively about him, as she has of Egyptian art.

Her husband Tom is the apparently still centre of this whirl of artistic and social activity. Very much his own man, whether running his family business, farming in Sussex or devoting long hours to hospital administration, he is no less so in Fleur's world. How often one has seen him sitting quiet but bright-eyed – away from the centre of activity the better to observe it – watching with pride his wife among her guests; ready to contribute his knowledge and humour and protection if needed; but if not, quite content to be a spectator.

Since 1970 we have spent every available Christmas with them. When possible they come to our first nights.

Another unclouded friendship. Another blessing to count.

XI
1969

Michael and Howard and Wyndham – a brave campaign ends in defeat – Felix Aylmer and a presidency avoided – Celia Johnson and Peter Fleming – a musical seduction – 'Holy Week'

Early in 1968 Peter Donald had invited me to become Play Adviser to the production side of Howard and Wyndham on a generous retainer. It was the nearest to security I had ever been and I gratefully accepted.

My principal initiative was to suggest that John Neville would be the ideal person to do for Howard and Wyndham what he had done for Nottingham. After all, few, if any, of his successful and distinguished classical revivals had toured or been seen in London. Given his zeal and experience his contribution could be tremendous, and complementary to Peter Bridge's.

Alas for my theories. I had overlooked the fact that after his idealistic battles against political currents in Nottingham he would want a change. No more pioneering, no more provinces, no more revivals – even no more acting for the time being. He wanted – and who shall blame him? – to indulge himself by directing new plays of his own choosing in the West End and to give starring opportunities to some of his Nottingham favourites. (My personal responsibility was minimal, but in view of the consequences I blame myself for not having assessed the probable effect on John of the 'Battle of Nottingham'.) In the event the plays chosen were esoteric and defeated talented casts; the public stayed away, and much money was lost.

It was one of a number of unrelated disasters which struck Howard and Wyndham over the next couple of years, crippling Peter Donald's imaginative attempts to move from theatre ownership into production, television and publishing, and leading successively to a take-over, Peter's resignation and personal bankruptcy.

It was a nightmare reversal of fortune for Peter, Cleone and the

191

children, which they weathered with exemplary resolution and dignity. Friends stood firm. A past Captain of Sunningdale Golf Club, he had to resign as a bankrupt. He was unanimously re-elected at the next Committee meeting. And now at last after more than a decade of anxiety the financial clouds have lifted – and Peter and Cleone in retirement are themselves again.

Apart from giving us our first joint engagement – £15 a week with a guarantee of six weeks (in Aberdeen in 1939) – which enabled us to get married, and then proving his friendship repeatedly throughout our lives, his 'gift' of the advisory job with Howard and Wyndham had one unexpected result.

After twenty years as President of Equity, that great servant of his profession Felix Aylmer decided this spring to seek election no further. (I proposed, with the support of Charles Farrell, that this called for a portrait rather than the statutory photograph of past presidents. The result is a marvellous likeness by John Gilroy, which is very much at home in the Council room.) I was nominated by Dickie Attenborough to succeed him. It was a position I did not want; but I could offer little resistance to the Attenborough technique, which has wrung millions of pounds, dollars, rupees, etc., out of men who would have claimed to be hard-headed beforehand, and more often than not, given the success of his pictures, have been able to resume their claims with added assurance afterwards. So I agreed to stand, provided my financial relationship with PD was not felt to disqualify me. Fortunately for my peace of mind, my fellow-councillors felt that it did; and so I was spared from that honourable bed of nails. (A further and final attempt to draft me in 1976 was happily frustrated by the management of *The Black Mikado* perversely deciding to have matinées on Tuesdays – Equity Council days – an experiment which lapsed soon after the Presidential election!)

Meanwhile, until the middle of July when Gladys, John Roberts, Dulcie and I agreed for various reasons to call it a day, *Out of the Question* ran happily on.

Lucy brought her parents, Peter Fleming and Celia Johnson, from their Chiltern hill to lunch on ours. At this time I had known Peter slightly for thirty years and Celia rather better for nearly fifty – the explanation for the latter unlikely statistic being, as already recorded, that her father had been our family doctor.

I have a clear mental photograph of her as a schoolgirl in Dr

Johnson's house in Richmond – wearing the unbecoming black stockings, blue 'gym-slip' and white blouse which was the regular school uniform of the day. Dominating her appearance, as they did throughout her life, were those enormous eyes – seen then through outsize horn-rimmed glasses. Cool but not unfriendly, amused yet withdrawn, loving but never gushing, they were a perfect instrument for communicating both the humour and the deep emotions of her peculiarly English art – though needless to say this assessment formed no part of a small boy's 'mental photograph'.

For a star of her eminence, she was a perhaps uniquely devoted wife and mother – ready to demand (and even more remarkably, able to achieve), as a condition for her services, engagements far shorter than her drawing power could have ensured.

As for Peter, he was on the surface even cooler, even more withdrawn; but his love for Celia, for his children and for his brother Ian was indeed 'an ever-fixéd mark'. For strangers and acquaintances it was not easy to get under his guard. My success was only partial; Dulcie's was swift, complete, and rewarding, for the solitary traveller, the trenchant and witty *Times* leader-writer, the brave soldier had much to tell.

We last saw him – as indeed did Lucy – on her wedding day in 1971. It was a splendid Fleming occasion, with the band of the 'Ox and Bucks' Light Infantry on the lawn and the bride and groom going away by helicopter. 'And then,' as Celia wrote to me, 'he went to Scotland which he loved and died on an instant. One can only be glad for him that he who never wasted one minute of his life, was not forced to waste any of it in dying.' Celia herself died equally suddenly when still at the height of her powers in 1982; and I was glad to be able to quote this letter to her children.

Ever since *Where Angels Fear to Tread*, we had been trying to win a place in the queue for Glen Byam Shaw's services as a director. This was more difficult than ever now, for he was turning himself, in spite of – or was it because of? – a complete ignorance of opera, into a distinguished opera director. We went down to lunch with him and his wife (Angela Baddeley) at Wargrave during the early stages of this process, and found him in headphones in a hut at the bottom of the garden trying to relate strange operatic sounds to story-lines that were even stranger. The successes at the Coliseum that followed were based on telling those stories simply, and were enhanced by the design skills and personal devotion of 'Percy' Harris (the last of the famous Motley trio still working in the theatre) who has been Glen's artistic partner for nearly fifty years, and, since the death of his beloved Angie, in even greater demand than before as friend and chauffeuse as well. His operatic schedule provided no space for a play in 1969 but he promised us a slice of his time in 1970.

We therefore decided to build a progamme round *Village Wooing*, preceding it with Barrie's untypically astringent little piece, *The Will*, and following it – most unwisely – with Noël Coward's *Ways and Means*. The first two worked well – *Wooing* particularly so – but when Barbara Murray, who had her showiest part of the evening in the Coward, decided she didn't want to come into London with it, we had no alternative but to think again.

At this moment there came to us, from Peter Willes at Yorkshire TV who seemed at this period to have become our last remaining link with television, a play by Hugh Whitemore aptly called *Unexpectedly Vacant*. It was the story of married stage partners reduced to playing *Private Lives* on the pier, when twenty years too old for the parts. He wanted to quit and buy a tobacconist's shop with their savings; she had not lost hope, and was particularly concerned to rekindle his ambition by arranging an interview for him with a West End manager. Nothing would come of it obviously, but in order not to disappoint her he agreed to soldier on. They were wonderful parts; and to increase our pleasure in them, the only other character – a very 'refeened' digs landlady – was played by Alison Leggatt, who had been one of our most influential teachers at drama school, thirty years before.

For London's theatre world, the end of the decade was dominated by 'Holy Week' – as Noël nicknamed the celebrations of his seventieth birthday. For us, certainly, the climax was *A Talent to Amuse*. This was a midnight gala in which every note and every word was his. As a consequence – and also because a cast of many talents was meticulously drilled by Wendy Toye – it was not only highly emotional, but also for the first, and I hope not the last, time in my experience of such performances, it didn't go on a moment too long. The New Year brought the glad tidings of his knighthood, followed by a telegram in mid-January inviting us to a celebration at the Savoy – 'just family'. A large, happy and united family.

* * *

Finally, a confession and a revelation. Yielding to none in our love and admiration for Noël, we never called him 'Master'; and were indeed embarrassed to hear others do so, particularly those who affected a hushed and reverential tone. When this happened in his presence, we were astonished that he allowed it – it seemed so out of character.

In 1982, I was invited to write his 'notice' for the Dictionary of National Biography. I was determined to get to the bottom of 'the "Master" mystery', which no work that I consulted referred to – merely accepting it as a fact of life. Eventually I rang Graham Payn at the Chalet Coward (pronounced 'Covar') in Switzerland.

'Who called him Master first and why?' I asked him.

'Oh it was Lornie – as a *joke*. And somehow it stuck.'

A joke! How splendid.

'Lornie' was Lorn Loraine, his adored and adoring super-secretary and 'one of the principal mainstays' of his life, for forty years. That he should accept an element of mockery in her love is totally in character – even if on other lips it got out of hand.

III The Seventies

Statistics are notoriously susceptible of conflicting interpretations; but they appear to confirm, in Dulcie's case and mine, our conviction that the Seventies were a more ambiguous period in our careers than the previous decade. For instance, in the Sixties, out of eight joint appearances in the West End we had long, or at least respectable, runs in seven; the comparable figures for the Seventies were two out of five. And yet in the Sixties Dulcie had no individual appearances in London at all; in the Seventies three successes out of three; and my individual tally moved from one out of one to three out of five.

The vital statistic however, which there is no gainsaying, is that in the new decade we only worked together in London in four years of the ten. And this was a disappointment for a partnership such as ours, particularly after the successes of the Sixties.

Fluctuations are of course part and parcel of most theatrical careers and are usually a source of mystery to those involved. After all, one does not suddenly become more – or less – talented; but it is as difficult as it is important to hang on to that conviction, particularly when the going is tough.

There is no doubt that with the financial eclipse of Peter Donald, and the gradual decline – through ill health – of Peter Bridge's energy and flair, we had lost the architects of our recent successes; but we were not suddenly friendless. We began the Seventies in fact with the highest hopes. We were immediately involved, with a young manager, Martin Tickner, in the formation of a new venture, the Play Company of London, backed by two men whose wealth was derived from shipping – Viscount (Tony) Furness and Eddie Kulukundis; and Glen would at last direct us in a classic, *The Wild Duck*, for the company's first production.

Next, Richard Todd introduced us to Duncan Weldon, who, with his then partner Paul Elliott, was an active touring management. A much valued and enduring friendship with Duncan resulted, and in the ensuing years we have worked more for his management than for any other. Our friendship and our working relations with Duncan have known their ups and downs, but I would like to think that the barometer is now set Fair.

Dulcie's writing maintained its remarkable productive rhythm, with a further eight titles – achieving in *Ride on a Tiger* the best of her thrillers – and, finally breaking the mould of crime and turning most eloquently and successfully to the subject of conservation, with *Butterflies on My Mind*. I flew solo for the first time as a writer, with *Overture and Beginners*, and with a commissioned but unfinished – and now I fear unfinishable – biography of Gerald Croasdell.

We were both subjects of *This is Your Life* – Dulcie in 1973 and I four years later.

Theatrically, the decade was nominated for Dulcie by her Mary Wilson figure in *At the End of the Day* and her long run in *Bedroom Farce*. For me, the high points were Captain Hook; the joyous, if at times agonising, experience of *The Black Mikado*; and joys and agonies of a different sort during a year with Prospect at the Old Vic.

Equity as usual demanded much of my time. I worked closely and happily again with Gerald in attempts to mitigate the effects on our union of the Heath government's Industrial Relations Act. I was finally rejected by the Equity electorate at the Council elections of 1977 – perhaps because I steadfastly refused to allow my name to appear on any of the rival lists of candidates. It was briefly hurtful but soon a relief to us both. I did a stint on the Drama Panel of the Arts Council and – as already mentioned – chaired a working party on touring and the future of the Old Vic. I became a director of the New Shakespeare Company, and played my first two leading Shakespearean parts in London for them (Prospero and Malvolio) in the challenging environment of Regent's Park.

We changed flats in the Buckinghamshire house, and acquired an apartment consisting of the drawing-room, the library and the ladies' boudoir of Robert Adam's plan of 1758, together with some rather *un*usual offices – a home which, with its half-acre private garden, still gives us daily joy.

There were no films and little television for either of us in the decade, causing friendly taxi-drivers and passers-by to enquire whether we were enjoying our retirement – this more often than not in front of theatres displaying our names in lights.

Of our friends, Rebecca West, Dick Francis and Frankie Howerd came more strongly into our lives; and we had the pleasure of introducing Rebecca to the other two; and Frankie to Jack Priestley.

We were, thank God, as happy as ever in each other's company. To our great delight we were both awarded the Queen's Jubilee Medal.

I
1970

Euan and Beatrix Rabagliati – Shaw triple bill – a storm at Windsor – Glen Byam Shaw's dramatic swan song

We spent Christmas and New Year with Euan and Beatrix Rabagliati at their lovely house below Grasse. From there I wrote to Noël with an idea which I shall always regret did not come off. It was that a record should be made of famous stories illustrating his wit (Queen Salote's 'lunch'; his 'kangaroo' response to the drunken Australian, etc., etc.) and that, in the interest of his favourite charities, these should be told, up to and excluding the punch-line, by world-famous stars who were his friends. Noël's contribution would be to add the punch-line, and then say whether or not the story was true. This could have been done in a brief recording session in his home or at the Savoy: and the result would surely have been a box-office sensation. Dickie Attenborough (who had succeeded Noël as a dynamic fundraiser for the Actors' Charitable Trust) added his appeal to mine, but sadly to no avail. How one would have loved to have a similar disc of Oscar Wilde. How much richer the anecdotes would have been in their authentic voices.

We had met the Rabagliatis with the Normans. They were in fact both related to Anthony – on his mother's side – and the introduction was to prove not the least of the many delights that have sprung from that friendship.

I tried to persuade Euan to write his life story; I tried to persuade *This Is Your Life* to 'do' him. Let the reader judge if I was wrong.

Euan was born of Scots-Italian parentage in Bradford. Moving to Wharfedale, where my parents did their courting, his first inamorata was one of my father's beautiful sisters; he then joined the army and was posted to Singapore, where he fell in love with a girl called Dulcie who was to be Dulcie's godmother. Transferring to the RFC at the beginning of World War I, he was

201

credited with being the first British aviator to 'shoot down' an enemy aircraft. (He was armed with a pistol, and six bricks for dropping through the enemy's wings when ammunition was exhausted.) The war survived, as the youngest Colonel, he represented the Air Force at the Armistice Commission; then logically enough went into aircraft insurance – in Berlin (a job which began a long association for him with MI6); and later drove for the Talbot racing team at Brooklands until, in a handicap race, a supercharged Baby Austin (!) came out of the slow lane into his path. When he came to, a few days later, with a broken neck, he was told that his love life and his driving were over. They weren't. Next came a period as a film producer – one of his productions employing the young Laurence Olivier and his first wife Jill Esmond. All this time he was still in aviation insurance, and notably refused on behalf of his firm to cover the airship R101 which crashed in France on its maiden voyage in 1930. Recalled to the colours in 1939, his posting to Finland came to nothing owing to the collapse of the Finnish resistance in the winter war against Russia. Instead he became a much-decorated Liaison Officer with the Dutch Resistance (and was later 'played' by Edward Fox in the film *Soldier of Orange*).

When we first met him, he and Beatrix, whom he had waited many years to marry, were living in most active retirement in the South of France. He was in his late seventies and the pattern of his days varied little. Eighteen holes of golf in the morning; then drinks before a luncheon party, which might be home or away; a close study of *The Times*, followed by a siesta; and then at least one but often two social occasions in the evening. This programme was modified slightly in his eighties, but the golf remained sacrosanct until a few months before his death at eighty-six.

I adored playing golf with him. First there was the early morning drive to the course – Mougins, Valbonne or Mandelieu – in whatever magnificent car was Euan's current choice. I remember a Rolls, a Jensen, a Ferrari, an Aston Martin, a Mercedes and a BMW. Having myself driven since my seventeenth birthday I am not at my most relaxed in the passenger seat. With Euan, my relaxation was total; his driving was a thing of beauty – swift, sure and safe – a happy blend of ballet and ski-ing, flowing round corners, smooth in response to emergency, up to a hundred or more whenever the opportunity offered.

Euan was short, neat and of a (usually) controlled intensity – so was his golf. Mine is the reverse. Much as I have loved the game for more than sixty years, the many preoccupations of my life have effectively stunted my golfing talents. But Euan and I had some marvellous games, often my only ones in a year. He would normally be five or six up before I was really awake; and though I often made inroads into his lead it was rarely enough to beat him. My extra length was no match for his demon accuracy.

After a major operation in his eighties, he woke up in his hospital room at night to find his bed a mass of blood. The tubes to which he was attached had come adrift. Calmly he rang for assistance; and then, using his instinct for mechanical principles, reconnected himself correctly before the arrival of the nurse.

He died some months after being hit by an opponent's ball at golf. The poor opponent was shattered of course, but Euan characteristically won not only the hole but the match. One day as normal he went to sleep in his chair after lunch – and didn't wake up.

I felt an extraordinary bond with him, partly I think because he reminded me of my surrogate father – my uncle Jack de Caynoth Ballardie, by coincidence another Scots-Italian with Yorkshire connections. They never met but they would have had much in common. They were both romantics and would both have denied it. They tried to conceal it by self-discipline and the soberness of their apparel; they gave it away by their addiction to flying, when to fly was still a romantic adventure, by finding in danger a natural and stimulating element, by an unshakable patriotism, above all in a brand of chivalrous devotion to their wives, who were not unworthy of it.

Beatrix Rabagliati – the sole survivor of the quartet – is now back in her native Scotland. Approaching ninety, she looks at least twenty years younger; she is an ardent reader, theatre-lover and dog-lover, gardener, bridge player and race-goer; and she has about her the special aura of a woman who has been much loved.

Before we went on holiday, we had decided with Martin Tickner that we would transform the triple bill into a Shaw evening. *Wooing* again would be the filling in the sandwich, preceded by *How He Lied to Her Husband* and followed by *Press Cuttings*. Nigel Patrick, who had directed the whole of the previous programme, was no longer available, so I directed *How He Lied*, with Bobby Flemyng, June Barry and Clive Francis, all admirably suited to their parts. *Wooing* by now had its own momentum; but for the rarity, *Press Cuttings*, Martin had the inspired idea of inviting Ray Cooney, who was taking a hard-working sabbatical from a decade or more of Whitehall farce.

Press Cuttings is a good joke set in a Whitehall so suffragette-dominated that the only safe way for Prime Minister Ballsquith to consult with General Mitchener at the War Office is to go dressed as a woman. Not so safe, as it turns out. He finds the gallant soldier being held at gun-point by a female Major-General. The reason why it is such a rarity in performance is that the little play is roughly twice as long as the joke will hold.

Ray asked me to cut it; and we then of course had to get per-mission for the cuts from the Shaw estate, which in those days de-pended for such decisions on the judgment of the distinguished critic, Ivor Brown. Ivor approved my cuts, and went so far as to say that if GBS were still alive he would have made similar ones.

It was a happy if not unduly long engagement at the Fortune. I had first met June Barry and admired her work in a *Boyd* episode; with Bobby, Dulcie and I are always happily at home, whatever the fate of the enterprise. In Clive Francis, we were meeting for the first time a young actor of versatility and style – equally effective as the dandified poet-hero of *How He Lied* and the revolutionary cockney batman of *Press Cuttings*. Clive has recently – in addition – become a witty and affectionate caricaturist of his contemporaries (not exclusively theatrical), with a strength and economy of line which invite comparison with Spy and Beerbohm, and a sparing use of colour which is uniquely his own.

Glen would not be ready for us until the late summer, so there was a gap to be filled. Ray, who had taken a lease of the theatre at Southend and who shared our enthusiasm for Pinero, agreed (or did he suggest?) that we should do *Dandy Dick* for him there. We managed to add a week at Brighton and three weeks at our be-loved Windsor.

There we had one memorable night. Early in the performance the most monumental thunderstorm struck the royal borough; and soon water began to pour into the stalls. John Counsell, the theatre's devoted owner since 1938, took command. He assured his patrons from the stage that there was no danger of the theatre sinking, and advised those worst affected to move to higher ground, even if it meant standing, until the waters subsided.

As already mentioned, British audiences love a crisis – it evokes the spirit of Dunkirk – and on this occasion their sense of adventure was fuelled by John's frequent announcements about the activities of the Fire Brigade, the level of the Thames and other related matters.

In the second act, as students of Pinero will know, there is a thunderstorm in the play. Inevitably it was a poor affair compared with the real thing that night, but when I as the Dean had to speak the line, 'What dreadful flood threatens to engulf the deanery!' we all took some time to recover.

And so to the Play Company of London, a title deliberately chosen because we intended to spend much of our time on the road. In one respect we made theatre history – we managed to take out an insurance policy to cover something like 80% of any production losses for a premium of £6000 or so.

Rehearsals of *The Wild Duck* with Glen were such total joy that we almost dreaded allowing the public access to what we had so lovingly created. In fact, things went particularly well on the road. Young Hayley Mills, as the innocent tragic Hedvig, demonstrated that she had acquired more than film technique from her father – already then a veteran of twenty-five West End productions as well as seventy-seven films. Glen had, as usual, gone deeply into the text and had discovered, to the delight of his cast (and subsequently of their audiences), that it was as inappropriate to play Ibsen for gloom as it was Chekhov. (Both great playwrights are masters of dramatic irony and broad comic effects, as well as of heartbreak and catastrophe; but, whereas Ibsen's characters are devised to hammer home lessons to society at large, Chekhov tells stories of highly individual men and women, and leaves the playgoer to draw his own conclusions.)

Then, misfortune struck us. The West End that autumn was going through one of those phases which are thought of as solid success by those with a theatre, and stagnation by those who want one. We were in the latter category, and had to wait a month – paying the cast retainers to keep them together – before the Criterion became available. A charming theatre, it was as wrong for *The Wild Duck* as the Ambassadors had been all those years before for *The Fourposter*. Our performances, which had become acclimatised to the large provincial houses, had to be scaled down to satisfy Glen's unswerving devotion to theatrical reality; but – as can so easily happen – in achieving intimacy we lost energy, and I fear did less than justice to Glen and ourselves, though Harold Hobson did say that Dulcie's and my performances were 'almost unbearably poignant' – a view echoed in Dulcie's case by Larry and Joan Olivier and Peggy Ashcroft.

The first performance was followed by a lavish party at the Savoy – eventually paid for, as were the production losses, by our insurers. It was the end of the Play Company of London and – as far as I know – of our brokers' interest in theatrical production. Sadly for British theatre – though not for opera at the Coliseum – it also marked the end of Glen's distinguished directorial career. I have the unique distinction of having appeared in both his first and last drama productions. He will always be a 'bright particular star' in my theatrical firmament. (Now, at eighty, he bears a staggering likeness to the last of Dulcie's white-haired and rosy-cheeked uncles, the late Dr Lionel Bailey; looking after him is his widowed sister-in-law, Muriel, who has a strong family look of Angie.)

It was during this year that we had our most extraordinary stroke of luck on the domestic front. We had already fallen irreversibly in love with the Buckinghamshire house. Now, our neighbour, Elspeth Hoare wanted us to take over her maisonette of seventeen rooms when she moved to Bath. We explained that we had neither the money nor the wish to encumber ourselves with such responsibilities; but I suggested, more to show willing to a friend than in any expectation of results, that if the owners were willing to divide her accommodation into three and name a price we could afford we would take her three main ground-floor rooms and her beautifully planned private garden. To our acute astonishment, they offered us a ninety-six-year lease for £9000. Perhaps they thought that any other potential purchasers would be frightened off by the problem of keeping eighteen-foot ceilings clean – something which has worried us no more here than at Chester Terrace. The offer was clearly not to be refused; and despite various vicissitudes with dry rot, and problems of human relationships inevitable in a small community whose only bond is the accident of living together in the same house, our love affair with our home continues unabated.

We were sad to leave Regent's Park after twenty-one years, but Cumberland Place sold sufficiently well for us to acquire a mews flat off Albany Street including a bedroom so small that, though we could both lie down, only one could stand up at a time. This breeze-block pied-à-terre cost precisely the same as our country splendours; and was extremely useful until we had to sell it to pay the tax on *The Black Mikado* – an ironical consequence of my most successful year.

II
Equity Interlude

*The Arts Council Theatre Report – the mysterious birth of TIF –
the battle to amend the Industrial Relations Act – a letter to the
Attorney General – collision course with the TUC – Gerald
Croasdell's devotion to Equity*

1970 and the following three years provided for me and others a
period of intense activity on behalf of Equity. First came the
campaign to ensure implementation of what we approved of – a
good deal – in 'The Theatre Today', the report of the Arts
Council Theatre Enquiry, and to be constructively critical where
the document seemed to us wrong or unnecessarily cautious.

An invitation to air my views on 'Touring in the Seventies'
came from the editor of the Arts Council house magazine. With
my general philosophy on the subject the reader is already
familiar; but in two respects my comments and proposals had a
new emphasis and urgency and they are still, fifteen years later, in
the realm of unfinished business.

The authors of the report believed that there was likely to be
only enough 'product' (at the minimum level of forty weeks per
theatre per year) to keep twelve large provincial theatres in
business. The Equity view was that twenty theatres was the
minimum, if a majority of citizens (and taxpayers) were to have
the opportunity of seeing major touring productions within a
tolerable distance of their homes. (Even this left the north of
Scotland, the extreme south-west of England and Northern
Ireland unprovided for.) I set out to prove that, given more
generous payments to artists from managements (to offset the
expenses of touring) and more generous guarantees against loss
to managements from local authority theatre owners, the theatre
(including drama, opera, ballet, pantomime and amateurs) had
the capacity to provide the necessary eight hundred weeks,
almost double that envisaged in the report.

An important element in this enhanced total could be

208

provided, I argued, if selected provincial companies were affiliated to the National Theatre, with the privilege of an annual visit to HQ and the duty to tour among themselves as well as playing seasons at home. (A spin-off from this would be that if there were, say, four companies spending three weeks each on the South Bank, the National would for that period not only have the stimulus of friendly rivals under its roof but an occasion for reciprocal visits to the home theatres of the visitors.) Frank Dunlop, then with the National, came up with a similar idea for 'National Provincial Companies' – the only difference between us being that he visualised his companies as radiating outwards from HQ, whereas I saw mine rooted in the regions and periodically visiting the metropolis.

The 1984 Arts Council strategy of switching some resources from the metropolis to the regions – which broadly I welcome, though quarrelling with certain specific decisions – makes the Dunlop-Denison plan highly topical. The truth is and has always been that London and the rest of the country are theatrically interdependent. Performers working out of London need to test their skills in the metropolis; audiences living out of London need to see what standards are being set in the capital. I believe that West End and South Bank audiences would also benefit from bracing draughts of country air. (But even if that is a long-term dream, it is encouraging to note that *The Stage* of May 1984 shows twenty-seven major provincial theatres in operation.)

The enquiry came up with one most imaginative brainchild, a 'Theatre Investment Fund' (TIF) 'to encourage and assist reputable managements to increase the production of new plays of interest and revivals of quality and to cause such productions to tour as widely as possible.' This was printed in block capitals in the report.

The Film Finance Corporation had established a precedent for public assistance to commercial producers. TIF, with its special emphasis on touring, reflected the committee's awareness that there was at this time five times as much touring by unsubsidised managements as by the Arts Council's clients.

In spite of the enthusiasm with which it was welcomed on all sides, its funding – £100,000 from the Arts Council and £150,000 from unnamed private sources – seemed and still seems quite inadequate for its job of helping to keep a score of provincial theatres and various deserving managements in business. Harmar

Nicholls, a member of the committee, made this point most strongly in a memorandum printed with the report; and – not for the last time – we at Equity had reason to be grateful for the strength and clarity of his views in matters that concerned us.

Conceived in 1970, TIF did not begin to operate for six years, and its birth pangs and early activities were shrouded in mystery. Although I was by 1976 chairing my Arts Council Working Party, and although the Council's Chairman, (Lord) Pat Gibson, whom I consulted, was one of my oldest friends, the only information forthcoming was that the organisation of TIF was complete, and that touring was not considered a priority. As its board of twelve included three West End managers, three repertory directors, a playwright, a critic and only one touring manager (who has since resigned), this is scarcely surprising.

After two years of operation, it was reported confidentially (why?) that TIF had invested in more than fifty productions and still had four-fifths of its capital intact. This was a less remarkable performance than it might seem, as its investment per production averaged less than £2000. New and young managements were its principal concern, it claimed; and yet half those hand-outs of under £2000 went to long-standing members of the Society of West End Theatre. What did they do with such largesse? What indeed did the new young managements do with the rest of it?

By the end of 1981, TIF had invested in roughly one hundred productions; it had committed all its funds, and recovered approximately half the money invested. Not bad housekeeping in a theatrical context.

The choice of productions, however, though inevitably subjective, strikes me as wayward. In particular, some of the 'new plays of interest' and 'revivals of quality' must have surprised TIF's founding fathers, as they would readers of these pages were I to list them.

Sad. An opportunity so far missed.

The other major preoccupation of Equity at this time was the mortal danger to our union from the Heath Government's Industrial Relations Act as originally drafted. One fundamental principle of the proposed legislation was the individual's right to belong or not to belong to a trade union. The latter opinion would inevitably destroy our union 'shop', and evoked a virtually united front of opposition not only within Equity but also from the profession's employers, whose interest in the status quo was almost as strong as ours. We even gained some stalwart support on the government side of the House, predictably from Harmar Nicholls, surprisingly from Norman Tebbitt and probably crucially from our great friend Peter Rawlinson, QC, by now the Attorney General.

The latter asked me for a brief on Equity's attitude. I replied on 25 November:

> Our position is poignant. A profession casually employed and individually contracted – like your own – is especially in need of protection. Yours is protected by entrance qualifications – you can only practise if you have them. Mine cannot be. Our only 'qualification' can be an offer of professional employment, our only protection the right to refuse to work with non-members (as propounded by Dames Marie Tempest and May Whitty in 1934) and therefore by implication with individuals even more vulnerable than ourselves to every sort of exploitation, from undercutting to one-way tickets to Buenos Aires.

> Our trade union record is I believe exemplary. No unofficial strikes. And our major official action against the then all-powerful ITV companies was only called after months of negotiation; and was won without one member being called upon to break a contract. As you know we are non-political and have been so in deed as well as name for more than twenty years.

> Equity's chosen instrument for serving its members is the Standard Contract. In 1934 we had one – for the West End. We now operate 75. But – and here we come to the crunch – these only work if they are enforceable, and they are only enforceable, by both sides, if there is the strength and discipline resulting from 100 per cent membership by both sides of their respective associations. And don't forget, the actor's 'side' in any contract is not the union but the individual actor.

> The temptation, because of our record and special circumstances, to try to make a deal with the government, in the interest of survival, is great. But we cannot do it, because – one of many reasons – it is only as a trade union that the organisation and protection of actors has worked. Equity's thirty-five years of advance was preceded by fifty years of frustration and

periodical retreat, based on mediaeval craft guilds and other Utopian expedients.

... I cannot help feeling that the onus is on the government to ensure that organisations which are 'fair and responsible' are not damaged by too rigid an application of its fundamental principles.

Gerald, sending a copy of this letter to Harmar Nicholls, said gratifyingly, though quite untruthfully, that it was expressed 'with a cogency which I could never hope to equal'.

This delicate exercise in making friends and influencing people was not to the taste of Corin and Vanessa Redgrave, who at successive special meetings argued that Equity should break with its tradition and join the TUC's proposed one-day General Strike. This was unhelpful not least because the overwhelming defeats they suffered on each occasion may have caused the government to underestimate the Union's solid opposition to the Bill.

In the event, our representations proved successful, in so far that the government recognised that we and the seamen's union could not live without a form of closed shop. But we could only qualify for this vital concession if we remained on the 'register of approved trade unions'. This proviso was to prove bitterly divisive within Equity, because the TUC instructed all its affiliated unions under pain of suspension or expulsion to de-register, in order thereby to hamstring the operation of the Act. We thus found ourselves divided into two camps – those who saw our TUC affiliation as sacrosanct, and those like myself and (to his infinite credit) Gerald, who while having no desire to sever the TUC connection recognised that if they remained inflexible in their opposition to the Act, Equity would have no choice but to disobey the Instruction and use the Act to achieve the union shop without which it would perish.

But first we obeyed the Instruction and came off the register – a gesture of loyalty to the TUC which puzzled many of our members. I have no doubt it was the right thing to do. It put the onus on the TUC to find a substitute acceptable to them and to us for the closed shop which our gesture would deny us. This they were quite unable to do.

This failure cleared the air, making the case for our return to the register unanswerable. At a Council Meeting in March 1972 I said that the government, the TUC and Equity each had 'a fundamental principle No. 1'. The government's was the right of the individual to belong or not to belong to a trade union; the TUC's was opposition to the Act; and Equity's was the preservation of its union shop. 'It is sad but certain,' I went on, 'that for all the faults of its legislation the government has been readier than has the TUC to abandon its fundamental principle and accept that we are a special case.'

Gerald was at his very best: 'No matter what are the dictates of one's own conscience, the interests of the membership come first and the decision must be taken for their welfare and not on the grounds of personal philosophy.' We all knew his personal philosophy, and that he was addressing himself as well as others in recommending that, in the interests of survival as an effective trade union, we must disobey the TUC and go back on the register. The Council endorsed his advice by 23 votes to 16; as did the membership in a referendum called as part of the decision.

Armed with this support, Gerald went before Congress to appeal against our suspension in 1972, and our expulsion in 1973. Both speeches failed in their immediate purpose – the block vote saw to that – but as I read them now I find myself deeply moved. There is the formidable skill of the advocate marshalling and presenting a good case and making it better. But transcending the technique, and making the case into a cause, is his passion – the more effective for being expressed without hyperbole – for our profession and for its union, which he did so much to make effective.

Although his Equity 'monument' is the mass of agreements and contracts for which he was our chief negotiator, in personal terms these two TUC speeches were perhaps the finest hour of his twenty-five years' service to the union, not only because they reveal the quality of the man but for their practical effect. When the time came to return to the TUC fold we could do so with dignity, because Gerald had explained so eloquently the reasons for our defiance.

This same year, physically and mentally drained by the tensions, complexities, successes and frustrations of his work for Equity, he resigned. Peter Plouviez, his assistant, succeeded him, and is no stranger himself now to those same pressures. It was through Peter's 'machinations', according to Gerald, that the latter became Secretary General of the International Federation of Actors.

When Gerald left Equity, officers of the union past and

present paid tribute to him in the Equity journal. I wrote:

> When I was very much a new boy on the Council, a new boy on
> the staff made an instantaneous impression on me. Neatly
> dressed, softly (sometimes too softly) spoken, he went cogent-
> ly and economically to the heart of any matter under
> discussion. No stranger to tension, I suspect, though out-
> wardly relaxed and courteous – let us have men about us who
> can smile! – his contributions to debate were always eagerly
> awaited. From his brilliant and devoted predecessor Gordon
> Sandison, who deserves our gratitude not least for having
> 'found' Gerald, he picked up the delicate art of leading and
> serving the union – 'leading' in the sense of being more
> articulate, more clear-sighted, better informed than his em-
> ployers, tougher than the faint hearts, more flexible than the
> hotheads, more consistent than all of us in putting Equity
> first.

No wonder I wished to write his biography. I shall always regret
that, having received the permission of this most private man, his
departure from Equity, my sloth in research and the necessity to
earn my living combined to halt *The Quiet Revolutionary* at the
half-way stage.

III
1971

A Girl from the Golden East – *a happy package – a sad home-coming – first tour for Duncan Weldon – a production that didn't start – enter David Conville – second tour for Duncan – a low ebb*

The public image which Dulcie had acquired in the days when the press and film publicity departments first began to take an interest in her was a travesty of the truth. When I got back from the war, and our marriage became a stage-and-film partnership untouched by scandal, the conviction became widespread that we were a humdrum bourgeois couple – obviously with considerable private means – whose success could only be attributed to the identification with us of humdrum bourgeois audiences.

If the cap went some way to fitting me, it totally obscured Dulcie's features, and I was determined to set the record straight. I accordingly began to write the story of her extraordinary childhood and adolescence, under the title *A Girl from the Golden East*; and thanks to the enthusiasm and know-how of Bertie van Thal – Dulcie's first publisher, it may be remembered, and by now her literary agent – it was serialised in *Woman's Weekly*, for what I considered an extremely generous fee.

Before I began, it seemed to me important that I should see Dulcie's Malaya with my own eyes and not be totally dependent on her own descriptions. She too was longing to go back; and so we shopped around the travel agents, and found a package tour which would take us out and back and give us seventeen days bed-and-breakfast in hotels of our choice for an *aggregate* of £499.

The only 'price' I had to pay for this bargain was one sleepless night on the way out, because in a totally full Boeing 707 I had the one seat that wouldn't recline. I therefore spent the interminable hours of darkness sitting bolt upright, cradling in my lap a little lady's head from the seat in front.

Apart from price, one of the great advantages of this package

215

was that from arrival in Kuala Lumpur to departure from Singapore we were our own masters.

We spent four or five happy days in KL. We found Dulcie's unexplained birthplace – the Police Officers' Mess (a sprawling single-storey building on the side of a hill) – and the site of the family home, overlooking the race-course in Kia Peng Road. We lunched with George Zachariah, an Indian official of the British Council, at the Selangor Club – known as the Spotted Dog because of its white walls and pseudo-Tudor beams. George was an old boy of St Mary's School, at which Dulcie had once been the only white pupil; he arranged for us to give a very hot and un-air-conditioned Shakespeare recital to the pupils, whose welcome was most touching. We explored the Lake Gardens – the most beautiful public park I have ever seen – which show so dramatically their jungle origin; and we dined at the Lake Club with a colleague of Arnold Savage Bailey, Dulcie's father. We made a pilgrimage to the red-brick Gothic St Mary's Church – totally English in atmosphere apart from its grove of jacaranda trees – where there was a plaque to him. I learned that in 1935, when he was killed in an accident, he was only fifty-four, and that he died well loved, having spent his life in the service of others. This service, as I knew, had been as solicitor, advocate and judge, and as a member of the Federal Council to which he was elected by the Malay, Indian and Chinese communities as their special representative.

There was only one initial disappointment. In 1962, when playing Higgins in Australia, I had been presented to the Sultan of Selangor, who, on learning that Dulcie had been born in his capital city, invited us to call on him if ever we came to Kuala Lumpur. I had accordingly written to him giving our itinerary and dates. No letter awaited us and so we assumed that His Highness had no wish to pursue the matter.

We were wrong. On the evening before we were to leave Kuala Lumpur for a trip in our hired car, we received a telephone call from the Sultan's ADC. If we were still intending to visit Fraser's Hill – the jungle hill station which had been the scene of Dulcie's teenage teaching and journalistic exploits – would we have a drink with the Sultan who would be spending the weekend there playing golf? We accepted with delight.

The drive to 'the Hill' was for me a new joy and for Dulcie full of nostalgia. First came the cultivated lowlands with their paddy fields and rubber plantations, then gradually the jungle took over. A surprisingly open and benevolent jungle it seemed to me, its giant trees often festooned with brilliant blossoms, the sunlight breaking through the canopy giving a glimpse of the wah-wah monkeys at play and striking down to the ferns and flowers of the jungle floor. Like the sea, the jungle has contrasting moods and dangers; this was its smiling face.

At the Gap, the real climb begins up a fiercely twisting gated road, reserved for upward traffic at odd hours and downwards at even. The hill station, though its buildings are at best unobtrusive and at worst downright ugly, has a powerful period charm. It is one of the countless Shangri-Las created by the British all over the world to appease the homesickness of long exile in the pre-jet age. This one is a miniature jungle Sunningdale. The centrepiece, inevitably, is the nine-hole golf course laid out in a brilliantly green little valley – a sort of grassy crater – with steep jungle slopes lining its fairways. (Dulcie may not be a champion golfer but she has always been rigidly straight. Having seen the 'rough' at Fraser's Hill, I understand why.) Up the crater's slopes and ringing its crest, looking both inwards and outwards, are the bungalows for visitors (mostly belonging to business concerns or government departments) and a few private houses. From those on the crest there are magical views of blue jungle hills, sometimes – in the morning and evening – with white clouds creeping into the valleys below you.

Our visit to the Sultan's bungalow was a happy and relaxed occasion, as was the small dinner party to which we were invited later at his palace of Klang outside Kuala Lumpur. We had by then become accustomed to being served food and drink by servants kneeling in the royal presence. But when the Sultan suddenly and disarmingly said 'I am happy tonight. This is so like England,' his two grateful English guests felt that the differences outweighed the resemblances. What chance was there of his clapping his hands in Buckinghamshire and saying 'This is so like Malaysia!'? And so the counter-invitation that trembled on Dulcie's lips was stifled.

Between these royal occasions we drove across the peninsula to Kuantan, on the exquisite palm-fringed white-sanded east coast which has always been Dulcie's idea of an earthly paradise. Back in Kuala Lumpur we did a performance of *Village Wooing* (without decor) for the British Council and were visited backstage by a fine old Indian lady who introduced herself as Nellie Ghouse – Dulcie's nanny for the first three years of her life! A brief visit to Singapore completed this most satisfactory 'package'.

We returned to a sharp sorrow, no less painful for being expected. Titus, now approaching sixteen and the oldest Labrador his medical advisers had come across, had reached the end of the road. Stupefied with jet lag we were called upon to make the decision immediately. Ian Nicol, the local vet – a man so dedicated that he gave me advice and a prescription for Prospero (the current Labrador) on his own death-bed a few years later – was always greeted by Titus with a quite distinctive bark. This last occasion was no exception. Eileen, who loved him and had nursed him devotedly while we had been away, was there too. And so, much moved, we said goodbye to the old boy; and buried him under an oak tree near the house.

I have referred before to the strange power of old newspapers to draw attention to themselves. There now occurred something quite as extraordinary. We were all three desolate; and the next day Dulcie at the graveside offered up a small prayer for a sign that the current of love which had flowed so strongly between him and us was not irrevocably broken. Nothing happened.

Back in the house I had decided, with no great originality, that what Eileen and the pair of us needed was a job to take our mind off our loss. We had not yet moved to our new flat and were using its drawing-room as a store for a mass of furniture, books, kitchen utensils and other chattels from Regent's Park. In the middle of the room the pile rose to a height of eight or nine feet. We were hard at work trying to bring order into this chaos when the moving of something at floor level dislodged a book from a kitchen chair at the summit of the pile. The book fell to the floor open, spine upwards. I picked it up. It was our engagement diary for 1955 – my year at Stratford. Before closing it I glanced at the open page. It had two entries: Wednesday: Titus Andronicus opens. Friday: Titus (the puppy) arrives. Dulcie had had her sign.

For some months we had been discussing a possible national tour of a revival with Duncan Weldon. Knowing our attitude to the provincial theatre, Duncan was keen to enlist us under his banner, for at this time he was serving his managerial apprenticeship exclusively away from London. Our only condition was that the choice of play should be reasonably adventurous. And so we set off on a twelve-week tour of David Garrick's *Clandestine Marriage*. The enterprise might have been more successful had we been less adventurous, but at least we had the satisfaction of performing a rarely seen classic and of establishing a good relationship with Duncan.

The rest of the year was a strange mixture of events – with one exception, fairly depressing. First we were invited to star in the latest of George Ross's and Campbell Singer's business plays, entitled *The Sacking of Norman Banks*. As a genre they had had a formidable track record of West End success under Peter Bridge's management in the Sixties. This one seemed well up to standard, and – to add to our enthusiasm – our old and trusted friend Charles Hickman was to direct. All in all it was the ideal contrast with *Clandestine Marriage*. We came back for rehearsals after a holiday with the Normans and Rabagliatis to find the whole production cancelled at the eleventh hour, leaving our autumn programme in ruins.

Into the breach came David Conville, of whose New Shakespeare Company in Regent's Park I had recently become a director. He invited us on behalf of John Counsell to play Sir Peter Teazle and Mrs Candour in *The School for Scandal* for the Windsor Festival. With the lovely and talented Gabrielle Drake as Lady Teazle, and Richard Goolden and Jonathan Cecil as Crabtree and Backbite, the production was strongly cast – Gabrielle in particular being the best Lady Teazle in my personal experience of the play.

As a director, David has proved a worthy successor to Robert Atkins at the Park. Separated in age by almost half a century, of course their styles were different. What they shared was a simplicity of approach, a readiness to let their authors speak for themselves, and an ambition to be interpreters rather than manipulators. In speaking of Glen Byam Shaw, Murray Macdonald and Frank Hauser, I have already indicated my enthusiasm for this style of direction. David is of their company.

As soon as Duncan knew of the débâcle of our London plans he suggested another tour for us. There were still some dates where we had not played *Village Wooing* – they included Weston-super-Mare, Rosehill and Swansea, which we played in that order – but Duncan wanted another two-hander to put with it. All we could think of was *Unexpectedly Vacant*, which in fact transferred quite well to the stage from television, but still made an uneasy companion for *Wooing*. Playing that failed theatrical couple to a handful of people in the tiny theatre at Lytham was, I think, the nadir of our joint careers.

IV
1972

The Dragon Variation, *Mark I – a summer in the Park – the two Prosperos – encounters with a third –* Dragon Variation, *Mark II – an agonising decision*

This was another strange amorphous year for us. In the dying days of 1971 Peggy Ramsay, that most dynamic of play agents, sent us 'on spec' a very strange piece called *The Dragon Variation*. Briefly, it was the story of a rich widow living as a recluse in the country, whose husband has died in mysterious circumstances, and who employs an out-of-work actor to portray a variety of men in her life. To interrupt this bizarre idyll there comes the nephew of the dead husband, an investigative journalist, who believes his uncle was murdered by the widow. These unlikely ingredients were graced with such excellent dialogue that we sent it to John Counsell for a second opinion. He had a gap after the pantomime and immediately agreed to give it a whirl, with Joan Riley directing.

Joan had been the most attractive and efficient stage manager on our hard-working honeymoon in Aberdeen in 1939 and has been a lifelong friend. This was I think the first time, but happily not the last, that we were directed by her. Still a very pretty woman, and a conventional dresser, she appears (and indeed is) a pillar of 'the establishment'. With these social graces goes a deep practical knowledge and love of the theatre, an effervescent sense of humour – and the unexpected capacity to swear like a trooper in moments of crisis, which are not unknown in our world.

Joan and we shared an enthusiasm for the dialogue, and reservations about the construction of *Dragon Variation*, and set to work, with the naturally hesitant co-operation of the author, to improve things. In this we were so successful that it was bought for commercial presentation by John Gale in a deal in which Duncan Weldon was to manage the initial tour. They both stated – in the phrase we all use – that there was 'still a bit of work

221

to be done on the script'; but as I had agreed to play Prospero and Malvolio for David Conville in Regent's Park, this gave us six months or so to get it right. This was in fact the high point of our connection with *Dragon Variation* – from then on it was down-hill all the way.

But first, for me, came the rich experience of the Park – scene of Dulcie's first London appearance thirty years before. In an ideal world (which would not have denied me the opportunity to play Shakespeare or indeed anything else between the ages of twenty-four and thirty-one), I would not have chosen Prospero with which to open my Shakespearean account in London. At the age of fifty-seven, however, I was extremely lucky to have the opportunity of grappling with that intractable character, and more than lucky in David's choice of director (Richard Digby Day) and cast – Wayne Sleep, in his first speaking rôle as Ariel, being one of those who remain vividly in the mind.

We had our adventures, inseparable from a Park production. It was the coldest June for a hundred years; and when I made my first appearance at the summit of a forty-foot cliff not unlike the Mappin Terraces, in a strong gale, with the cloud cover about six feet above my head, I looked down on my public who were huddled in rugs and pixie hoods, their heads bowed against the elements. There was no question of their seeing me, and I did fleetingly wonder what the hell I was doing there.

Then there was the night of the fire. I was standing half way up my cliff superintending the Masque which I had conjured out of the air when I noticed a thin column of smoke rising from a spotlight below me. Soon there was a small but healthy fire in progress, accompanied by a most unhealthy smell. To put it out should have been well within Prospero's powers, but was alas outside mine. Suddenly, from the entrance to my cell high up on the escarpment, there appeared a heroic figure in dungarees with a fire extinguisher. He struck it sharply on the ground as instructed; but nothing happened, except the hysterics of the audience and the rapid withdrawal of Prospero. The fire was finally doused with a bucket.

Embarrassments came in various guises from out front, parti-cularly at matinées which are heavily dominated by school-children. You see them of course only too clearly from the stage; and it is disconcerting, to put it mildly, when you have them, as you think, in the hollow of your hand as you discourse of cloud-capp'd towers, to see three giggling members of the fifth form at St Trinian's set off in search of ice lollies. One otherwise well-attended matinée had an entirely empty front row during the first half of the play. Early in the second half, however, the cast noticed that there were two small boys sitting together in the old-fashioned deck chairs which preceded the construction of our new auditorium. Their legs couldn't reach the ground and they were sprawled in attitudes suggesting an agony of boredom. We had reached the scene where Prospero forgives his usurping brother (played by the commanding figure of John Quentin) in language both stately and obscure. Suddenly a penetrating trans-atlantic voice came from below us, 'Do you understand one word of this?' 'Nope,' was the reply.

My favourite moment of the play came at the end. I bade farewell to Ariel and watched Wayne dart away into the shadows and on, it seemed, into the night sky. Most nights my eyes were full of tears as I dropped my magic cloak to the ground preparing to speak the epilogue. One evening the silence was shattered by an authoritative Cockney voice on a loud-hailer. 'The park is now closing. The park is now closing. Kindly make your way to the nearest exit.' My next line was, 'Now my charms are all o'erthrown.' Indeed.

In describing these minor disasters I run the risk of making the Park operation sound a shambles. In fact, in every department – not forgetting the catering – it is highly professional; and in good summers gives much pleasure to many thousands of people, as well as fulfilling the important educational function of intro-ducing Shakespeare to the young, and to tourists from overseas.

Despite this, we have now no Arts Council grant; and our landlords, the Department of the Environment, having built us splendid dressing-rooms and rebuilt them after a fire, were forbidden by some quirk of the legislation to play any part in building the new auditorium – an operation which we directors were forced to authorise ourselves with hearts in our mouths and cheque-books at the ready, and which aged us all considerably.

David captains this capricious craft with flair and enthusiasm, whether shooting rapids, heading for the rocks, feverishly baling or gliding through pools of sunlit calm. It will be a sad day for the Park and for London when he decides to hand over command.

Meanwhile Dulcie was giving an excellent account of Judith Bliss in *Hay Fever* – much encouraged by a telephone call of good wishes from Noël, the last time either of us heard his voice, which for a moment Dulcie didn't recognise, so ill did he sound. I caught up with this production in Bath, but sadly was unable to see her Mrs Alving in *Ghosts* in York, which much impressed that most versatile, enthusiastic and erudite of directors, Richard Digby Day.

Anne Norman had been very fond of Titus and had asked if she might give us a successor. And so it was that in May I went to view a litter of Labradors at her request. Dulcie was on tour so I sent her the puppy's 'audition' photograph, which she found irresistible. *The Tempest* opened its prior-to-London tour in York on 11 April. Prospero had been born in Leatherhead two days earlier, and by the time the production reached the Park in June, had joined me back-stage – and more than once, with the elusive mobility of the very young, almost on stage.

One evening, giving him his last outing in the mews behind Chester Terrace, I was aware of a space-helmeted figure on a very large and softly purring motor cycle bearing down on us. It was immediately identifiable as Ralph Richardson. The vast machine was stabled in a garage, the helmet removed, and we exchanged civilities. Then – 'What a lovely puppy,' said Sir Ralph. 'What do you call him?' 'Prospero.' 'Ah. Difficult part.' I could only agree; and so we went our separate ways.

A year or so later the meeting was repeated in every detail, except of course that Prospero had grown. 'Whatever happened to your puppy?' said Ralph suddenly. 'That is my puppy,' I replied. 'That's what I mean,' he said earnestly.

In midsummer we began rehearsals for the revised *Dragon Varia-tion*. To our regret and Joan Riley's, the powers-that-be decreed that we should have a new director. Tony Sharp, with whom I had worked so happily on *Hostile Witness*, agreed to direct, but was never really happy with the play. However we toured quite successfully for ten weeks; but John Gale appeared to have lost interest and, with Duncan not yet ready to chance his arm in London, the production seemed destined to end at Southsea in December. However Duncan appeared before we disbanded to ask whether we would start up again in the New Year with a view to coming in to town. We agreed in principle, as we were already booked to revive the musical, *Alice Through the Looking Glass*, at Croydon over Christmas. This turned out to be most exhausting, as I was in pain from a strained back and Dulcie badly injured a shoulder in a ludicrous tug-of-war with the circus company, which had been planned as a publicity stunt.

Also during this period we were invited by Michael Codron to appear for him in the original West End production of Alan Ayckbourn's *Absurd Person Singular*. We had as yet no new contract with Duncan, but we felt we had to tell Michael Codron that we had a moral obligation to continue with *Dragon Variation*, particularly as it was proposed to bring it into town.

V
1973

An unhappy tour – Dulcie's This Is Your Life *– Binkie and Noël: double end of an era – playing politics – two parties at Chequers – authorship for the author*

It was perhaps quixotic of us to turn down *Absurd Person Singular*; it was certainly an agonising decision, and may have had incalculable professional consequences. For not only was the Ayckbourn play an enormous success at the Criterion, but our management failed to bring *Dragon Variation* (Mark III) into town at all.

They never explained their reasons; and our only clue is that when, four years later, Paul Elliott presented the play – very briefly – in the West End, it was with a different cast. In all of this we were treated with less consideration than we had shown the management, and a rift (happily long since healed) opened between Duncan and ourselves.

Knowing Duncan better now than we did then, and having more than once been beneficiaries of his unique and still expanding contribution to theatre in the English-speaking world, we recognise and understand the conflict in him between head and heart.

His genuine love for theatre people leads him to dream – and sometimes communicate – extravagant dreams. And when his head tells him that a particular dream can't be realised he finds it an agony to tell the people concerned. But just as Peter Bridge filled the Sixties to overflowing, so has Duncan the Seventies and early Eighties. In a period when the lot of the unsubsidised manager has been more hazardous than ever, British playwrights, players, and public have been blessed indeed to have at their service two such dynamic, warm-hearted, broad-minded, successful yet dissimilar men. To join them in the Eighties with his theatre of Comedy has come Ray Cooney – playwright as well as impresario – a whirlwind generator

226

of laughter for the public and of work for the profession.

Unaware of what was to come we set off on the resumed tour of *Dragon Variation* (now directed by Richard Digby Day) in good heart, and were immediately rewarded with a sensational reception at Stratford-on-Avon. Jack and Jacquetta Priestley came to see it and were amused – which enabled me to pay a tribute to Jack in a curtain speech from the stage of the Memorial Theatre.

Also during the week, I received a guarded phone call from *This Is Your Life* saying that they wished to 'do' Dulcie and requesting my assistance. I arranged to meet a researcher at Amersham station the following Monday when we would be en route for our next date in Bournemouth.

(Dulcie never suspected anything, any more than I did when my turn came four years later. The organisation by Eamonn and his team is superb and if individual programmes occasionally topple over into sentimentality the aim of presenting a life with warmth and humour and gratitude is far more often achieved.)

Getting her to the starting line was not easy. My rendezvous at Amersham station was on a day of continuous downpour. I had said that I was walking Prospero, whom I took in the car with me. Fifty yards from the house on the way back, I realised that we were both bone-dry – so that had to be rectified in the interests of my cover story. A projected radio series for me (about which Dulcie became most enthusiastic) had to be invented to justify various clandestine meetings for me with the researcher.

At my request it was agreed that the 'pick-up' should be on stage at the Richmond Theatre at the end of a performance of *Dragon Variation*. To explain the presence of cameras in the auditorium, a television series on historic theatres was invented. I asked that we should be jointly informed of this the night before, and that no one should be surprised if I objected strongly on the grounds that our audience might be inconvenienced. The ruse worked. 'Oh, for God's sake, Michael,' said Dulcie, 'I think it's a splendid idea. Can't you forget Equity for once?'

So, all unsuspectingly, she was presented with her red book. Her brother and sister were there; and among theatre friends were Pete Murray, Alan Melville, Barbara Mullen, Hayley Mills and Dickie Attenborough, with filmed messages from Hermione Baddeley, Tito Gobbi and James Mason. After the initial shock, Dulcie much enjoyed herself.

* * *

There was much sad news for us during the tour. First came the death of Binkie Beaumont, the most famous of West End theatre managers, who had played an important part particularly in the early days of our careers. I should like to record here what I wrote of him in *Overture and Beginners*:

> He was one of the most unchanging human beings I have ever known. Always fastidiously neat, with an office to match, and speaking with hushed courtesy, he projected without apparent effort and even simultaneously the most conflicting impressions – relaxation and high tension, the wisdom of the ages and boyish enthusiasm, the hard-headed man of business and the idealist, the dangerous enemy and the most solicitous and loyal of friends.

Within a week, we were mourning Noël. To say we were stunned and desolate and miss him still is to suggest a degree of intimacy which we did not enjoy. And yet stunned and desolate we were, and we do miss him still. In my piece on him for the DNB I quoted a sentence from Gertie Lawrence's last letter to him – 'It's always you I want to please more than *anyone*' – adding that I thought this a 'sentiment that would be widely echoed among those who knew him'. Certainly it was by us. In addition to missing the fun of his company, the sound of his voice and the speed and generosity of his mind, there is the irreplaceable loss of a unique arbiter of theatrical taste from the performer's standpoint, someone whom we indeed wanted 'to please more than anyone'.

Lastly came the death of Lord (Tim) Nugent. Tim, like Norma Gwatkin (my fellow usher at Rosie Headfort's memorial service), was a regular soldier turned courtier, who was charged with administering the often ridiculous rules of theatrical censorship from the Lord Chamberlain's office. They both gave censorship a human, if not always acceptable face; and were much loved by theatre people.

I consider myself now as something of a connoisseur of memorial services. Binkie's, Noël's and Tim's, which came close together, could not have been more different. Binkie, of course, knew everyone in the theatre; but not everyone knew Binkie. To many, even of those who worked for him, he remained an enigma only seen at interviews, auditions and first nights – all occasions of panic for performers, however successfully they may conceal it. There was, therefore, scope for revelation of the unknown at

Binkie's service, and this was most charmingly supplied by Paul Scofield reading a piece about him by Enid Bagnold. A great success.

This was in fact the first of countless services (and All-Star-Galas) organised by Martin Tickner, who is now the acknowledged chef-de-protocol to the profession in such matters. Quite how it came about I don't know, but we all owe him an enormous debt of gratitude.

Not all of them have been equally successful. Noël's service at St Martin's on Empire Day had all the makings of an unforgettable occasion. Like Binkie, Noël knew everyone – and everyone was there; but unlike Binkie, everyone knew Noël or felt they did. And this made things much harder for the organisers – how to reconcile in one portrait the affectionate, individual and perhaps even conflicting memories of that large congregation? It was rather like the film of a well-loved book which can enhance or jar on one's private picture of the characters. 'My' Noël did not emerge from that star-studded gathering. (Fortunately that is not the end of the story. In 1984 there was a Celebration at the Abbey, also organised by Martin and Graham Payn. The Queen Mother, in purple velvet, flanked by the clergy in scarlet and gold, unveiled a memorial tablet to him; Dickie Attenborough gave a eulogy with exactly the right balance of humour and emotion; and some of Noël's music was beautifully played and sung. This was more like it.)

Tim's service was at the Guards' Chapel. No razzmatazz. Royalty represented. Meticulous, apparently impersonal ritual, in memory of Lt. Col. The Lord Nugent, GCVO, MC. Then at the end, as we knelt, the Chaplain said, 'O Lord, we commend to thy fatherly care thy servant Tim' ... That little monosyllable was incredibly moving.

Putting *Dragon Variation* firmly behind us we faced the familiarly uncertain future. Soon, to our joy, John Gale and Ray Cooney in partnership offered us excellent parts in Willie Douglas Home's political comedy, *At the End of the Day*.

Set in Downing Street in the then recent past, the action concerned a socialist administration presided over by a pipe-smoking northcountryman with a devoted if homely wife, being defeated by a silver-haired Tory bachelor with an idiosyncratic way of walking along looking to right or left but never where he was going. Both gave television interviews to an astringent character wearing a spotted bow tie. Any resemblance to persons living or dead was coincidental.

John Mills played the Labour premier (Henry Jackson), Dulcie his wife (Mabel) and I the incoming Tory (Lew Trent). We had great fun with the play, which ran successfully at the Savoy through the autumn and into the spring of 1974.

It opened therefore in the apparently carefree last summer of Edward Heath's government, ran through the confrontation with the miners and the three-day week, and ended shortly after Heath's defeat by Harold Wilson in the spring of '74.

The reactions of our audiences changed with the developing political situation. Laughter still came in the same places, but what had been uninhibited in the autumn was uneasy in the New Year. Whatever Willie's original intentions, our audiences cast Johnnie, Dulcie and myself in the rôles of the real-life protagonists.

There was one particular exchange between Johnnie and myself, set on the morning of the play's Tory victory, which when played against the impending Tory defeat in real life was clearly spell-binding to our audiences. It went like this:

Jackson: You're going to bring down prices, reduce unemployment and curb inflation?

Trent: That's right – at a stroke.

J: How, Lew?

T: By Leadership.

J: I see. So you're going to bash the unions?

T: I'll legislate of course.

J: And if they won't play?

T: They'll have to won't they? It'll be the law.

J: And if they break it?

T: They'll have to pay the penalty.

J: Or you will, Lew.

T: One thing I won't do, Henry, is what you did – and that's back down.

J: Like a bet on it?

T: Right – the pound in your pocket.

Willie's political spoof had become a play for all seasons.

Dulcie had a deserved success as the voice of decent, harassed, impotent common sense lost in the political jungle. 'How did you manage to drop your behind?' enquired Rebecca West. 'I didn't know I had,' said Dulcie.

We never discovered whether the actual protagonists came to the play; but certainly streams of politicians of all parties and both houses did. Among them were Peter and Iona Carrington, who are neighbours in Buckinghamshire and had become close friends.

Was it perhaps through Peter that we were invited, before rehearsals began, to the Prime Minister's birthday party at Chequers, also not far away?

A wonderful smokey July night heavy with roses; Gina Bachauer playing in the Great Hall; and a special tape of great operatic voices singing, 'Happy Birthday dear Te-ed.' Among our fellow guests was a cheerful rubicund little man in a smoking jacket which matched his complexion. 'Are you enjoying yourselves?' he asked us. 'Enormously.' 'I'm so glad. You see,' he went on proudly indicating our host, 'he's my son.' No problems of communication there. But what a lovely civilised evening it was.

We asked Ted back and he accepted, but when we were able to tell him that we had run Tito and Tilde Gobbi to earth in Chicago and they were coming to England especially to meet him, he enquired if we would mind switching the gathering to Chequers which he felt the Gobbis might like to see. We could hardly deny them that pleasure, so back we went to Chequers for the second time. By now, *At the End of the Day* was on, and Ted enquired of Tilde whether it was true that I was 'a subversive character'. 'Oh no,' she replied. 'He lives in a beautiful house.'

In October, to my intense excitement, *Overture and Beginners* was published, with the accolade of a Foyle's Literary Luncheon at the Dorchester. Johnnie Mills made a most generous speech about the book and ourselves; and other top-table guests included Felix Aylmer, Livia Gollancz, Derek Nimmo, Terry Rattigan, the Rabagliatis, Rebecca West and Bertie van Thal – who (with Livia's 'maternal' contribution) had been the book's 'onlie begetter'. Sybil Thorndike cried off in heart-rending terms: 'I think I'd be idiotic to come, in case of collapse which would be very awkward and I'd be accused of "stealing the thunder". Going to the theatre is easy because it's no effort. God bless you for understanding – and Dulcie too, the darling. Good luck to your beautiful book. Your very affectionate old pal Sybil.'

A few days later, in a letter which crossed our thanks to her,

Christina Foyle described the luncheon 'as quite the most delightful we have ever had', and went on – 'I know the book will be the season's best seller.' In this sadly she was mistaken, though Harold Hobson of the *Sunday Times* made it his Book Choice of the Year.

On the Sunday in question I read his theatre review first. It was one of those historic occasions when Harold was fighting a lone battle in favour of a play which his colleagues had dismissed. 'Harold's really gone round the bend today,' I called out to Dulcie. And then my eye caught his book choice.

VI
1974

*A rescue attempt – a short-run thing – a Berkshire lunch party –
a long run begins – Hook performed – Pooh-Bah offered*

On 2 January 1974 I went as part of a small Equity deputation to
meet the Russian cultural attaché. Our aim was to intercede on
behalf of Valery and Galina Panov, the married ballet dancers,
whose attempts to emigrate to Israel had received much sympathetic coverage in the media of the free world.

'Panov? Panov?' said the Soviet official. 'It's not a name I
know. Why are you interested in these people?'

We explained – to his astonishment – that Equity had no
political affiliations and that our motivation was artistic. We
were concerned with the freedom of professional colleagues to
practise their art, wherever that freedom appeared to be en-
dangered; we emphasised that regimes of the right could be as
guilty in this respect as those of the left.

He promised eventually to pass on our request to the ambassador, but said that if by any chance these unimportant
dancers were allowed to leave, it would not be because of our
representations.

If this was intended to depress us it failed in its purpose, and we
repaired to the nearest pub with quiet confidence. Within seven
months Dulcie and I were meeting the Panovs in London – a
most heartening occasion, whatever caused the Soviet authorities to relent.

It may be remembered that in 1971 we had been invited to appear
in *The Sacking of Norman Banks*, only to see the production
disintegrate before rehearsals began. Now, even before *At the
End of the Day* closed, Ray Cooney, who never lets the grass
grow under his feet, asked us to do *Norman Banks*, which had
been re-named *The Sack Race*. We still thought it a good play;
Charles Hickman was again to direct and so we happily agreed. A

233

talented and outstandingly friendly company (who included Tony Nicholls, Ewan Roberts, Terence Longdon, Anna Dawson and Deborah Watling) were engaged, a highly successful tour followed and all seemed set fair.

Then sadly we came into the Ambassadors, which *The Mouse-trap* had just quitted after the first eighteen years of its run – one effect of which had been to remove that charming little theatre from the consciousness of London's theatregoers, while making it as much a part of the tourist scene as Nelson's Column or the Horse Guards. And so it was that in spite of good notices the play was withdrawn ten days later – the decision being communicated to the company in the half-hour gap between the Saturday performances. There was not even time to see our colleagues to commiserate; so we had the strange experience of giving that final show to a large and enthusiastic house with death in our hearts.

The ensuing vacuum was filled with publicity functions connected with Dulcie's latest book (*Dead Give Away*); and with various social junketings, the happiest of which was driving Rebecca West down to lunch at Blewbury with Dick and Mary Francis. Dick and Dulcie had become great friends at meetings of the Crime Writers' Association; he and Rebecca admired each other's work but had never met. It was a particular joy to introduce them.

The Francis home is a luxurious bungalow planned to be run with the minimum of difficulty by Mary, who was suffering from polio when it was built. Happily she recovered and became not only a pilot with her own air-taxi firm, but a first-class photographer as well. She also makes a major contribution to the phenomenal success of Dick's writing. In America they no doubt call her 'a lovely person' – I can think of no better way to describe her.

As for Dick – whether as jockey, journalist or novelist he is a winner. His skill, his enthusiasm and his interest in others win him friends at all levels of society and in all walks of life. Not surprisingly he and Rebecca were in instant rapport.

Soon Dulcie embarked on *The Pay Off*, an ingenious if mechanical thriller by Bill Fairchild, in which her co-star and director was Nigel Patrick. It was to run for nearly a year. Nigel was a consummate director and play-doctor; he was also a most incisive player of comedy. Unfortunately (in my view), he liked to do both, and when he did, as in *The Pay Off*, both main facets of his talent were put at risk. Many distinguished players have directed themselves of course – Gielgud, Olivier, Redgrave, Quayle, to name a few – but I would contend that they have been at their best as actors when directed by others and as directors when they were not playing. The functions are separate: they demand that you should be 'out front' and on stage simultaneously. Paradoxically it is only when the actor-director is the playwright as well – I think of Noël and Emlyn Williams – that all functions can be successfully combined.

Meanwhile I had been approached to play Captain Hook and Mr Darling in *Peter Pan*. There had been more than one attempt in the early Fifties to get us both to do it, but the long provincial tour which in those days always followed the London season had made it impossible. This time Susan Hampshire was to play Peter and the engagement would be confined to five or six weeks at the Coliseum. I enjoyed Hook, loathed Darling (chiefly for his attitude to dogs) and much admired Susan's Peter. The pretty girl who had had problems getting across vocally when she played in *On Approval* with us in the little Yvonne Arnaud Theatre in 1966 now commanded the stage and the 2500-seater auditorium of the Coliseum with strength and grace and assurance.

Playing the villain to those vast audiences of children, letting the braver spirits try on my hook in the dressing-room afterwards, and following in the footsteps of so many famous Hooks stretching back seventy years, was a memorable experience. The Coliseum has two strange walk-ways which protrude from the stage towards the stalls and pass immediately in front of the boxes. I decided to use one of these, when Hook was at his most villainous, as though I was coming down into the auditorium. One afternoon as I advanced, ghastly pale in my black costume lit by my green follow-spot, a small voice from the box at my elbow said urgently, 'Mummy, I don't like that man.'

Just before Christmas I was invited to tea at the Savoy by James Verner and Braham Murray – both then strangers to me – and told of their plans for *The Black Mikado*. It would use all Gilbert's dialogue and lyrics and all Sullivan's music; but the rhythms would be those of reggae, calypso and blues, the setting would be Caribbean and the cast would be black except for Pooh-Bah. Would I play Pooh-Bah?

'I don't sing,' I said.

'That doesn't matter,' they said.

That exchange was the only familiar part of the interview. The justification for the one white performer was that Pooh-Bah would be the political sophisticate, the fixer, whose know-how is essential to the emerging black nation.

I was fascinated by the idea, and also comforted that there was to be a six-week tour. The show – inevitably at this stage an unknown quantity – would only be brought into London if it worked.

And so, after talking it over with Dulcie and Ronnie Waters (our agent) I decided to take the plunge. Rehearsals would start early in the New Year.

VII
1975

*Learning to be a minority – traumas and triumph in Titipu –
Rebecca in the stalls – an airborne birthday – two journeys with
Frankie – farewell to a silver lady*

I set off for the first rehearsal of *The Black Mikado*, excited but
somewhat daunted by the prospect of being an ethnic minority
for the first time in my life. (True, there were some white faces
around – James Verner, the manager, Braham Murray, the
director, Johanna Bryant, Murray's wife and the show's designer,
and two members of 'Juice', the group who were adapting the
score and would perform it as the Titipu Town Band – but the
spotlight did not beat upon them in performances· as it did on
me.)

No sooner were introductions over than we were plunged into
the first of a number of financial crises. James Verner, not being a
member of the Society of West End Theatre (now SWET instead
of SWETM), was under the standard obligation to deposit with
the Society the equivalent of two weeks' salaries for the cast (in
this case £5000) before the production could proceed. The
money was not forthcoming, so the rehearsal was cancelled
before it began. Eventually Braham and his mother gallantly
stepped into the breach – the former raising a mortgage on
his house, the latter lending her son the balance. And so with
the occasional hiccup we got under way only one or two days
late.

It was a punishing routine. The days began with an hour's
'class' under the inspiring control of Amadeo, choreographer son
of the Philippine Ambassador to West Germany. He was most
solicitous towards me, not for my whiteness, but because I was
thirty-two years older than any other member of the 'corps', and
he feared for my life and limbs. 'Go to the back, Mr Pooh,' he said
to me at the first class, 'and don't attempt anything you feel is too
difficult.'

237

If I had followed his advice to the letter I would have had to remain immobile, for almost everything was too difficult. To my astonishment this also applied to the majority of my black colleagues. True, they had the inestimable advantages of youth and the apparently congenital sense of rhythm of their race, but only a handful were trained dancers. For the rest of us it was an adventure, agonisingly but joyfully shared.

People are either racially prejudiced or they are not. If you are not, count it a blessing rather than a virtue – a state of original grace, something difficult if not impossible to learn. Fortunately we none of us had to learn it. *The Black Mikado* was not without tensions – what production is? – but none had a racial element.

Minorities – unless eliminated Stalin-style – have always been a problem in human affairs. The onus of behaving in a civilised manner is of course on the majority, but the minority can help or hinder them in that delicate task. Looking back on my days as Pooh-Bah I can say that, if all minorities were treated as I was by my black colleagues, the world would be a happier and less dangerous place. What, I wonder, was my contribution to this happy situation? I can only think that it was my patent (and successful) readiness to make a fool of myself in class and refuse the easy way out offered by Amadeo. One not-to-be-forgotten day I had my reward. 'Mr Pooh,' cried Amadeo, 'come to the front. You're the only one doing it right!'

Class, of course, was only the beginning of the day. We then scattered like schoolchildren after assembly to various parts of the South London boys' club we had taken over. In one room there would be musical rehearsals – we weren't all trained singers either; in another, Braham, a most astute and encouraging director, would be taking dialogue scenes; Amadeo would be staging the musical numbers up in the main hall, while those not immediately involved played snooker underneath. The air vibrated with the efforts of Juice to complete their enormous work of adaptation.

I can't speak for the younger generation, but my days ended in a Radox bath in which I more than once fell asleep.

It was during this phase that I began to identify the personalities and talents of my colleagues. They came from three main areas – West Africa, the West Indies and the United States, though a few in the first two catagories had been born in England.

There was Val Pringle (the Mikado) from Washington, a former prize-fighter and footballer, who, when dressed in his three top hats and tiger-skin, looked as formidable as Idi Amin, but was in fact a gentle giant with the most glorious voice. Anita Tucker (Katisha) was another larger-than-life figure. A blues singer from Memphis, Tennessee, who had worked with Louis Armstrong, Duke Ellington and Count Basie, she was also the granddaughter of an Ethiopian princess, and claimed to have 'seen the Lord'. You never knew which rôle was going to be dominant, and so she was easily affronted; but she wanted to be loved and in due course we came to love her. She too was a superb artist.

What but unstinted praise can be applied to Norman Beaton (Nanki-Poo), a good singer and even better actor; to Vernon Nesbeth (Pish-Tush), who put his gleaming ebony athleticism to the service of his profession; and how describe Derek Griffiths (Ko-Ko), except in terms of genius, as an actor-mime-dancer-singer, a combination of talents at a level unique in my experience? And so finally to the three little maids from school – Jenny McGusty (Peep-Bo), Floella Benjamiyn (Pitti-Sing) and Patricia Ebigwei (Yum-Yum). Jenny was, I think, the baby of the company and very inexperienced, but she was a bundle of energy and an intensely hard worker; Floella, from Trinidad, had begun singing with her father's jazz band in London at the age of twelve, then became a bank clerk and a promising athlete, until one lunch break when she decided to audition for *Hair* and was accepted. She is now, like Derek, nationally famous with the young for her children's programmes on television, and is a most appealing personality – warm, exuberant and highly intelligent. Pat, from Nigeria, was yum-yum indeed – a beautiful long-legged creature with a lovely voice, who used to stop the show with 'The Sun and I', and is now a great success in cabaret, under the name of Pattie Boulaye.

The 'Ladies and Gentlemen of Titipu', each in a witty and colourful individual costume, were much more than a chorus line – Glenna Forster Jones, a high-born lady from Sierra Leone, remaining firmly in the mind for her earthy humour and the lithe intensity of her dancing.

We moved in due course to the Adelphi to acclimatise us to working in a theatre, and it was there that we suffered two more shocks – one then new in my experience, the other still happily unique.

We had all been aware that there was tension between Braham and Jimmie Verner, which I put down to the latter having so far failed to repay the £5000. Nothing certainly prepared us for Jimmie's announcement that Braham had been sacked and that he was taking over.

Swift action was called for. The principals assembled in our flat, and it was agreed that we would all leave the show unless Braham was reinstated. We asked Jimmie to meet us at the Adelphi next day. Our argument – not strictly accurate in law – was that we had signed our contracts on the understanding that Braham was to direct, and that they were nullified by the change of plan.

In the event the argument was unnecessary. After a look at our sombre expressions – and Val Pringle in particular could lower like a thundercloud – Jimmie said, 'On my way to the theatre this morning I realised I had made a mistake.'

So Braham was back; and a disturbed but still enthusiastic company buckled to once more. It was at this stage that Dulcie came to a run-through – and her excitement at what she saw on a bare stage with the company in rehearsal clothes was a special tonic for me.

A regular spectator of our rehearsals was the house manager of the Adelphi – the theatre was dark at the time – who was sufficiently enthused to invest in the show. On the last Saturday of our rehearsal period (we were to open in Edinburgh in four days' time), the company was informed by the two Equity representatives who had been in frequent attendance from the outset that there was no money to pay the week's rehearsal salaries. We were accordingly instructed not to travel to Edinburgh.

Providentially I had my cheque book with me – why, I can't imagine. It was a Saturday and I had no inkling that it might be needed. I asked the Equity people how much was the total sum involved. It was in the region of £230 for around twenty-six people. (If so small a sum was unavailable, the production must be in a very bad way.) I went to our friend and investor the house manager. Had he any funds, in the theatre? And if so, would he take my cheque for £230. He would. So that was straightened out. For me it was a painless altruism. I was reimbursed by Equity as soon as the office re-opened on Monday.

Meanwhile there was worse to come. Neither the scenery nor the costumes had been paid for, so there might still be an embargo on our travelling to Edinburgh.

I was planning to drive up, spending Sunday night with the Reynolds at Leighton Hall near Kendal. I determined to continue with my plan and asked to be rung at Leighton by noon on the Monday with instructions to proceed or return. Helen Reynolds decided that the only way to wait for such news was with a glass of champagne in one's hand. The celebration was justified: on the stroke of noon I was told to proceed.

What had happened was this. Clive Perry, then in charge of The King's, Edinburgh – already a civic theatre, incidentally, since its sale to the Corporation by Peter Donald – had arranged a guarantee against loss for the production during its ten days in the city. A suggestion that we should do the show without scenery or costumes did not appeal to him, so he set about persuading his committee to turn the guarantee against loss into an unconditional 'up-front' guarantee. In this he was miraculously successful, and so funds were immediately available to persuade the costumiers and scene-builders to release their wares.

The set, half-finished and unpainted, arrived the day before the opening. It was constructed with a rake, to sit at an advantageous angle on the flat stage of the Cambridge Theatre – our intended London home. Unfortunately the King's Edinburgh has a rake of its own, so having rehearsed our complicated dance routines on the flat, we had to perform them for the first time on a splinter-strewn hillside. There had only been time for a truncated technical rehearsal – mostly for lighting and sound – which ended an hour or so before curtain up. We had no dress rehearsal at all. We were to play to an Edinburgh Charity audience (black tie), in an irreverent send-up of a cherished masterpiece. I knew better than most what we might be in for.

But we had a triumph, the like of which I had never experienced before, and which was only to be surpassed six weeks later in London. The finale of the show was a reprise by the entire company – in stomping reggae rhythm – of Derek Griffith's Tit-Willow song. One reprise was not enough for the London first-night audience, and soon a sizeable proportion of them had left their seats and were dancing with us in the aisles – a mood echoed next morning by the press.

There followed a year's run. All in all, a fitting reward for a hard-working company that had been through so much.

A word about Jimmie Verner. I have no knowledge of what lay behind the financial traumas that I have described. Perhaps he was more sinned against than sinning – the company certainly were. But he did have the idea for *The Black Mikado*; no less important, he chose Braham to direct – and for that and all that flowed from it I shall always be in his debt.

There was one hilarious postscript on the financial front. Braham (and his mother), who had still not been repaid their £5000 when we opened at the Cambridge Theatre, instructed their solicitor to 'attach' that sum from the box-office receipts. He duly attached it, not from the Cambridge Theatre but from the theatre in Cambridge (The Arts), much to the astonishment of its director, Richard Cotterell.

Dulcie had seen the show a couple of times in Newcastle, while *The Pay Off* was moving theatres, but inevitably missed the London opening. I decided to make a special occasion of that year's wedding anniversary. 'Just pack an overnight bag, and come to the Cambridge after your show,' I told her. I had booked at the Dorchester, where we had spent our one-night honeymoon in 1939. 'Where are we going?' she asked me as we drove through Mayfair; and then, as we turned down Park Lane, heading for the Dorchester, she murmured sadly, 'I had hoped we might be going to the Dorchester.' With such a sense of direction no wonder she needs a husband.

During the early stages of my London run, Dulcie suffered for a while a bout of insomnia and depression, with ominous echoes of her breakdown in the early Fifties. This time it was perhaps a reaction from her long stint in *The Pay Off*, combined with the demands of *Ride on a Tiger*, her most ambitious novel to date. Fortunately the gloom lifted after a month or two as suddenly as it had descended.

Ride on a Tiger was the story of a professional actress who was enamoured, as a dilettante, with revolutionary politics. The story had a certain topicality – there were and still are members of our profession in many countries who behave like Dulcie's Coralie – but it was not a portrait of any individual. It was a serious – and thrilling – cautionary tale of the dangers of playing with fire, or of riding tigers; and it had a gratifying success not only at the time but since, on the evidence of Public Lending Right borrowings.

Eight *Mikados* a week were indeed tiring, but I believe I have never been fitter. Not only was I one of only four members of the

At home with the Rolls, early 1970s

left Mrs Alving, 1972

below Miss Marple, 1977

Pooh-Bah on stage and in rehearsal with the Three Little Maids, 1975

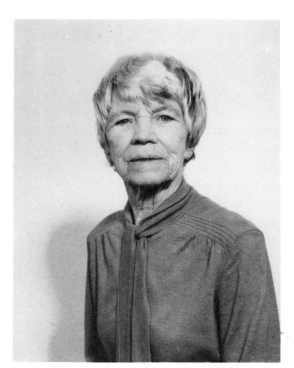

right Eileen Leahy

below Prospero

company never to miss a performance – the others were Floella, Jenny McGusty and inevitably the super-fit Vernon Nesbeth – but I was still an Equity Councillor, had joined the Drama Panel of the Arts Council, and had been invited on to a Tory committee whose task was to work out a much-needed party policy for the Arts. Merely to study those engagements today is more exhausting than I found them then.

At least I had the good sense finally to retire from cricket. In June I was non-playing captain of the World Wildlife XI on our local ground. As we were losing, in spite of Bill Edrich's captaincy on the field, I decided that the situation called for the non-playing captain to go in twelfth. The captain of the opposing club (of which I am a member) agreed, and I duly hit the last boundary of my career. It was also my first, since playing for Magdalen College 'A' against the Church Army Press in 1937. I know a good exit when I see one.

The good things in the *Mikado*'s London run were many; but the high spots must suffice.

An early visitor was a charming elderly lady who announced herself as the granddaughter of George Grossmith senior, the original Ko-Ko. 'How he would have loved it,' she cried. 'And my father too.' (George Grossmith junior.) Members of the D'Oyly Carte Company were equally enthusiastic. 'It's never going to be the same again,' said the current Yum-Yum. I bet it was though; that tradition was not so easily to be broken.

My favourite 'notice' came in a letter from Rebecca West:

Dear Michael,

I was watching you last night and enjoying every minute of it. I marvelled that Whitey could keep up with the Niagara flow of African energy, and Whitey certainly did, though I quaked to think what the two matinée days must be like. I loved your Macmillan look and voice ... What miracles they are, miracles of loveliness, miracles of skill, miracles of grotesquerie, and what *industry*, what perfectionist passion there is behind it. The Mikado has the presence of Chaliapin, he roars for all the bull bisons that ever were created. And that Tit-Willow song is marvellous, so absolutely right, and ungreasy, if you know what I mean.

And then as a postscript:

What a chancy business yours is. There you are, in a most unlikely milieu doing a lovely piece of work, part of a lovely whole. I saw Paul Scofield the other day playing Prospero – the island being converted into a Drill Hall with Ariel standing in the gallery and wearing tight pants and looking like the caretaker – and I suppose Scofield like myself could never have thought that any production of *The Tempest* could work out that way – anyway his spirit died.

Quite early in the run Princess Anne came to a Sunday Charity Gala, which included an excerpt from our show. Val, Derek, Anita and I were to be presented to her. Anita – granddaughter of an Ethiopian princess, it may be remembered – had demonstrated her membership of the international royal set by kitting herself out from head to foot while in Edinburgh in a costume and matching bonnet of Royal Hunting Stuart tartan. (It looked unlikely, but magnificent.) Dressed on this occasion in Katisha's finery, she was clearly nervous as the Princess approached. 'What do I call her?' she whispered to me. 'You call her Ma'am and you do a little bob,' I replied. Anita looked at me in outrage. 'Don't tell me what to do, man.' In response to Princess Anne's outstretched hand Anita all but disappeared through the floor in a curtsey of operatic splendour. 'Do you think I might shake your hand as well?' said the Princess. 'Certainly Madam,' said Anita on the way up. And then: 'It might interest you to know, Madam, that I too am of royal blood.' 'I thought you must be,' said the Princess, keeping an exemplary straight face.

That November I had my sixtieth birthday. I had told no one in the company; but they had found out, and presented me with a handsome attaché case – still in use – and a card, criss-crossed with affectionate messages, which has survived nine years of my filing system. Derek came to me in my room to say that he had not contributed, because he wanted to give me a special present of his own. 'I want to take you and Dulcie to lunch at Le Touquet.' 'But how, Derek? We'd never be back for the show.' 'Oh yes we will. I'm going to fly you there. I'm a pilot you know.' 'How very kind. I'll discuss it with Dulcie and let you know tomorrow.'

Now, I have already called Derek a genius. His performance thrilled me; but his superabundant energy overflowed his performance. Back-stage he was often like a mischievous child, dashing up to the flies to sprinkle water over the girls as they waited in the wings in their diaphanous costumes, thinking up every sort of practical joke. How was I to entrust Dulcie and myself to him as a pilot? How was I to refuse, without hurting that beguiling character? Dulcie would solve my problem, I had no doubt.

And Dulcie did. 'How marvellous,' she said.

I should have had faith in Derek's versatility. The pilot who met us at Biggin Hill that November morning had only enthusiasm in common with the Derek we knew. 'Bad news, I'm afraid,' he said. 'There's fog over the channel. We'll have to go to the Isle of Wight instead.' And so, instead of a gourmet meal in France, it was fish and chips at Bembridge. But the flight was longer – which was a bonus for both his passengers. Dulcie had never known the joy of being in a light aircraft before, and for me it brought back happy memories of the early Thirties. Our pilot gave us complete confidence.

And that was not all. In the evening, after the show, Floella and Pat were our hostesses in an excellent West Indian restaurant – a happy birthday indeed.

One final illustration of the spirit of that company, and indeed of what was expected by them of 'Mr Pooh'. During a very cold snap the theatre's heating failed. I received a deputation in my room ten minutes before curtain up, bringing a thermometer which showed the temperature on stage to be in the middle forties Fahrenheit. 'We cannot go on,' they said. (It must be remembered that most of them came from the tropics and were very scantily dressed. I was 'all right Jack', with the built-in central heating engendered by a Public School education, and in any case was dressed in white serge from head to foot.) A quandary. We could hear the growing hum of the audience over the tannoy. 'It seems a pity to disappoint them,' I said. 'After all, they'll be colder than we are – just sitting out there. Why don't we get the house manager to apologise to them and say that the company would be quite entitled to refuse to perform, but that, not wanting to disappoint them, we have agreed to go ahead, but with extra clothing over our costumes.' This was greeted with whoops of delighted agreement – and in the event was equally popular with the audience. The variations on Johanna Bryant's brilliant costumes were hilarious. Floella, I remember, who has a Churchillian love of bright colours, added to her peacock-blue leotard thigh-long woollen leg-warmers in the scarlet and yellow of the MCC. The audience's good humour was shared by the cast as each new apparition appeared – but after all, it had been a real crisis, and it was much better than no show at all.

Dulcie's summer had had its surprises. The first was a request from our good friend Frankie Howerd that she should write him a television who-dunnit with a military background. Frankie had apparently much enjoyed his military service – particularly the time spent in the empty expanses of the Gower Peninsula in South Wales, where he was a clerk in the Quartermaster's Stores. He felt it was important that Dulcie should get the feel of that untrammelled solitude, so an elaborate expedition was arranged. Frankie would be driven from his house in Somerset; Dulcie would go by train to Cardiff. They would meet for lunch at the Angel Hotel and drive on together. Frankie was in his most expansive mood and became highly excited as they approached journey's end. 'It's just round this corner, Dulcie, and over the brow of the hill, and there's this wonderful view stretching to the horizon.' What actually stretched to the horizon were serried ranks of post-war bungalows.

Dulcie wrote the script nevertheless, and very good it was. But though Frankie was delighted with it, it was never done. For Dulcie it was that sort of year.

The abortive effort had one unlikely spin-off. I had been reading Jack Priestley's *Particular Pleasures*, which contains a glowing essay about Frankie. Frankie hadn't read it but was very thrilled because he greatly admired JBP. And so the idea was born of arranging a meeting. Jack was agreeable, provided it took place at Alveston. 'Bring him to lunch,' he said. I was unavailable to take them; neither Dulcie nor Frankie drive; so a car and chauffeur was hired. Frankie in a very smart pale-grey suit became progressively more nervous as they approached Stratford. They only had three miles to go and were half an hour early, so Dulcie suggested a drink. Frankie gratefully accepted a large brandy and ginger ale; but someone promptly poured most of it over his suit. Willing hands mopped him up in return for autographs, but Dulcie's hopes that a drink would relax him had not been fulfilled.

Kissing Tree House is a substantial and attractive white Regency house in a beautiful garden. It is approached by a circular driveway covered with that loose gravel that crunches so seductively under the tyres of expensive cars. A marble-floored passage leads through the centre of the house with shallow steps raising its level to a french window. Jack's library is at the end on the right, and it was his habit to emerge from it and stand in unmistakable silhouette in front of the window to welcome his guests. Though a relaxed enough routine for old friends, it could be, I dare say, disconcerting to strangers – the great man standing above you, his face in shadow. (His greetings and farewells were always very formal – handshakes accompanied by endearing little bows.) On this occasion Jack was still at his most formal and Frankie not yet at his ease as the trio, now joined by Jacquetta, stood round the fire in that lovely library. Dulcie accepted the proffered sherry. 'Sherry for you, Mr Howerd?' enquired Jack. 'Could I have a brandy and ginger ale?' 'I've only got Napoleon brandy,' said Jack. 'I'm not putting ginger ale into that.' So poor Frankie was given two glasses, one with Napoleon brandy and one with the offending ginger ale.

Over lunch, however, the author of *Lost Empires* – a book which, for my money, far outshines *The Good Companions* – and Frankie, a refugee from those Empires and one of the greatest comics of our day, really got together. ('He is, I think,' Jack had written, 'a very clever man pretending not to be.') Jacquetta and Dulcie were an enthralled audience. What a pity there was no tape recorder at work.

Dulcie's next assignment, though brief, had considerable fascination. It was to read the Edith Sitwell part, with Gordon Jackson and Joe Melia, in *Façade* – that collection of her poems written to be spoken to music specially composed by William Walton. Technically extremely difficult, for the rhythms of poems and music rarely coincide in a conventional manner and some of the most obscure and tongue-twisting passages have to be read at lightning speed, it was a thoroughly rewarding exercise. They performed it in Nottingham and in the Queen Elizabeth Hall.

Her year ended with a production of *Time and the Conways* at Guildford. Her Mrs Conway was splendid – I managed to see a matinée – and I determined, if a management could be found, to redirect it myself for London in the New Year. Antony Andrews and Christopher Cazenove not only gave excellent performances but won our gratitude for taking it in turns to drive Dulcie home every night.

Before *The Mikado* began we had reluctantly decided to sell the Rolls – the camel's back finally giving way under a bill for £550 for a new exhaust. We sold her for roughly three times what we had paid for her ten years before – she was now twenty-four years old and had done 217,000 miles – but in the fullness of time I was charged Capital Gains on the transaction. I have a conviction that this could only happen to me.

VIII
1976

I meet my model – and Dulcie her uncle's pupil – Palm Sunday on Nevis – JBP's blessing in vain – a busy summer with Anna and Boo – Duncan pulls the strings

In the letter quoted, Rebecca referred to my 'Macmillan look and voice'. It had been a deliberate plan – my idea, but enthusiastically embraced by Braham. It seemed to us quite in keeping with Gilbert's addiction to political satire that the one white character in our version should suggest a contemporary figure. Why Harold Macmillan? Not to make fun of him, but to make fun with him. The appearance and voice of the Edwardian toff, allied so unexpectedly to the quick mind, the humour, the ready and practical sympathy for victims of circumstance whatever their race and generation, helping to speed 'the wind of change' simply by formulating the phrase – all these characteristics, placed in Pooh-Bah's situation in *The Black Mikado*, could enhance the comedy without distorting Gilbert's intention. Such was our thinking, and it seemed to work well in practice.

The word must have reached Macmillan as to what I was up to, for a few minutes before curtain up one evening I was told that he was in front with a family party. I took a Librium and wrote him a note saying that I hoped he would forgive me, and that if he was enjoying himself would he come and have a drink with me afterwards. At the end of the interval my note was returned to me. For a heart-stopping moment I thought it was unopened; and then I saw the envelope had been slit with surgical precision. On the back of the note was written: 'I had heard great accounts of your performance but it has far exceeded my best expectations. Splendid. HM.'

He and his party were in my room so quickly at the end that, though I was out of my costume and in my dressing-gown, I still had my Macmillan make-up on – which did really make me look

249

quite like him. For me it was a marvellous encounter. He was so enthusiastic about the show.

'Are you thinking of having a holiday?' he asked eventually, the lips all but immobile, humour lurking in the hooded eyes.

'Eventually, sir, yes.'

'Well do let me know, I'll come and take over.'

And then with a charming technique of asking you questions to which only he knew the answers: 'I've always loved the theatre, you know. Do you know what my mother was doing a hundred years ago? She was crossing the Atlantic from America. And how, do you think? In a paddle steamer. And why, do you think? To go to Paris to train as an opera singer. She had a lovely voice – I remember it as a child – but it was not powerful enough for opera. So then what do you think she did? She became a sculptress. Adventurous, don't you think?'

Sadly Dulcie missed this occasion; but in 1984, on the day on which he had taken his seat in the Lords as Earl of Stockton, Fleur Cowles gave a dinner party for him, attended by the Queen Mother – a gathering which we were invited to join after our performance of *The School for Scandal*. Dulcie's Uncle Cyril had been his tutor at Balliol; Macmillan was enchanted when Dulcie identified herself as Cyril Bailey's niece, and he talked long and affectionately to her of 'that dearest of men'.

The holiday duly came – most appropriately, in the West Indies. We went first to Montpelier on the island of Nevis, where the delightful hotel was run by George, a former (black) Governor of Nevis, and his consort, Mary. (They had been in office when the Queen had visited the Caribbean. 'Fifty-eight minutes,' said Mary ruefully, 'was all her schedule allowed her on Nevis. But we made the most of it!') Among the delights of friendly people, a verdant landscape bright with hibiscus, cannas and plumbago, and a mile-long empty sandy beach backed by soaring palms, one particular occasion sticks out in my mind – Palm Sunday. George was a Methodist, and Mary Church of England; so we asked the latter if we could come with her to church.

We went in a Jeep, driven by the young barman, over dusty tracks through the fields. We saw the church from some way off, and suddenly the landscape was alive with its congregation converging on it from all directions. They were in their Sunday best – no cliché in the West Indies, nor indeed among those of our own black communities who have not rejected their roots.

The children in particular looked ravishing – reflecting their parents' strong and joyful conviction that only the best was good enough for the Lord. (A conviction which when shared by the Anglo-Saxon is so often the reverse of joyful!)

The church – of grey stone with a sturdy wooden roof – was almost full when we got there. Its 'windows' had no glass, so the sights and sounds of the countryside mingled with those of the service. For the moment they were drowned by the happy hubbub of the congregation. As a former first lady, Mary rated the front pew, and so did her guests. We would sooner, in Norman Gwatkin's phrase, have 'hung on at the back' – but it was at least a Church of England service, so no confusing bells would be rung. In the event it seemed like three Church of England services. We had Matins and Communion, and anything else that didn't irrevocably belong to Evensong. The clergyman, the only other white-skinned person present, preached for a good half-hour – he knew that his flock expected no less. It was a great occasion – so I suspect was *every* Sunday – and they didn't want it skimped. Nor, in that moving atmosphere, did we.

As a devotee of the language of King James's Bible and the Book of Common Prayer, no less than of Shakespeare's; I have always regarded their occasional obscurities as part of the scenery – after all we are in the realms of mysteries, which should not be too clinically spelled out. However, if there could ever be a case for modern simplifications, I reflected, waiting for that service to begin, it would be to make things easier for the simple folk of Nevis. Wrong. I have never heard a congregation more in tune with the prayers in which they joined, relishing the words as something well loved and familiar, and yet finding in them 'newness of life'.

Before we started back our driver was asked by a friend whether he would be playing cricket that afternoon. 'No. Not today,' said the young man sadly. 'Why not?' asked Mary when we were on our way. 'I'm on duty this afternoon.' We assured Mary that none of her guests would expect drinks in mid-afternoon – so he was given the rest of the day off. His joy was elemental. How had he done, we enquired later. 'I took three wickets and made twenty-eight runs,' he said proudly.

I returned for one week to *The Black Mikado*, by now not much lighter in skin than the rest. There was one calypso number which I danced and sang with the girls. I ended with them swarming all over me as I sat in a chair. Glenna's 'business' was to roll up my trouser leg and examine my strange white calves. Confronted with my new mahogany ones, she let out a squeak. 'Man,' she said, 'that's real sick!'

And so I said farewell to the old *BM*, after my longest West End run of more than 450 performances, my regrets tempered by the fact that some of my best friends were leaving too. 'One more time' was the general theme as we said our goodbyes; and indeed there was a flicker of hope that it might have been filmed in Ghana – which came to nothing. Sad. It would make spectacular television.

Duncan had agreed to present *Time and the Conways*, JBP had given his blessing, and so, true to my conviction that directors should come to the first rehearsal with a detailed plan, I had been plotting the moves and making a close study of the text while on holiday.

I told the company that, while we couldn't 'command' a London theatre, we could at least deserve one. And that I think we did. Jack thought so too when he came to the show in Wolverhampton. He was particularly pleased with Dulcie's matriarch and gave his permission for the production to be seen in London. However, by the time the tour was completed, the heat of that hottest of summers had stifled all thoughts of investment on the West End scene. And so that was that. Disappointing, but at least we had both been deeply involved in a play of Jack's – which hadn't happened since *Dragon's Mouth* – and, more important, we had won his approval for both our contributions.

While the tour was still in progress, Duncan begged me to take over from John Clements in a tour of *The First Mrs Fraser*, which starred Anna Neagle. It had played to enormous business in all the dates within reach of John's home in Brighton, but now it was planned to take it to the Midlands and the North and perhaps to London. The brave and adorable Katie Hammond was still alive; and John, the most devoted of husbands, was still insisting, as he did throughout the twenty years of her incapacity, that he would get home at the end of the day.

I enjoyed working with Anna tremendously. Her professionalism and her good manners go hand in hand. 'Michael,' she said to me early on, 'if you did so and so you'd get an entrance round.' 'Thank you,' I said, 'but I don't want one.' The blue eyes widened. 'You don't want an entrance round?!' I might have been refusing a glass of Dom Pérignon. 'No,' I explained. 'Yours is fine at the beginning. But by the time I come on it would interfere with the story, and the rough character I want to portray.' Anna was unconvinced.

My return to Edinburgh – with a man-made Scots accent – was if anything more frightening than the first night of *The Black Mikado*. Audrey Cameron and her great friend Barbara Bruce Watt were encouraging, however, and next day *The Scotsman* confirmed that the accent was indeed located north of the border – although appearing to be on tour throughout the kingdom. I think I got off lightly.

Soon after I started *Mrs Fraser*, under Charles Hickman's direction, Dulcie said goodbye to her problem Conway children and started a tour of *Ladies in Retirement* with Evelyn Laye – also directed by Charles. We criss-crossed the country in the most bewildering fashion, but not only managed to meet at most weekends but even saw each other's shows.

We had never known 'Boo' Laye particularly well, though there had been a flurry of meetings in the late Fifties when she bought an option on Dulcie's musical. But *Ladies in Retirement* was the start of an enduring friendship with that beautiful, talented and indomitable woman. 'My mate,' she calls Dulcie, ever since they shared a dressing-room in Peterborough, something which hadn't happened to Boo in her fifty years of stardom.

Another special friendship started that summer. When playing Eastbourne, Dulcie was staying with John and Vanessa Wauchope. A fellow house-guest was Mary Anna Marten. She arrived while Dulcie was at the theatre and had gone to bed by the time Dulcie got back – to bed, but not to sleep until she had finished *Ride on a Tiger*, which impressed her so much that she delayed her return home the next day until she could discuss it with the author. 'You must come and stay at Crichel if ever you're acting in Bournemouth,' she said warmly. It is dangerous to say this to us. There was no sign of Bournemouth on the map for Dulcie at this June meeting, but by October she was there and staying with the Martens in their superb eighteenth-century house. (Toby Marten, a retired naval officer, was responsible for the famous victory of the individual against government bureaucracy after the war, known as the Crichel Down Affair.) Since that chance meeting, Crichel has become the most splendid of all the friendly 'lodgings' we visit on tour.

Next I had great fun at Windsor with *The Earl and the Pussycat*, a new comedy by Harold Brooke and Kay Bannerman which was directed by Joan Riley. Gwen Watford, a marvellous actress with whom I had twice appeared on television (in Turgenev's *Provincial Lady* and Barrie's *Twelve Pound Look*), was my daughter, married to a Socialist cabinet minister; while I was an irreverent Tory peer. The comedy demands, clearly, that there should be a Socialist government in power. The next time that happens I shall pull whatever strings I may still have to get it revived, but Neil Kinnock will have to hurry.

We toured briefly after Windsor but there was no London theatre then available; and with *The Black Mikado* tax looming, I was persuaded by Duncan to play Old Father Moulton Barrett in *Robert and Elizabeth*, Ronnie Millar's musical version of *The Barretts of Wimpole Street*. My co-stars were Sally Ann Howes (who as a teenager had tested with me for the part of Edie in *My Brother Jonathan*) and Jeremy Brett (our Marchbanks in *Candida* at Oxford). Ronnie had, as usual, shown great skill in adaptation; but to make room for the musical numbers, something had to give. And in my view it was the character of Dad, who had dwindled from a complex, pitiable monster into a conventional 'baddie' of melodrama. There was nothing to be done with him, or rather – to be fair to my old friend the author – let me just say that there was nothing I did with him. In consequence I was professionally unhappy. Luckily the cast was an excellent one – Sally Ann's beautiful voice the crowning glory of the show – and Duncan, knowing my feelings, had very kindly invited Dulcie to come to Canada with us in the New Year.

IX
1977

This was my Life – Butterflies for Dulcie – brief encounter in Bermuda – 'my' Pinero – Jubilee honours – a difficult decision – Miss Marple to the rescue – penalty of success

Before moving to Canada, *Robert and Elizabeth* played seasons at Guildford and Brighton. For the former I was able to work from home. One day Dulcie said she was going up to the London flat to have discussions with a butterfly expert about her forthcoming book, so would I join her there after my show? As it happened I had received an unexpected invitation from Ronnie Millar to lunch with him the next day at The Inn on The Park – unexpected because of the choice of rendezvous and Dulcie's exclusion from the party, and because of Ronnie's insistence that he should pick me up at the flat. 'Why The Inn on The Park?' I asked him as I got into the maroon Rolls which in those days he maintained as though it were a clapped-out banger. 'Is it a regular haunt of yours?' 'Never been there before,' he replied. 'But after lunch I'm meeting an American there who is interested in taking the show to the States after Canada; and I'm hoping to persuade you to go along with the idea.' I had no wish to make my American debut in my least favourite part, but this seemed no time to say so, so I made some non-committal reply.

Our arrival at the hotel had a VIP quality about it which seemed surprising for two people who had never been there before; but perhaps, I reflected, it was their normal way of receiving guests. I had a very heavy sinus cold that day and by the middle of the meal was feeling quite ill. 'Forgive me, Ronnie,' I said, 'but if I'm to give anything like a performance this evening I think I'd better go home now and lie down.' 'Please just wait till I've finished my lunch,' said Ronnie firmly. 'And have a brandy. I'm going to.' It was becoming a nightmare, and I still hadn't categorically refused America. A waiter came over to me. 'You're wanted on the telephone, sir.' 'But nobody knows I'm here.'

255

'Dulcie does,' said Ronnie smoothly. I was led to the middle of three call-boxes. 'Darling,' said Dulcie, 'if you look in the box beside you you'll see an old friend.' 'There's no-one there,' I said looking to the right. 'There *must* be,' said Dulcie. So I looked to the left and there was Eamonn grinning cheerfully with a red book.

So I had been caught as completely as Dulcie, and – my sinus forgotten – I enjoyed 'My Life' as much as she did hers.

Dulcie had done particularly well in the background, and I had a wide range of friends to greet me. There was Ron Randell, with whom a close relationship goes back to the strange affair of *Sweet Peril* in 1952 (he had flown in from America); Dorian Williams who had introduced me at school to the intoxication of acting; Pam Rose who, with her brother (Pat Gibson) and her parents, had persuaded me to go to the Webber-Douglas where I was to meet Dulcie; Rodney Millington who had enabled us to get married on the security of a six-week season in Aberdeen at a joint salary of £15; Sam Derry, a heroic figure in German-occupied Rome, who later became my Colonel (I had been on his 'Life' many years before); Cheerful Charlie Chester, reminiscing about *Stars in Battle Dress* in which I had spent the nine months between the end of the war in Europe and my 'demob'; Bob Lennard, the architect of my film career; Val Pringle – the Black Mikado in person; recorded messages from Juliet Mills and Richard Todd, and – apparently – from Tito Gobbi, until with a splendid coup de théâtre, it turned out to be the great man himself. Most touching of all was the appearance of Bobby Melvin and Bobby Blair, two of the squad of twenty-four (twenty-three of them from the Glasgow Post Office) with whom I had joined the Army in 1940, and with whom there had been a series of reunions whenever we played in Scotland after the war. Bobby Blair was the calmer of the two; Bobby Melvin was tremendously excited, and his accent became almost unintelligible except to fellow Scots and myself. His life, which ended prematurely some years ago, had been a tough one, but there was never a sign of a 'chip' when faced with the contrast in our post-war lifestyles. Dulcie loved him as much as I did. 'He's so proud of you, Michael,' she said to me after one of those meetings, 'it's as though he'd invented you.'

Dulcie's butterfly expert and Ronnie's American, though real enough, had been used to shepherd me up to the starting line.

Both were highly plausible, particularly Dulcie's, for she had been engaged in preliminary research for her butterfly book since the previous summer.

She had said from the outset of her writing career that she would write fourteen detective stories and then a book on British butterflies. Actually *Butterflies on My Mind* was her nineteenth publication. Macdonalds, publishers of most of her crime stories, were not interested in butterflies, so she had simply kept on writing thrillers for them until a publisher could be found.

One evening, at a Crime Writers' party in 1974 or '75, a young man asked her if she would be prepared to write for his firm as well as for Macdonalds. 'Only if you're prepared to publish a book on British butterflies,' she replied. He was not enthusiastic. They met again, however, at a similar function a year later and Dulcie understood him to say that he might be interested after all. She accordingly suggested he should get in touch with Bertie van Thal, her agent; and rang Bertie herself in great excitement saying not to drive too hard a bargain because she so much wanted to write it. The telephone call duly came, and a contract was signed with Ian Dear of Angus and Robertson; and only at a celebratory lunch at the printers in Aylesbury did it emerge that neither Ian Dear nor anyone from his company had met Dulcie at a Crime Writers' function. The mystery remains unsolved.

I am not sure how far the writing of the book had progressed when Dulcie joined me in Canada. Certainly when staying with the Martens at Crichel the previous autumn she had visited Robert Gooden's butterfly farm at Over Compton for the first time. (She was already a Vice-President of the British Butterfly Conservation Society which he had founded.) He advised her to get in touch with John Heath of the Institute of Terrestrial Ecology at Monks Wood in Lincolnshire. Heath was the first of many distinguished entomologists to give her unstinted help – something which, as Peter Scott said in his Foreword, redounded both to their credit and to hers. For the help would assuredly not have been forthcoming if she had appeared as a dilettante invading their world for frivolous ends.

Certainly, also, before the Canadian trip another vital link had been forged. Brian Hargreaves was at work on his beautiful illustrations – each butterfly, life-size, pictured on or around its food plant.

I had also asked the author, 'Why is a butterfly called a butterfly?' 'I don't know,' she replied. 'I think your readers might like to,' I said. 'I'll find out.' But when she came back from a visit to her new friends at the Natural History Museum she said, 'They don't know either – and what's more, they don't care!' I did. More than ever.

So once the show was safely launched in Canada we settled down to find out, from the (twelve-volume) Oxford Dictionary and its French, German, Spanish, Italian, Greek and Russian equivalents. For the results, I refer the reader to *Butterflies on My Mind*. I will only say here that the names given by the various peoples to this beautiful insect range from 'butter-shit' (Dutch) to 'the soul' or 'psyche' (Ancient Greek).

The late Norman Riley, then doyen of British entomologists, was another key figure whom Dulcie had to win to her side. He very kindly agreed to read the first draft of the book and then invited her down to his home in Wimbledon to discuss it, while Mrs Riley and I talked of other things.

To Dulcie's joy his verdict was favourable. Not only did he treat what she had written seriously, but he told her that in the wide-ranging literature on the subject there was room for her individual approach. A generous response indeed from a great authority.

On our return to England, Dulcie's continuing research provided many fascinating occasions. The Queen gave permission for her to visit Buckingham Palace garden and discuss its butterfly population with Mr Nutbeam, the Head Gardener (she splashed around with him in wellingtons during an investiture). The Revd A. A. H. Harbottle, then Her Majesty's Chaplain at Windsor, invited her to his house in the Great Park to talk about his speciality, the Clouded Yellow. And we lunched with Dr Miriam Rothschild when we were playing Peterborough.

'My house has a number of front doors,' she told Dulcie on the telephone. We found none of them and entered through the kitchen. Our hostess, a strikingly handsome woman with lustrous eyes and dark hair coiled high on her head, wore a scarlet and blue dress above green and yellow rubber boots. While she answered Dulcie's questions about the Monarch (that amazing butterfly which makes it to Cornwall from North America in suitable conditions), and about the attempts to reintroduce the Large Copper at neighbouring Woodwalton Fen, I took Prospero for a walk down to the village, where the pub is called The Chequered Skipper. A happy lepidopterous day.

* * *

Before all this there had been a poignant meeting of another kind. Terence Rattigan, for whom I had 'fagged' at Harrow, was dying in Bermuda. Some time during the previous year he had written – in a Sunday paper – a most dignified and moving farewell to life; and I – among countless others I'm sure – had written to thank him for his contribution to the theatre, for many kindnesses to Dulcie and to me (even though sadly we had never appeared in any of his plays), and to say goodbye. There was no response, and although of course none was necessary, I had worried in a typically British manner as to whether I had embarrassed him. Bermuda lay on our homeward path, so we decided to ring him from Toronto, only to find that, not surprisingly, he was ex-directory. 'Shall we go anyway?' I said to Dulcie. We were ready for a day or two of sun after a Canadian winter in which we had walked through canyons of hard-packed snow seven feet high on the sidewalks of Ottawa. And so we went to that excessively pretty island.

I rang the exchange as soon as we were settled in our hotel. 'I understand that Sir Terence Rattigan is ex-directory.' 'That's right, sir,' said a cheerful Bermudan voice. 'I'm a very old friend,' I said. 'Would you ring his number for me and ask ...' The friendly voice gave me Terry's number.

Living with Terry at this time were Harold and Peggy French. Harold had been our director in *My Brother Jonathan* thirty years before, and had come into Terry's life eleven years before that as director of his fabulously successful *French Without Tears*. Peggy answered the telephone, and, when she recovered from her surprise, invited us to drinks the following evening and said she would arrange a dinner party for us before we left. 'Terry's very well just at the present,' she said. 'But I'm afraid you'll miss Harold. He's in England.' 'Peggy, one thing before we come. Did Terry get my letter?' 'He did indeed. He was very touched.'

We had the most lovely evening with him and Peggy. He was in marvellous form and we gossiped away about matters theatrical for hours. He told Dulcie quite directly and compulsively about the plays he still wanted to write – plays with a background of fact, historical or contemporary. For instance, his new play had been based on the notorious Rattenbury murder case. Called *Cause Célèbre*, it was to be presented in the West End that summer, and would be his twenty-second – and last. Pressure was being put on him from London to change the title. What did we think? We thought he should resist the pressure. But I promised to bring him some possible alternative titles when we came back to dinner the following night. I duly returned with my few suggestions, but alas Terry was too ill to join us and our fellow guests.

At least our last sight of him had been with his charm and enthusiasm at their peak; *Cause Célèbre* was a great success – as *Cause Célèbre*; and he was able to attend its opening. We left Bermuda, thankful that he had Harold and Peggy to look after him, and thankful that we had come.

Duncan had promised that if I would do *Robert and Elizabeth* for him he would do his best to set up for us a production of Pinero's *The Cabinet Minister*. I had done a version of this forgotten piece, cutting minor characters, reducing the number of sets and removing an unpleasant streak of snobbish anti-Semitism which had no place in a cheerful near-farcical comedy concerned with the financial problems of an aristocratic family in Belgravia and a Scottish castle. It seemed a suitable offering for the Queen's Jubilee summer but it would cost a great deal to stage with the luxury it demanded. In the end a combination of John Counsell, Duncan's Triumph Productions and Arts Council Touring did the trick. We got together a splendid cast who included Boo Laye and Pat Kirkwood, and after a capacity three weeks at Windsor we had a happy time with it on tour.

The actual Jubilee found us in Darlington, a town linked (tripletted?) with both a French and a German town, each of which had sent a Mayoral party to join in the celebrations. All of them, with their Darlington hosts, came to our performance, after which there was a civic supper at which I was to propose the loyal toast. I decided to begin and end in three languages and the toast – Vive la Reine, Es lebe die Königin, God Save the Queen – had a vociferous response.

Shortly after this when we were at home – playing Richmond, I think – we each received through the post the Queen's Jubilee Medal. Dulcie's was awarded to Dulcie Gray and therefore, having been despatched in alphabetical order, came a few days after mine. So Her Majesty was presented with two heartfelt thank-you letters. I enclosed in mine the text of my Darlington speech and received a warm acknowledgement from HM Yacht Britannia, Cardiff.

It was also at Richmond that Dulcie was faced with a hideous dilemma. Gerald and Veronica Flint Shipman wanted *The Cabinet Minister* for the Phoenix but were contracted to another show, which might not get off the ground. They couldn't therefore give us the green light immediately. At this moment Peter Saunders offered Dulcie Miss Marple in his new Agatha Christie production, *A Murder is Announced*, with the virtual certainty of a long London run at the Vaudeville. Dulcie knew how much I loved the Pinero – and her performance in it – but we had both privately agreed that some of the casting was not quite right. The Christie adaptation read pretty turgidly, but Miss Marple was undeniably the best part, and Bob Chetwyn, with whom we had worked so happily on *At the End of the Day*, was to direct. We made one last agonised call to the Flint Shipmans to learn that the other show was definitely coming into the Phoenix. So that was that, and Dulcie gratefully accepted Peter Saunders' offer.

It was to be her longest West End run; a solidly successful and reasonably uneventful engagement – apart from her broken wrist. She was within twenty yards of the Stage Door one evening, carrying her enormous handbag and a carrier-bag of shopping in the other hand, when she tripped on the uneven pavement of Maiden Lane. Nobody in this age of chivalry volunteered to help her. Two men made a detour into the street to avoid her. A young girl was in the act of stepping over her when Dulcie, who was in considerable pain, asked for assistance. This was grudgingly given, until the Stage Door Keeper's concern identified her. 'Oh, Miss Gray,' said her unwilling rescuer, 'can I have your autograph?'

Dulcie's eyesight had been worrying her, and me, for some time. Floella – a devotee of soft contact lenses – had urged Dulcie to go to see a friend of hers, Philip Cordrey of the David Clulow organisation. Philip, it transpired, was a fan of Dulcie's and was eager to help. The broken wrist decided her to take up this friendly offer. By now extremely short-sighted without glasses, she was fitted with a trial pair of lenses and was asked to look across the consulting room to where there was a mirror. 'Who is that strange little woman in a woolly hat?' she enquired of her own unnaturally sharp reflection.

She has worn them ever since; they have transformed her life; and to complete a miracle, her first pair were presented to her free.

With me unusually idle, apart from an ever-agreeable return to Windsor, this time for *She Stoops to Conquer*, the Christie play provided much-needed income. My *Black Mikado* engagement had not only been the best paid of my life at that time, but it had fitted only too neatly into one financial year. I had accordingly reached the dreaded tax threshold of 83%; and with a return to normal earnings in 1976, and abnormally low ones in 1977 (in which, in fact, my legitimate expenses exceeded my income), how was this mountain of tax to be paid? We decided with regret to sell the little London flat – a decision put into effect just before Dulcie embarked on eighteen months' continuous work in the West End.

So we severed our residential link with London, not from choice but as an ironic consequence of success. It was certainly not evidence that we were 'tired of life'.

X
1978

A fair Prospect – at and from the Vic – a battle of words – end of a dream – forty years on – butterflies on the wing – Dulcie at the National – a party with Ted – a message from Margaret

This was a year of professional separation but of varied and rewarding activity for us both.

First, Adrian Rendle, who had been in charge of our young playwrights' scheme in the days of Allied Theatre Productions and was now teaching drama in Malta, invited me to give my 'one-man show' in Valetta. 'I haven't got one,' I replied; but he was persistent, so that difficulty had to be overcome. There was the basis of something in my 'solos' from our Shakespeare programme, and in *How the devil did they get together?*, a show we had devised for Rhoda Birley's Charleston Festival, which had consisted of autobiographical anecdotes and readings. Some of the latter presented problems; for instance, I required a Nina for my piece from *Dragon's Mouth* and an Alice for my scene as the White Knight. Undeterred by the presence of his students, Adrian was both. I gave two performances in the ravishing Manoel Theatre – smaller but as beautiful as La Fenice in Venice – and spent three or four days of gentle sightseeing and junketings with my host, reminding myself of the island I had last seen on my way to Russia in 1945.

The Arts Council Working Party which I chaired in 1976 had been required as part of its brief to make recommendations about the future of the Old Vic. We had unanimously chosen the plan put forward by Toby Robertson's Prospect Company as being the most imaginative and the most practical. It was also far the most detailed, and was most persuasively presented to us by Toby himself.

Prospect was committed to touring, he told us, reminding us that for fifteen years or more it had been the premier large-scale

263

touring company in the land. 'We shall not tour less if we have a London base,' he told us, 'but we shall tour more efficiently and more attractively, because to be able to offer engagements which include a season at the Old Vic will inevitably enhance the quality of our company.' The argument was – and is – unanswerable. We duly recommended Prospect as tenants of the Old Vic, and the Arts Council accepted our report, although in terms which gave my colleagues who formally presented it – I was absent at a matinée – some cause for concern. (I shall return later to the fate of the policy when it was put into effect.)

Dulcie and I had long wanted to work for Prospect. We felt instinctively that we should be more at home with Toby and more likely to get worthwhile classical parts with him than elsewhere in the subsidised field. So I was thrilled when he asked me to join Derek Jacobi, Eileen Atkins, Robert Eddison, Louise Purnell, Ronnie Stevens and my old friend Brenda Bruce for a programme of three plays – *Twelfth Night*, *The Lady's Not for Burning* and *Ivanov* – which would last through the year – half of which, a month at a time, would be spent on the road. Sad that Miss Marple put Dulcie out of the reckoning, but perhaps I could succeed, where I had failed at Stratford in 1955, to be a pathfinder for a future joint operation.

Toby wanted me to play Lebedev – a dear old boy, marinated in vodka – in *Ivanov*; the blustering Mayor, trying to stand on non-existent dignity, in *Lady*; and Sir Toby in the Shakespeare. I thought the first and last far too alike for comfort, if played by the same actor. Toby saw the point, and so for the second time in the decade I had the challenge of Malvolio.

Of all Shakespeare's comedies, *Twelfth Night* has the most 'star' parts; and therefore most requires ensemble playing. And yet, however loyal the parts are to the whole, one performer usually turns out to be primus inter pares. I can think of productions which have turned out to be Malvolio's (Olivier), Olivia's (Geraldine MacEwan), Sir Toby's (Roger Livesey), Viola's (Peggy Ashcroft), Aguecheek's (Michael Redgrave) and Maria's (Dulcie) – and if the last is evidence of bias, so are all the others. The production on which I was now engaged had many felicities, but was dominated by Robert Eddison's Feste – an Adonis eroded into a drop-out by time and the bottle, so that 'when that I was and a little tiny boy' was the real stuff of heartbreak.

Malvolio is a very lonely part. Every character in the play

dislikes him or at best laughs at him. He has nothing to sustain him but the wild rapture of his self-obsession and his infatuation for Olivia –which are two sides of the same coin, and lead inexorably to his come-uppance, surely the most merciless in comedy. The great set-piece of the letter scene is a solo with a 'backing-group' consisting of Toby, Aguecheek and Fabian, but curiously not the instigator, Maria. In Regent's Park there was no shortage of greenery to conceal the conspirators; at the Vic, Toby Robertson had waywardly ordained that there should be no concealment, but that the three should pose as statues with sheets for togas. My colleagues were the soul of discretion, but their visible presence throughout fatally split the focus at those points where Shakespeare intended that Malvolio should seem to be alone.

Toby, a most original and stimulating director, is sometimes ensnared by his own originality. This was a case in point. When it happens, his actors are major sufferers; but that it didn't happen often in the bright record of Prospect is obvious from the devotion, not only of those I have already mentioned, but of those many others (Ian MacKellen, Timothy West and Prunella Scales spring to mind) to whom he gave crucial opportunities in the formative years of their careers. From Gielgud in the Thirties and Forties and Frank Hauser in the Fifties and Sixties, Toby picked up a particularly individual torch – something quite different from that wielded by Peter Hall and Trevor Nunn at the head of their august empires. If he has a successor today I have not identified him.

I enjoyed myself as much with Prospect as I had at Stratford in the Fifties. It was the sort of theatre Dulcie and I had dreamed of working in when we were drama students, and again when we were reunited after the war. As a joint ambition it remains unfulfilled.

The reader may imagine what it meant to me, at last to play in Shakespeare at the Vic – that extraordinary building which has been the womb from which have sprung most of the great individual talents which have been the glory of our stage over the last sixty years. It had taken me forty years even to get there, but it seemed like the promised land.

We played in London as 'Prospect at the Old Vic', and on tour as 'Prospect from the Old Vic'. They were exhausting but happy days. But sadly, before the year was out, my promised land had wavered into a mirage.

The problem was this. What the Arts Council gave to Prospect with one hand they took away with another. Being under great –and legitimate – pressure even then to cultivate 'the glory of the (provincial) garden', they had refused to make any funds available for Prospect's operations at the Vic, although they accepted that the value of the company's work on tour had been 'greatly enhanced by the higher standards of casting and performance' attributable to a London base. What made the dilemma worse for everybody was that Prospect at the Vic was not nearly so successful as Prospect *from* the Vic. So deficits were mounting up.

Still a member of the Drama Panel, and with my working party report not yet totally forgotten, I was passionately committed to all that Toby and Prospect stood for. I had friends and contacts in all camps – including the Old Vic governors, who had obligations to the building but little or no financial power and hovered uncertainly between the main protagonists. I wrote letters in all directions – a rather good one, though I say it, to Kenneth Robinson who had succeeded Pat Gibson as the new Chairman of the Arts Council.

In his reply he reminded me that I had made my case for an ideal world – of course I had – and that there was not enough money to support all good schemes. If Prospect could not afford to play the Vic without subsidy, he went on, why should not its base be established outside London? 'Because,' I replied, '"Prospect from the New Theatre Hull" would not mean as much to playgoers up and down the country as our current title.'

Until the end of October all this activity and lobbying had been in private. An 'in-depth evaluation' of the whole situation had been promised by the Arts Council but all Prospect got was a discussion by the Drama Panel, which illogically had no juris-diction over the company, followed by a unilateral press con-ference announcing the Council's refusal to support Prospect at the Vic.

This caused six of us to write to *The Times* – or, to be accurate, caused me to write a letter and collect five signatures. We said:

Sir

During 1978 Prospect has presented nine major productions (Shakespeare, Shaw, Dryden, Fry, Chekhov and Sheridan) for a total of 22 weeks on the road, a unique achievement in the field of classical theatre.

Furthermore in the touring undertaken since the company has been able to describe itself as 'Prospect from the Old Vic' attendances have practically doubled. This is no coincidence, but a grateful recognition, out of town, that alone of major touring companies we conduct our try-outs in the metropolis under the eyes of the national press – which is seen as a happy reversal of the old tradition of first trying a production on the provincial dog. This improvement in the company's fortunes springs directly from the Vic connection ... The national and the RSC are subsidised at base, and get extra if they tour. Has not Prospect, which glories in being a touring company, an unanswerable case for some support at base?

The Arts Council is Prospect's best friend – and we have no wish to give more than an admonitory nip to the hand that feeds us on our travels – but is it not ironical that, given the Council's pressing financial problems and the great and justified pressure on it to give the regions a fair share of the cake, the company currently best suited to bake an acceptable cake at a fraction of the cost of the other major companies may find itself without a kitchen?

The Arts Council recently re-affirmed that there was no money available for another major metropolitan company. We sympathise with that decision but cannot see that the cap fits Prospect, who are dynamic in their hopeful travelling, not static in any complacency of arrival in the Waterloo Road. We are continually poised for flight, as witness our philosophy and the simplicity of our staging.

We submit that the evidence shows (a) that the regions want Prospect more than ever, and (b) that Prospect needs the Vic (to say nothing of the Vic's need for Prospect); and we ask the Arts Council to think again.

Only so will Prospect be able to give full value as a touring company for the considerable investment made in it by the Council over the years.

We are, Sir, yours sincerely and alphabetically, Eileen Atkins, Brenda Bruce, Michael Denison, Robert Eddison, Derek Jacobi, Ronnie Stevens

It was in vain. We were battering against a door that was bolted and barred. But I'm glad we battered.

As my final throw I even tried to effect a 'marriage' between Prospect and Duncan Weldon's Triumph Productions who were now established at the Haymarket and in a string of provincial theatres. I could do no more than bring the parties together; but the complexities of such a plan defeated an early solution, and soon it was too late.

Prospect, now ironically re-christened 'The Old Vic Company', lingered on for another year; but with its financial needs still unprovided for there could only be one end. The dismissal of Toby, as a ritual sacrifice, when he was actually with the company in Peking, was appropriately followed by total débâcle. A sad end to a vision and an achievement, as much needed today as ever.

(We are all in the debt of Ed Mirvisch of Toronto for rescuing the fabric of the Vic from dereliction and bringing the theatre back to life. Is it too much to hope that with his enthusiasm and resources, at least part of the year might be devoted to a Prospect-like operation, in keeping with the Lilian Baylis tradition, but with a firm emphasis on touring here and overseas?)

Meanwhile, back in the West End, Miss Marple held sway until the autumn. *Butterflies on My Mind* came out, was much praised, and its author was guest of honour at 'the first literary luncheon in South Bucks' (so she was assured by Lawrence Evans our dynamic local bookseller). Later in the year the book was awarded the 'Times Educational Supplement Senior Information Award for 1978' – one of the most cherished successes of Dulcie's literary career, recently enhanced by her election as a Fellow of the Linnean Society.

In August we celebrated my forty years on the stage, with a party much enjoyed by the host. Jack and Jacquetta Priestley were absentees, as were Glen and Larry; but John Gielgud was there, with fifty others who had contributed to my life – stretching from Michael Macowan who had directed my first London appearance, to Toby Robertson and my then colleagues at the Vic. Peter Bridge, Peter Donald, John Gale, John McCallum and Duncan were there as managerial friends; Harold Hobson and John Trewin as respected critics. To Dulcie's dismay I was determined to thank all fifty; to her relief I managed to squeeze them into fifteen minutes.

Late in the year came a great excitement for Dulcie – and, vicariously, for me. Alan Ayckbourn's *Bedroom Farce* – an enormous success at the National and due to open on Broadway in the New Year – was to transfer to the West End for a commercial run with a new cast to be directed by Peter Hall and the author. Would Dulcie take over the part of Delia, which Joan Hickson would continue to play in New York? She would indeed.

All this meant that she missed one very special party in the winter – an invitation from Ted Heath to dine at his London house. So I went alone. My fellow guests were Celia Johnson, Peter Ustinov and Dave Allen and our host was at his most relaxed. The two 'comics' made no attempt to hog the evening and the result was a wide-ranging and often hilarious conversation in which politics were never mentioned.

In the summer I had had my first contact with Mrs Thatcher at a Tory seminar on the Arts, and after a brief meeting had sent her the two articles which I had contributed to the AUEW magazine. They came back with a handwritten letter and some interesting sidelinings in the same coloured ink. For instance, these paragraphs:

> Government in a democracy has no right to buy the arts with subsidy. If theatre in this country ever became Socialist *or* Tory or indeed anything but liberal, with a small 'l', it would not matter how generous the Treasury grant . . . a giant step would have been taken away from art and towards propaganda.
>
> . . . I believe the danger of such a disaster is slight; but the arts of the spoken word . . . are a rich prize for those who see everything in terms of political advantage, and if they are not to win that prize, vigilance is required by artists and by the public – and that I hope includes the readers of these words.

In the accompanying letter she expressed surprise that the AUEW *Journal* should have accepted an article 'from someone advocating that politics be kept out of many activities. That happens to be my view too,' she went on, 'but then I am Conservative because I believe that politics should be limited in their effect, whereas my opponents want to politicise every decision.'

Her years in office – particularly 1984 – must surely have strengthened that conviction.

XI
1979

New girl and new boy – Rebecca and Frankie – Dulcie in the pulpit – The Fourposter *remembered – friends far above rubies*

Every human being who has been exposed to organised education has known, and probably remembers, the traumas associated with being a new boy or girl. For a few the shock is pleasurable, for the majority a nightmare, but for none is it a matter of indifference. It is not of course confined to schooldays; the start of a new job produces similar reactions. But whereas 'sensible' people may change their work say four or five times in their lives – and many professional people not at all – we in the theatre are often new boys and girls four or five times a year. It is as much an occupational hazard as lack of security, but for Dulcie and me, even after forty-five years, it still produces the old familiar symptoms – 'like love but without the pleasure', I once described it – not only on first nights but at first readings as well.

Add to this, for the first reading of *Bedroom Farce*, the presence of the Director of the National Theatre and his acolytes, and of the country's most successful writer of comedy, and of a young company who seemed relaxed and assured, and Dulcie's state of jitters may be imagined. And that was not all. Lurking behind the familiar strangeness of the start of a new job, was an ingredient new to Dulcie in her unsubsidised career – the institution of the National Theatre itself. She had nothing but kindness, co-operation and encouragement from the individuals involved, Peter Hall in particular going out of his way to ease her into this unfamiliar environment, but she was, I think, lucky – as I was to feel later – that her introduction to the National was in the West End and not on the South Bank. (I am one of those who feel that for all the technological skills that went into the planning of the building, the many triumphs of the Company since it moved from the Vic have been achieved in spite of the expense and uncompromising nature of its new home.)

270

I don't know what Peter Hall's expectations were for the West End run of *Bedroom Farce*, but there is no doubt that when it closed at the end of September it had far exceeded them. Dulcie thoroughly enjoyed the part of Delia, and in Michael Aldridge's Ernest she had a most sympathetic foil.

Meanwhile, after one appearance as a 'Silk' on Granada TV's 'Crown Court' I had now been elevated to the bench, from which I 'won' two cases in rapid succession, one of them certainly in opposition to the scriptwriter's intention. Then it was back to Windsor for a favourite part in Willie Douglas Home's *A Friend Indeed* – one of his most skilfully crafted comedies, which, inexplicably to me, has twice died the death in the West End. At Windsor I had the joy of working once again with Mary Kerridge (Mrs John Counsell), and with an even older friend, the late Geoffrey Lumsden – with whom I had been sharing a dressing-room forty years before on the night when Jack Priestley had released me from my contract with him so that Dulcie and I could get married.

No sooner had I signed for Windsor than to our great excitement Peter Hall asked if I would join Dulcie in *Bedroom Farce*. I accepted with alacrity, even though it meant rehearsing during the Windsor run, and opening at the Prince of Wales forty-eight hours after *Friend Indeed* closed. By a happy coincidence it was forty years to the day since Dulcie's first professional performance in Aberdeen, which also marked the start of our joint career.

My initiation into the National was even more traumatic than Dulcie's, for I was taking over from Michael Aldridge and was therefore the only new boy that day.

The change-over had been too quick for the publicity department; Michael A's photographs continued to be displayed outside the theatre for quite a while, although a great effort had been made to get pictures of me taken. His name also still appeared on the bills, but since, in accordance with National Theatre ideology, all the cast names were in white on pink and very small, my absence was academic; in any case it was eventually, and invisibly, put right.

Peter Hall had been much preoccupied at this time with industrial relations on the South Bank so I had been rehearsed into the production by Giles Block – a most sensitive and efficient deputy. When Peter came he was enthusiastic about my performance and asked if we were prepared to go on into the autumn. Of course we were. If so, he would set about re-casting the other parts.

This, frankly, astonished us. Our young colleagues were all, to the best of my recollection, making their first West End appearances – and in wonderful parts – yet they clearly felt, after five or six months, that if they didn't get out when they could they were in danger of life passing them by. How attitudes had changed since we were in their position.

We suggested – tactfully I hope – that, as this was a West End operation, it might be helpful to the show to feature our names on the bills in a conventional commercial manner. (It was in fact our twentieth joint starring appearance in London.) Peter, I think, saw the strength of the argument and promised to make the change when the show was re-cast. The change was duly made, but as our names on the new posters were in white on pale yellow they were if anything harder to identify than before. (I was glad to see that when *Amadeus* came from the National to Her Majesty's – we were across the road at the Haymarket – the front-of-house display featured the names of the leading players as strongly as that of the Company.)

One of our fondest memories from the West End run was a private dinner after the show with Rebecca West and Frankie Howerd – mutual admirers who were meeting for the first time at our instigation. By the time we reached the restaurant, they looked and sounded like old friends. Frankie can be very serious; Rebecca could be very funny. That night they both were both. 'Thank you for a most joyous evening,' Rebecca wrote. 'I always love you two, and I certainly hope Frankie will let me love him.'

In December, *Bedroom Farce* was recorded for BBC television. The National very properly tried to get their original cast. Michael Gough, the first Ernest, was not available. Nor was Michael Aldridge, my predecessor; so I had the good fortune to get in by default. Dear Joan Hickson was most apologetic that her own availability had denied Dulcie the chance to join me.

Back in the spring, when I was rehearsing at Windsor, Dulcie was asked to give the address at the memorial service at St James's Piccadilly for the distinguished author and former film producer, R. J. Minney – who had been a friend of hers since the days of her contract with Gainsborough Pictures. Virginia McKenna (star of R. J.'s film, *Carve her name with Pride*) was to recite some poetry, and Harold Wilson was to read the lesson. Alarmed by this distribution of duties, Dulcie determined to be there in good time; and was in fact so early that she decided on some window-shopping in Piccadilly. Accosted by a tramp, she found she had no silver in her bag – only a £20 note. 'Don't go away,' she said to him, 'I'll get some change in Fortnums.' But what with the distracting atmosphere of the shop and her preoccupations with the impending service, she forgot all about him, left Fortnums by the back door and walked along Jermyn Street to the church. In due course she solemnly and nervously climbed the long curving staircase into the pulpit, and as she waited for the congregation to settle her eye was caught, through a plain glass window, by a figure frenziedly jigging about and doing the rude version of the V sign. It was 'her' tramp, whose darkest suspicions of the pious she had unwittingly confirmed.

That summer we were asked to take over from Jessica Tandy and Hume Cronyn in *The Gin Game*. The reader may remember that it was this talented pair who had acquired *The Fourposter* in 1950, when the negotiations to present us in it on Broadway finally broke down. It would have been pleasant if after all these years we could have picked up a success from them. There was, however, in our view, one insuperable obstacle. *The Fourposter* was of no fixed nationality; *The Gin Game* was all-American. It was also so superbly played by the Cronyns, and so effortlessly American, that we knew that, however well drilled our accents, our innate Englishness would have been a stumbling-block.

We had a happy meeting with them after the performance, and exchanged memories of *The Fourposter*. They didn't know we had been asked to take over from them. 'I've got an idea', said Hume. 'Why don't you two take over from *us* this time?' We explained that we had just seen perfection and had no wish to tamper with it.

On the social front, the high spot of the year for us was our Ruby Wedding on 29 April. 'I count myself in nothing else so happy as in a soul remembering my good friends' – and good friends were there that day in numbers and variety. Of our fifty guests, many of whom the reader has met in these pages, thirty had come into our lives through the Stage Door or from the world of books; the rest were unconnected with the theatre, though not unsympathetic to it – the kind of friends who have broadened our horizons and thereby enriched our work and leisure. The gathering thus represented many of the strands of our lives, and it was fascinating to see the interaction of personalities from different worlds meeting for the first time.

For instance, I remember watching with gratitude as Peter Carrington, with his unflappable sense of fun, coaxed Jack Priestley into a good mood. Indeed, there was only one discernible cloud. We had known for some time that there was a rift between Jack and Rebecca. We knew no details, but Dulcie, a tactful hostess, thought that perhaps we should not invite them both. 'No,' I said, 'we love them both; and, who knows, they might make it up under our roof.' Sadly it was not to be.

So our fourth decade was celebrated, as the beginning of it all had been, with us both in rehearsal with excellent parts for a play by the foremost comedy writer of the day – then it had been Noël in Aberdeen, now it was Alan Ayckbourn in the West End.

In our twenties that prospect would probably have seemed quite appropriate; in our sixties we can recognise it as the most tremendous luck.

A Song at Twilight, 1983

right *See How They Run,* 1984

below *Cold Warrior,* 1984

Lady Sneerwell (Saturday) and
Mrs Candour (Monday), *left*,
Duke of York's 1984

Investiture, 1983

STOP PRESS

The five succeeding years have not been empty.

On the professional front, a meeting with Gerard 'Secret Army' Glaister (arranged for me in a moment of inspiration by our agent Ronnie Waters) led to my return to BBC television after twenty-one years, as the (I hope) mysterious Captain Percival in *Blood Money*, *Skorpion* and *Cold Warrior*; and – my favourite-ever small part to date – Wobbly Massingham in Molly Keane's *Good Behaviour*. Dulcie also returned to the BBC fold with a two-minute scene as a *vendeuse* (selling widow's weeds to Dorothy Tutin in *Life After Death*), which had an unbelievable critical response. We both appeared as genteel brothel-keepers defended by Leo McKern in *Rumpole* – an idea which for some reason came to John Mortimer when he was lunching in our Buckinghamshire home; and Dulcie joined me in an episode of *Cold Warrior*, playing a former colleague of mine in MI something.

We had a long and happy relationship with Willie Douglas Home's *Kingfisher* – first with Bobby Eddison at Windsor, then with Bobby Flemyng on tour. The final unlikely chapter saw Dulcie, as an expert witness, helping Willie win his case against a charge of plagiarism – a victory swallowed up in more than £30,000 of legal costs unrecovered from his opponent who was legally aided. (Partial recompense was eventually obtained from the Legal Aid Fund, but only after further proceedings.)

In 1981 we were able to accept Derek Nimmo's invitation to take part in one of his Dinner Theatre Tours. We were lucky in the choice of play – Alan Ayckbourn's already classic comedy, *Relatively Speaking* – and lucky too in our young colleagues, Simon Williams and Lucy Fleming. (Lucy had just suffered an appalling personal tragedy; and though our trip could not be a cure for grief it seemed as though our colourful adventures in the

275

Far East and the Gulf helped to prepare her, by their un-familiarity, for her eventual return to the familiar.)

Derek's contribution to the Dinner Theatre empire, whose boundaries seem to be growing wider still and wider, is not the least remarkable achievement of a career of enviable versatility and success. Conjured quite literally out of the air – by courtesy of British Airways – Dinner Theatre is dedicated to the serious business of making people laugh. This is combined for its fortunate actors with luxurious living, mainly in Hilton and Intercontinental Hotels, and an off-duty social programme of a splendour that for me will be forever Nimmo – luncheons with rulers, governors and ambassadors; cruises on yachts, power-boats, junks, dhows and landing-craft belonging variously to navies, merchant banks and mere millionaires. If Barbara Cart-land were a member of Equity it is a milieu in which she would feel triumphantly at home. For simpler folk like the cast of *Relatively Speaking*, it provided continuous surprises and de-lights. As Lucy said, 'There are so many firsts.'

One such was the never-to-be-forgotten day when we visited an aged Malaysian Sultan, who, after graciously taking us on a guided tour of his palaces, polo clubs and motor cars, old and new, gave us a splendid meal. As we sat at table, our host (at Derek's instigation) requested me to read aloud a letter which His Highness had received from Beverly Nichols some years before, which stated categorically, but without evidence, that *Oh Calcutta!* had been financed by the USSR in order to rot the moral fibre of the West. I read it with a conviction that I scarcely felt – not helped by the giggles of my colleagues down the table – but I reflected afterwards that, even if the show did not fulfil Mr Brezhnev's highest hopes as propaganda, he must have been well satisfied – in his unlikely debut as a theatrical 'angel' – with the box-office returns and the lack of wardrobe expenses.

I think we had all expected the Gulf to be an anti-climax after our Far Eastern adventures. Not at all. We roamed the soukhs of Sharja, Dubai and Muscat. We went up to 7000 feet in a helicopter with the crack paratroopers of Dubai and watched them jump – the last out of the aircraft closing the great door from the *outside*, when he noticed Dulcie leaning apprehensively away from it! We relished the five-star simple life of Jebel Ali and Abu Dhabi; and last – and perhaps best of all – the romantic forts and harbours and mountains of Oman. I particularly remember a long day's drive through the June heat up to an ancient village built with natural camouflage into an arid mountainside, with below it in a narrow valley its own oasis of palm trees and bright water. A magical place. The road to it savaged the tyres of the car, and there was a time around sunset on the homeward journey when the entire cast looked like being benighted in the desert instead of giving their last performance of the tour. The vital spanner required for a wheel change was missing from the tool kit, but a local inhabitant miraculously produced one; and while the job was being done the four of us were able to watch the gloaming flower and fade over those tawny silent hills. A fitting farewell to Arabia.

1981 also saw Equity's 50th anniversary dinner at the Cafe Royal – an awful fiasco. Speeches too long, no adequate tribute to Gerald Croasdell, although he was present, and, as an intended climax, the award of Life Membership to Athene Seyler – at which the adorable ninety-two-year-old recipient very properly giggled.

1982 found us twice on stage together at the Haymarket, though we only addressed a few words to each other in *Coat of Varnish* and none at all in *School for Scandal*. I also played the judge with Penelope Keith in *Captain Brassbound's Conversion* as part of this Haymarket season, and savoured again the delights of being directed by Frank Hauser. Dulcie meanwhile was at Chichester, playing Joan Plowright's mother in Keith Baxter's *Cavell*.

On 9 May 1982 the Queen Mother came to lunch; Sir Martin Gilliat, her genial private secretary, supervising everything for us by remote control. Her fellow guests were Luke Annaly, son of Lavinia, one of Her Majesty's greatest friends, Rebecca, Frankie, Dick and Mary Francis and Tony and Georgina Andrews.

No words of mine can adequately express the joy given us by her visit; and by her manner of returning our hospitality.

On 15 July we were both involved in a public royal occasion when the Queen and Prince Philip came to a Gala Performance to mark fifty years of the Open Air Theatre. Only a few days before, there had been the extraordinary incident of the intruder in Her Majesty's apartments at Buckingham Palace. The play that had long been proposed and accepted for the occasion was Shaw's *Dark Lady of the Sonnets* – which concerns an intruder (who turns out to be Shakespeare) in the apartments of Queen Elizabeth I. We offered of course to change the programme, but a message came back that Her Majesty was quite happy with the existing arrangements. As the only director of the New Shake-speare Company who had performed at the Park, I had the privilege of sitting next to her, and can report that she did indeed seem happy with the performance, if a little thoughtful when the Queen in the play enquired of the Beefeater, 'Who keeps ward on the Queen's lodging tonight?' and, when told 'I do', replied, 'See that you keep it better in future.'

In the early autumn, with the publication of her first straight novel, *The Glanville Women*, Dulcie embarked on a new phase of her career as a writer. (It was the story of three generations of a family, and linked the theatre and Malaya between 1910 and the present day.) Rebecca West, in one of her last reviews, called the book 'fascinating . . . a solid Thackerayan read. I am enchanted by its great originality. This is a really rich book.' An accolade indeed.

Rebecca was very frail now, but she came to the publisher's lunch for the book. A few weeks later I went at her invitation to collect a brooch belonging to her mother, as a present for Dulcie. It was the last time either of us saw her; but I was glad to be invited to read at her memorial service in the spring of 1983 in support of Bernard Levin's admirable address. I introduced my contribution as follows:

> To choose a parting gift – an envoi – for Rebecca on behalf of her family and friends is a great responsibility. It would be easier if only she could send it back – accompanied by that marvellous hoot of derision – if it were not to her taste. But if her sword never slept in her hand, nor did her capacity for loving and accepting love. Please accept this, Rebecca.

A few months previously I had had the same duty to perform for her great friend and ours, Norman Collins; a few months later, for his great friend and ours, Leonard Simpson. A sad time.

The summer of 1983 was an extraordinary roller-coaster time for us. During rehearsals for what turned out to be a nightmare engagement in *Tartuffe* (planned for London and suddenly abandoned in Bromley), it was announced that we had each been made CBE. The warmth of our friends' reaction added enor-mously to our own delight.

Meanwhile the collapse of *Tartuffe* – in itself bad enough – brought us into a technical dispute with Duncan which none of us wanted, but which took some time to clear up. Advised by one

Equity official (correctly) that it was our duty to get work, to mitigate our 'claim' against Duncan, we duly signed a contract to do Noël Coward's marvellous *Song at Twilight* at Worthing and Windsor. This we were told by another Equity official (incorrectly) was in breach of a current Instruction not to accept work in the provincial field, and therefore placed us under threat of suspension or expulsion from the union.

It was against this background that we reached the great day of the Investiture – 26 July. We had been offered a bed the night before, and lunch afterwards, by John and Elizabeth Higgs. John is now the Prince of Wales's Secretary for the Duchy of Cornwall and has a flat facing the Palace in the Duchy building at the corner of Buckingham Gate – a marvellous starting point, which even enabled Dulcie to make an eleventh-hour change of wardrobe on a very hot day.

As we waited in the CBE 'pen' in the Picture Gallery, Johnnie Johnston (whose job on these occasions is to hand the appropriate decorations to the Queen) appeared and beckoned to us. 'As you're going to be "done" together', he said, 'perhaps a little special rehearsal might be helpful. Let's go somewhere quiet.' And he led the way into the deserted Throne Room, where he had arranged chairs to represent the lay-out in the Ballroom where the ceremony takes place. He explained apologetically that I had to precede Dulcie when our names were called, and showed us where and when to bow; and under his friendly eye we rehearsed until he declared himself satisfied. 'Keep in step if you can. Good luck,' were his final words.

Now, in normal life, Dulcie takes two steps to my one, so we had a problem. We were the sole representatives of the theatre that day, among heroes of the Falklands and other men and women of courage and distinction. The large audience (our personal guests were Peter and Cleone Donald, and Robert and Kay Lennard) would expect a polished performance. But if I shortened my stride to Dulcie's I would, in Robert Atkins' immortal words, 'arouse the gravest suspicions', and if I walked normally I would condemn her to the gait of Groucho Marx.

I hope we achieved a decent British compromise. Dulcie in the excitement put in an extra curtsey, and got an extra smile from Her Majesty.

Johnny waylaid us on our way out of the Palace. 'You passed,' he said to me, 'but I'm afraid it's back to the drawing board for Dulcie.'

Meanwhile it was back to John and Elizabeth's flat to drink quantities of champagne in the company of our first employer, Peter Donald, and Robert Lennard, the architect of my post-war career. How appropriate – and what fun.

EPILOGUE

One of the cardinal rules in human relationships is never to take another person for granted. True. And yet, paradoxically, one essential of a long and close relationship is to be able to do just that, and to have it done to you in return – in other words, to trust and be trusted; to take comfort – 'infinite heart's ease' – from the process of growing together. That is true too. I know from my own experience.

At the end of *Overture and Beginners*, I quoted from a poem of Maurice Baring's – written I believe to Laura Lovat. It spoke, and still speaks, more simply and eloquently of my feelings for Dulcie than I ever could, and I make no apology for repeating it here:

> I have known beauty and I once was young,
> But you are more than all the poets sung;
> Varied in beauty, versatile as flame,
> And never, save in constancy, the same.

The first two lines are melodious and deeply felt, but of general application. In lines three and four, however, Baring sharpens the focus and begins to paint an individual portrait. Let us examine my claim that they could be applied to Dulcie.

Varied in beauty? In real life, certainly – a model for Modigliani when I met her, and for Rubens now! (For the record, the author has far less cause for illusion than she as to the effect of Time's wingéd chariot. Now so thin on top that he salutes the diminishing survivors individually each morning, he is alas less thin than of yore around the middle; the bags under his eyes are becoming portmanteaux; the jowl thickens, the chins multiply. After a recent television screening of *The Importance*, there were cries from fans of 'You haven't changed at all.' Very touching but, fortunately for *The Importance*, very untrue.)

But back to Dulcie. 'Varied in beauty' is particularly true of her in the intensely 'real' life of the theatre. I think of the infinite

281

variety of her characterisations: of her Dream Child in *Dear Brutus*, and of Rose, the pathetic trusting cockney waif, in *Brighton Rock*, the serene shimmering Nina of *Dragon's Mouth* and the elegant little tigress of her Duchess in *Let Them Eat Cake*. Three of her Shavian characters are for ever fresh in my memory – Candida, illustrating so effortlessly woman's superiority over man, Lady Utterword, the languid upper-crust predator, and by contrast, 'Z' in *Village Wooing*, the country girl unhandicapped by experience, who can trust the life force and a sense of humour to achieve what Priestley once called woman's 'adamantine purpose'. There was the joyous awakening to the sun of Italy of her prim Edwardian spinster in *A Man About the House*, an effect transposed to a subtler key in *Where Angels Fear to Tread*; and latterly she has played Evelyn in *The Kingfisher* and Carlotta in *A Song At Twilight*, performances which though not (as yet) seen in the West End have filled her partner with pride and gratitude.

Since the middle Fifties there have also been notable character studies: her White Queen as surely drawn in lovable dottiness and her Miss Marple in sharp-eyed eccentricity as Margaret Rutherford's; her Mrs Conway, a loving but child-devouring matriarch, much approved of by Jack Priestley her creator; Mrs Banger, the female Major-General in Shaw's *Press Cuttings*, propounding the theory that Napoleon's notorious lack of enthusiasm for Josephine was because he was really a woman; Mrs Candour despatching her poisoned arrows with the relish of an unshakeable do-gooder.

'Varied in beauty' indeed. 'Versatile as flame'? Let the evidence speak. Having weathered a virtually homeless and parentless childhood, and in adolescence the simultaneous demands of teaching and journalism in the Malay jungle, Dulcie successively won scholarships to a surrealist art school and to the drama school where we met. She then laid the foundations of her career – and mine – quite alone, while I was away for six years in the army. Her first book was published in 1957, a year after the débâcle of her play, *Love Affair*. In the twenty-seven succeeding years she has produced a further twenty-two books; has been on tour forty-six times; and has starred in eighteen of those productions in the West End – making forty in all.

The case for 'versatility' is clearly proved. The case for 'flame' depends on my subjective judgement. For those who know her, if not as well as I, the metaphor might seem to accord ill with her sincere concern for others and her gentle friendliness, which people occasionally and unwisely interpret as weakness. I will only say that, present her with an intellectual problem – a part to absorb, a book to write, a cause to promote, even a crossword to solve – and her reaction is bright, intense, swift and surprising, each an attribute of flame.

All this has made forty-six years of her company a stimulating, if periodically exhausting, experience. To put up with me for that period is surely the apotheosis of 'constancy'. I can only say I would ask her again. I hope that she would make the same response.

CHRONOLOGICAL CHART

Note: B, Book; F, Film; L, London; M, Musical; O, Overseas; P, Play; R, Radio; T Tour; TV

Michael	Joint	Dulcie
Born Doncaster, Yorks. (Mother dies three weeks later. Father, wartime soldier.) Goes to live with mother's sister and her husband		Born Kuala Lumpur, Malaya. Daughter of Lawyer. (Birth not registered!)
Boarding school, Broadstairs (age 8½)		Boarding school, Wallingford (age 3¾). (Parents still in Malaya except for rare leaves)
Harrow (with scholarship). 'Fags' for Terence Rattigan. Plays female parts in school plays		Returns to Malaya. Becomes schoolmistress and journalist in jungle at 16
Magdalen College, Oxford. B.A. Modern Languages. Member of University Dramatic Society (OUDS). Death of aunt who brought him up. Decides to become actor		(Father killed in accident in Singapore.) Returns to England. Wins scholarship to surrealist art school; then Webber Douglas Drama School

284

	Michael	Joint	Dulcie
1937	Enrols at Webber Douglas	First meeting	First public performance: Maria in *School for Scandal* (Lord Bessborough's private theatre, Stansted Park)
1938	First professional engagement: Lord Fancourt Babberley in *Charley's Aunt* at Frinton P First London engagement: *Troilus and Cressida* LP *Dangerous Corner* LP & OT *Marco Millions* LP (all at Westminster Theatre)	First performance together as Parnell and Kitty O'Shea in *Parnell* (at drama school) 11 Nov. Secretly engaged	

1939	*The Doctor's Dilemma* LP
	Candida LP & OT
	Marco Millions TV
	
	3 Sept.: Volunteers
	Told to go home
	
	October: *Music at Night* LP
	Major Barbara LP
		11 March: Officially engaged
		29 April: Wedding
		1 May: Begin work in Aberdeen
		Plays include:
		    Hay Fever
		    On Approval
		    Arms and the Man
		    Outward Bound
		    Dear Brutus
		    The Young Idea
		Night Must Fall (for the troops)
		    TP	

285

	Michael	Joint	Dulcie
1940	*Tilly of Bloomsbury* (first film)	F H.M. Tennent Company (Edinburgh & Glasgow) *Plays* include: *Music at Night The Silver Chord Biography Musical Chairs Spring Meeting Last of Mrs Cheyney*	White Rose Players (Harrogate). *Plays* include: *The Importance of Being Earnest The Shining Hour Ma's Bit of Brass The Middle Watch* (Trevor Howard in company)
	June: Joins R. Signals Whitby Huddersfield Ossett		
1941	Halifax (attached Duke of Wellingtons) Bodmin (attached D.C.L.I.) Bulford (OCTU) Commissioned into Intelligence Corps (Oxford) Posted to Northern Ireland		*Front Line Family* R (395 broadcasts)
1942	In Northern Ireland Promoted Captain	Film test for Dulcie F (Michael plays scene with her while on leave)	Composes and broadcasts 'Singapore', for beleaguered garrison. (Her mother killed at sea during escape)

	Michael	Joint	Dulcie
			First London performances (Open Air Theatre, Regent's Park):
			Twelfth Night (Maria) LP
			'*The Shrew*' (Bianca) LP
			'*The Dream*' (Hermia) LP
			The Little Foxes LP
1943	Posted to Middle East (as an interrogator) Stationed near Cairo		*Brighton Rock* T & LP (given co-star billing with Hermione Baddeley and Dickie Attenborough after first night). Contract with Gainsborough Pictures.
			Landslide T & LP
			2000 Women F
			Madonna of the Seven Moons F
1944	With liberating forces to Greece. Besieged by Communist guerillas in Athens		*A Place of One's Own* F
			They Were Sisters F
			Lady From Edinburgh
			(i) OT to liberated Europe
			(ii) Tour in UK
			(iii) LP

	Michael	Joint	Dulcie	
1945	Siege of Athens lifted. To Russia (via Naples, Malta) to collect Allied POW's at Odessa and accompany them to UK		Outstanding notices for *They Were Sisters*. Sacked by Gainsborough – engaged same day by 20th Century Fox.	
	Transfer after VE Day to Stars in Battledress. Stationed in London	Reunion (late March).	*Wanted for Murder*	F
			The Years Between	F
1946	Long term contract with Associated British Pictures. Loaned to Rank for		*Dear Ruth*	LP
			The Wind is Ninety	LP
			Signed up by Korda.	
	Hungry Hill F		*Fools Rush In*	TP
	Demobilised (April).		*A Man About the House*	F
	The Petrified Forest (Windsor) P		*Mine Own Executioner*	F
	Ever Since Paradise TP			
1947	*Blind Goddess* F (Death of uncle who brought him up)	*My Brother Jonathan* F		
1948	Refuses Hollywood offer to star in *The Fan* (Lady Windermere's)	*The Glass Mountain* F *Rain on the Just* T & LP (first joint West End appearance).		

288

	Michael		Joint		Dulcie	
1949	*Landfall*	F	*The Will*	TV	*Crime Passionelle*	TV
	First elected to Equity Council		*Queen Elizabeth Slept Here* (until April '50)	T & LP		
1950			*The Franchise Affair*	F		
			The Fourposter	T & LP		
1951	*The Tall Headlines*	F	(British delegates to Film Festival in Uruguay.)		(Delegate to Venice Film Festival.)	
	The Importance of Being Earnest	F	*Angels One Five*	F	*See You Later* (Revue)	L
			Milestones	TV	(*Writes Take Copernicus*	P)
1952	Vice-President of Equity		*Dragon's Mouth*	T & LP		
			There Was a Young Lady	F		
			Sweet Peril	T & LP		
1953	*Second Man*	TV			(Breakdown)	
	Bad Samaritan	T & LP			*Art and Opportunity*	TV
	Alice Through the Looking Glass	T & LMP			*A Fish in the Family*	TV
	What's My Line?	TV			*The Distant Hill*	TP

289

	Michael		Joint		Dulcie	
1954	*Contraband Spain*	F	*We Must Kill Toni*	T & LP	*Diary of a Nobody*	LP
	Waiting for Gillian	TV	*Olympia*	TV		
			Fourposter and	OTP		
			Private Lives			
			(South Africa)			
1955	Stratford Season (with Oliviers):				*Writes Love Affair*	P
	All's Well (Bertram)				*September Revue*	TV
	Twelfth Night (Aguecheek)					
	Merry Wives (Dr Caius)		*Alice Through the Looking*			
	Titus Andronicus (Lucius)		*Glass*	LMP		
	(Motor Accident)					
	Directs *Love Affair*	P				
1956	*Rain on the Just*	TV	*The Sun Divorce*	TV	*Lesson in Love*	TV
	Who Goes Home?	TV	*Love Affair*	T & LP	*South Sea Bubble*	OP
	Village Wooing	T & OTP			(South Africa)	
	Fanny's First Play	T & OTP			*Tea and Sympathy*	OP
	(Edinburgh and Berlin Festivals)				(Australia)	
	Festival Fever	TV			*Writes Murder on the Stairs*	B
	Boyd QC	TV				
	(1st of eighty episodes					
	24 December)					

	Michael		Joint		Dulcie	
1957	*Boyd* QC (Series I) continues	TV	Dulcie does a *Boyd* episode	TV	*South Sea Bubble* (return to South Africa)	OP
	The Truth About Women	F			*The Governess*	TV
	Meet Me By Moonlight				*Murder on the Stairs* published	B
		T & LMP				
1958	*Boyd* QC (Series II)	TV	*Double Cross*	TP	*Double Cross*	LP
	Inside Chance	TV	*The Importance*	TV	*Take Copernicus* re-christened	TMP
	Frankie Howerd Sketch	TV			*Love à la Carte*	
	Late Extra	TV	*Candida* (Oxford)	P	(music by Charles Ross)	
					Writes *Murder in Melbourne*	B
					Epitaph for George Dillon	TP
1959	*Boyd* QC (Series III)	TV	*Let Them Eat Cake*	T & LP	*Baby Face*	B
	Faces in the Dark	F	(Made Duke and Duchess of Redonda)		*The Best Cellar*	TP
	(Paintings exhibited)					
	(Death of father)					
	Dear Octopus	TV				
1960	*Boyd* QC (Series IV)	TV	*Candida* (breaks London record)	T & LP	*Winter Cruise*	TV
					Murder on the Stairs	R
					Epitaph for a Dead Actor	B
					The Letter	TV

291

	Michael	Joint	Dulcie
1961	*Boyd QC* (Series V) TV (Equity negotiator with ITV)	*Candida* TP *The Chairs* TP *Heartbreak House* T & LP	*The Bald Prima Donna* TP *Murder on a Saturday* B
1962	Higgins in *My Fair Lady* (Australia) OMP Compère for Joan Sutherland TV	*Village Wooing* OTV & OP *A Marriage Has Been Arranged* OP Shakespeare Recital (Berlin) OP *Royal Gambit* TP	*Murder in Mind* B *Virtue* TV
1963	*Boyd QC* (Final Series) TV	*Where Angels Fear to Tread* T & LP	*The Devil Wore Scarlet* B
1964	*Hostile Witness* T & LP	*Where Angels Fear to Tread* TP *Merely Players* OTP & TP (Shakespeare Recital) *The Actor and His World* B	*The Seagull* (Birmingham) TP *No Quarter for a Star* B
1965	*Hostile Witness* (until September) LP *The Citadel* R	*An Ideal Husband* T & LP (Formation of Allied Theatre Productions) (Sale of Essex cottage)	*Beautiful For Ever* TV *A Man Could Get Killed* F

292

	Michael	Joint		Dulcie	
1966	(Equity: Resignation and re-election over South African policy)	*Ideal Husband* (continues)	LP		
		On Approval	T & LP		
		We Beg to Differ	R		
1967		*On Approval*	L & TP	*The Murder of Love*	B
		Happy Family	LP		
		No. 10	T, OT, LP		
1968	*Funeral Games* TV	*Vacant Possession*	TP	*Died in the Red*	B
	(Play adviser to Howard & Wyndham)	*Confessions at Night* (Nottingham)	TP		
		Out of the Question (with Gladys Cooper)	T & LP		
1969	(Nominated for President of Equity)	*Out of the Question* (continues)	LP	*Murder on Honeymoon*	B
		Trio: *The Will*			
		Village Wooing	TPs		
		Ways & Means			
		Unexpectedly Vacant	TV		

293

	Michael	Joint	Dulcie
1970	'Touring in the 70s' (Article for Arts Council)	Three:	*For Richer, For Richer* B
		How He Lied to Her Husband *Village Wooing* *Press Cuttings* } LPs	
		Dandy Dick TP	
		Both directors of Play Company of London	
		Wild Duck T & LP	
		(Accept offer of country lease: leave Cumberland Place)	
1971		(Holiday in Malaysia)	*Deadly Lampshade* B
		(Death of Titus)	
		Clandestine Marriage TP	
		(Sacking of Norman Banks collapses)	
		School for Scandal TP	
		Village Wooing TPs	
		Unexpectedly Vacant }	
1972	*Tempest* (Prospero) T & LP	*Dragon Variation* (Windsor)	*Hay Fever* TP
	Twelfth Night (Malvolio) LP	*Dragon Variation* TP	*Ghosts* TP
	Becomes a director of New Shakespeare Company (Regent's Park)	(Prospero born 9 April)	*Understudy to Murder* B
		Alice Through the Looking Glass TP	

294

	Michael		Joint		Dulcie	
1973	*Overture and Beginners*	B	*Dragon Variation*	TP	*This is Your Life*	TV
	The Quiet Revolutionary (begun)	B	*At the End of the Day* (Two visits to Chequers)	T & LP		
	The Twelve Pound Look	TV				
1974	*The Provincial Lady*	TV	*At the End of the Day* (continues)	LP	*The Pay Off*	T & LP
	Peter Pan (Capt. Hook Mr Darling)	LP	*The Sack Race*	T & LP	*Dead Give Away*	B
1975	*The Black Mikado* T & LMP (Drama Panel, Arts Council)		Painted by John Bratby		*The Pay Off* (continues)	LP
					Time and the Conways	TP
					Ride on a Tiger	B
1976	*The Black Mikado* (continues)	LMP	*Time and the Conways* (D: Mrs Conway M: directs)	TP	*Carry On Jeeves*	TP
	(Visit of Harold Macmillan (Lord Stockton))				*Ladies in Retirement*	TP
	The First Mrs Fraser	TP			*Façade* (Recital with orchestra)	
	The Earl and the Pussycat	TP				
	Robert and Elizabeth	TMP				
	(Refuse nominations for President and Vice President of Equity)					

295

	Michael	Joint	Dulcie
1977	*This is Your Life* TV *Robert and Elizabeth* T & OMTP *She Stoops to Conquer* TP (Windsor) (Rejected as a Councillor by Equity electorate)	Visit Terence Rattigan (Bermuda) *The Cabinet Minister* TP (M's adaptation of Pinero) (Both awarded Queen's Jubilee Medal)	Writing Butterfly Book (Research in Canada) *A Murder is Announced* T & LP *Stage Door Fright* B (short stories) *Death in Denims* (for children) B
1978	One Man Show (Malta) Recital *Twelfth Night* } T & *Lady's Not for Burning* } LPs *Ivanov* (Prospect: Old Vic)		*A Murder is Announced* LP & T (continues) *Bedroom Farce* LP (for National Theatre) *Voysey Inheritance* TV *Butterflies on My Mind* B (awarded *TES* Senior Information Award)
1979	*A Friend Indeed* TP *Crown Court* (twice) TV	M joins D in *Bedroom Farce* LP (40th anniversary of joint career).	*Bedroom Farce* (continues) LP *Dark Calypso* B
1980	*Private Schulz* TV (return to BBC TV after 21 years) *Blood Money* TV *Venus Observed* (Windsor) TP *Bedroom Farce* TV	*The Kingfisher* (Windsor) TP *The Cherry Orchard* (Exeter) TP	*Lloyd George Knew My Father* TP

296

	Michael		Joint		Dulcie	
1981	*The Critic*	TV	*Relatively Speaking*	OTP	*Life After Death*	TV
	Sherry Commercial	TV	(Far and Middle Eastern tour for Derek Nimmo)			
			The Kingfisher	TP		
1982	*Capt. Brassbound's Conversion*	LP	*Coat of Varnish*	LP	*Pink Panther*	F
	Agatha Christie	TV	*School for Scandal*	TP	*The Glanville Women*	B
	Skorpion	TV	(The Queen visits Open Air Theatre)		Agatha Christie	TV
	Good Behaviour	TV				
1983			*School for Scandal*	LP		
			Tartuffe	TP		
			Song at Twilight	TP		
			Rumpole	TV		
			The Thirties (Stansted)	TV		
			(Both made CBE)			
			Are You Still Awake?	R		
1984	*See How They Run*	LP & TV	*School for Scandal*	LP	*School for Scandal*	LP
	Cold Warrior	TV	One episode of *Cold Warrior*	TV	(Switches from Lady Sneerwell to Mrs Candour overnight)	
					British Council: OTP 16 cities in 9 countries in 10 weeks	

297

INDEX

Plays and films in which Michael Denison and Dulcie Gray have appeared are listed in the Chronological Chart on pages 284-97.

Aarvold, Carl, 112
Ackland, Joss, 74
The Actor and His World, 38-39, 99, 137-138, 174
Adams, Polly, 129, 159, 161, 163
Adelphi Theatre, 239-240
Aherne, Brian, 122
Albery, Sir Bronson, 105
Aldridge, Michael, 271, 272
Alexandra, Princess, 176
Alexandra Theatre, Birmingham, 63-64
Allen, Dave, 269
Allied Theatre Productions, 143, 144-145, 158-159, 161-164, 182, 263
Amadeo, 237-238
Ambassadors Theatre, 18-19, 205, 234
Andrews, Antony, 247, 277
Andrews, Eamonn, 42, 227, 256
Angus and Robertson, 257
Annaly, (Lady) Lavinia, 14, 57, 68, 277
Anne, Princess, 244
Artists' Benevolent Fund, 90
Arts Council, 101-102, 172, 173-174, 200, 208-210, 223, 243, 260, 263-264, 266-267
Arts Theatre, 49
Ashcroft, Dame Peggy, 21, 48-49, 129, 206, 264
Ashcroft Theatre, Croydon, 128-129
Ashmore, Peter, 17
Asquith, Antony 'Puffin', 25, 26
Associated British Pictures, 6, 35
Associated Rediffusion, 71, 82-85, 118, 127, 143
Atkins, Eileen, 264, 267
Atkins, Robert, 81, 219, 279
Attenborough, Sir Richard, 9, 10, 36-37, 138, 187, 192, 201, 227, 229
Attenborough, Lady (Sheila), 9, 36-37
Atwood, Clare, 62

Auchinleck, Field Marshal Sir Claude, 179-180
Audley, Maxine, 53, 55, 64
AUEW, 269
Australia, 67-68, 119-122, 123-125
Australian Broadcasting Corporation, 123
Ayckbourn, Alan, 142-143, 225, 226, 268-269, 270, 274, 275
Aylmer, Sir Felix, 62, 117, 147, 153, 192, 231

Baby Face, 75, 94-95
Bachauer, Gina, 231
Baddeley, Angela, 53, 55, 193-194
Baddeley, Hermione, 227
Bagnold, Enid, 229
Bailey, Arnold Savage (Dulcie's father), 94, 125, 216
Bailey, Cyril, 170, 250
Bailey, Kate Savage (Dulcie's mother), 94, 125
Bailey, Dr Lionel, 206
Bailey, Robin, 122
Baker, Bernard and Valerie, 182-183
Baldwin, James, 186
Ballardie, Jack de Caynoth, 203
Bangkok, 124-125, 126
Bannerman, Kay, 254
Barber, John, 26, 33, 64
Baring, Maurice, 281
Barnes, Sir Kenneth, 14
Barnett, Lady Isobel, 41-42
Barr, Patrick, 50
Barrault, Jean Louis, 170
Barrie, Sir J. M., 194, 254
Barry, June, 203-204
Barton, John, 43
Bassey, Shirley, 83
Bath Festival, 102, 103, 104

298

Baxter, Keith, 132-133, 277
Baxter, Stanley, 70
Bayliss, Sir Richard, 139
BBC, 12, 28, 49-50, 62, 85, 95, 115, 137, 143, 159, 272, 275
Beaton, Norman, 239
Beatty, Robert, 22
Beaumont, Binkie, 75, 132, 135, 137, 138, 182, 228-229
Benjamin, Floella, 239, 243, 245, 261
Benson, George, 49
Berlin Festival, 69, 70, 128
Betjeman, Sir John, 129
Bird, Richard, 8-9, 131
Birkett, Lord (Norman), 76
Birley, Lady (Rhoda), 136, 263
Birmingham Post, 64
Birmingham Repertory Theatre, 139
Black, Kitty, 182
Black, Sir Robert, 125
Blair, Bobby, 256
Bloom, Claire, 28
Bogarde, Dirk, 92
Bond, Derek, 157
Boot, Gladys, 23
Borsi, Manfredo, 47
Boulter, Rosalyn, 16
Boulting brothers, 12
Boyd, Leslie, 71
Boyer, Charles, 30
Brett, Jeremy, 75, 87, 103, 163, 254
Bridge, Peter, 99, 141-143, 144-145, 158-159, 163, 164, 167, 191, 199, 219, 226, 268
British Butterfly Conservation Society, 257
British Council, 124-126
British Film Producers' Association (BFPA), 20
Brittany, 102-103
Britton, Tony, 82, 122, 139-140
Brook, Peter, 60-61
Brooke, Brian, 51-52, 67
Brooke, Harold, 254
Brooke, Petrina, 51-52
Brown, Irene, 60
Brown, Ivor, 8, 39, 204
Brown, Janet, 61
Brownrigg, Captain, 84, 85
Bruce, Brenda, 69-70, 264, 267
Bruce, Edgar K., 137
Bruce Watt, Barbara, 253
Bryant, Johanna, 237, 245
Burton, Richard, 12, 56
Butterflies on My Mind, 200, 257-258, 268
Butterworth, Peter, 61

Byam Shaw, Glen, 53-54, 56, 60, 63-64, 131, 132, 193-194, 199, 204, 205-206, 219,268

Calvert, Phyllis, 22
Cameron, Audrey, 61-62, 102, 135, 253
Cameron, Iné, 62
Campbell, Judy, 87, 113
Canada, 175-176
Carrington, Iona, 231
Carrington, Lord, 181, 231, 274
Casson, John, 187
Casson, Sir Lewis, 118, 135, 185-187
Casson, Pat, 187
Cazenove, Christopher, 247
Cecil, Jonathan, 219
Charles, Prince of Wales, 165
Chekhov, Anton, 205
Chelsea Palace, 64-65
Chester, Charlie, 256
Chetwyn, Bob, 261
Chipping Campden, 16
Christie, Agatha, 77, 106, 261-262
Churchill, Sir Winston, 25, 93, 170, 171, 178, 190
Clark, Ernest, 115
Clark, May, 6
Clark, Robert, 6-7, 12, 15, 20, 21, 25, 35 84
Clark, William, 175
Claude (au pair), 76-77
Clements, Sir John, 14, 105, 252
Clements, Mrs, 160
Cleveland, Kenneth, 127
Clulow, David, 261
Clunes, Alec, 105
Codner, Maurice, 48
Codron, Michael, 225
Collins, Norman, 115, 168-169, 278
Collins, Sarah, 168, 169
Compton, Denis, 41
Compton, Valerie, 50-51, 52
Condon, Dick, 163
Connor, Kenneth, 35
Conville, David, 219, 222-223
Cooney, Ray, 114, 204, 226-227, 229, 233
Cooper, Lady Diana, Duff, 25
Cooper, Sir Duff, 25
Cooper, Giles, 142, 163-164, 166
Cooper, Dames Gladys, 23, 106, 183-185, 192
Copley, Peter, 149-150
Cordrey, Philip, 261
Cotterell, Richard, 242
Counsell, John, 34, 204-205, 219, 221, 260, 271

Couper, Barbara, 95
Courtneidge, Dame Cicely, 144
Coward, Sir Noël, 24, 38, 46, 50, 60, 67, 95, 114, 159, 188, 194-195, 201, 224, 228-229, 235, 274, 279
Cowles, Fleur, 188-189, 190, 250
Cowles, 'Mike', 189
Craig, Edith (Edy), 61, 62
Crawford, Anne, 25, 50
Creighton, Mrs Mandell, 107-108
Crime Writers' Association, 76, 234, 257
Crisham, Wally, 44, 65
Criterion Theatre, 205, 226
Croasdell, Gerald, 115-117, 138, 141, 147, 149, 151-155, 200, 212-214, 277
Cronyn, Hume, 19, 273
Culver, Nan, 144, 185
Culver, Roland, 144, 185
Cunningham family, 176
Currer Briggs, Michael, 71

Daily Express, 26, 64, 114
Daily Telegraph, 95
Dali, Salvador, 190
Daniel Mayer Company, 37
Dare, Zena, 185
Dark Calypso, 123
Daubeny, Sir Peter, 186
Davey, Pamela Ann, 129
Dawson, Anna, 234
Day, Richard Digby, 222, 224, 227
Dead Give Away, 234
Dean, Basil, 49
Dear, Ian, 257
Dench, Judi, 82, 87
Denison, Gilbert (Michael's father), 94
Denison, Marie Louise (Michael's mother), 94
Denison, Michael: on Equity Council, 5, 10-13; first London house, 5-6; South American film festival, 22-24; Vice-President of Equity, 35; paintings, 46-48, 90, 189-190; in South Africa, 50-52; car crash, 57-58; Equity 'strike', 83, 99, 114-118; Duke of Redonda, 92-93; Rolls-Royces, 93-94, 140, 247-248; in Australia, 119-122, 123-125; Far Eastern tour, 124-126; Silver Wedding, 135-136; and Equity's South African policy, 141, 146-157; Allied Theatre Productions, 141-143, 144-145, 158-159, 161-164; Buckinghamshire flat, 160-161, 200, 206; and Arts Council policy, 172-175, 208-209; visits Canada, 175-176; and Howard and Wyndham, 191-192; proposed as

Denison, Michael — *Contd*
President of Equity, 192; and the Play Company of London, 199, 205; Theatre Investment Fund, 209-210; opposition to Industrial Relations Act, 210-214; visits Malaysia, 215-218; holiday in West Indies, 250-251; *This is Your Life*, 256; Ruby Wedding, 273-274; awarded CBE, 278-279
Denning, Lord, 71, 130
Derby Evening Telegraph, 66
Derry, Sam, 256
Desert Island Discs, 35
Devlin, William, 55, 150
Died in the Red, 180
Dinner Theatre Tours, 275-277
Donald, Charles, 165
Donald, Cleone, 191-192, 279
Donald, Peter, 99, 101-102, 141-143, 159, 163, 165, 167, 172, 176, 191-192, 199, 241, 268, 279, 280
Donaldson, Frances, 162
Donat, Robert, 7
Dors, Diana, 92
Douglas, Felicity, 43
Douglas, Wally, 91
Douglas Home, Rachel, 38
Douglas Home, William, 38, 40, 42, 229-231, 271, 275
D'Oyly Carte Company, 243
Drake, Fabia, 110
Drake, Gabrielle, 219
du Maurier, Sir Gerald, 7
Dublin, 50
Dunfee, Jack, 13-14, 46, 126-127
Dunlop, Frank, 209
Dux, Pierre, 184

East Lynne, 137
Ebigwei, Patricia (Pattie Boulaye), 239, 245
Eddison, Robert, 62, 264, 267, 275
Edelman, Maurice, 69
Edinburgh Festival, 69-70
Edrich, Bill, 243
Elizabeth, Queen Mother, 14, 57, 229, 250, 277
Elizabeth II, Queen, 137, 139, 189, 250, 258, 260, 277-278, 279
Elkins, Margarete, 129-130
Elliott, Paul, 199, 226
Emrys Williams, Sir William, 172
Equity, 5, 10-13, 35, 53, 83, 99, 114-118, 132, 137-138, 141, 146-157, 172, 186, 192, 200, 208, 210-214, 233, 240, 243, 277, 279

Evans, Dame Edith, 21, 26, 28, 62, 82, 136
Evans, Laurence, 127-128
Evans, Lawrence, 268
Evening Standard, 13-14, 123
Every, Sir Edward, 5-6, 88-89
Every, Lady (Ivy), 5-6, 88-89, 135

Fairchild, Bill, 234
Faith, Adam, 147
Farebrother, Violet, 135
Farrell, Charles, 149-150, 192
Faulds, Andrew, 59, 150
Ferrer, José, 19
Fielding, Fenella, 63
Finch, Peter, 129
Finney, Albert, 99, 143
Fleming, Lucy, 185, 192, 193, 275-276
Fleming, Peter, 192-193
Flemyng, Robert, 56, 115, 159, 162, 163, 173, 203-204, 275
Flint Shipman, Gerald and Veronica, 261
Fontanne, Lynn, 19
For Richer For Richer, 75
Forster, E. M., 132-133, 135
Forster Jones, Glenna, 239, 252
Fountain, Mr, 160-161
Fox, Edward, 202
Foyle, Christina, 232
France, 16-17, 42, 102-103, 106
Francis, Clive, 203-204
Francis, Dick, 76, 200, 234, 277
Francis, Mary, 234, 277
Frangçon Davies, Gwen, 21, 95
Fraser, Bill, 181
Fraser, John, 156
French, Harold and Peggy, 259-260
Fugard, Athol, 156
Furness, Viscount, 199

Gainsborough Pictures, 27
Gale, John, 40, 102, 105, 135, 221-222, 224, 229, 268
Gale, Lisel, 135
Gardner, Lord, 130
Garner, James, 143
Gawsworth, John, 92-93
Ghouse, Nellie, 217
Gibson, Pat (Lord Gibson), 210, 256, 266
Gielgud, Sir John, 20-21, 27, 55-56, 60, 62, 137, 162, 187, 235, 265, 268
Gilliat, Sir Martin, 277
Gilroy, John, 192
Gingold, Hermione, 69
A Girl From the Golden East, 215
Glaister, Gerard, 275

The Glanville Women, 278
Gluckman, Leon, 148
Gluth, Bill and Margaret, 122
Gobbi, Tito, 227, 231, 256
Gollancz, Livia, 137, 231
Gooden, Robert, 257
Goolden, Richard, 219
Goring, Marius, 148, 150-151
Gough, Michael, 272
Graham, Sonia, 75
Grand Theatre, Leeds, 175
Graves, (Lord) Peter, 137
Gray, Dulcie: first London house, 5-6; South American film festival, 22-24; Venice Film Festival, 25; a mistaken diagnosis and its consequences, 34, 37, 38, 42; in South Africa, 50-52, 73-74; plays, 61, 63-64, 66-67, 85; in Australia, 67-68, 123-125; Far Eastern tour, 124-126; Silver Wedding, 135-136; Buckinghamshire flat, 160-161, 200, 206; visits Canada, 175-176; MD writes *A Girl From the Golden East* about, 215; visits Malaysia, 215-218; *This is Your Life*, 227; suffers depression, 242; holiday in West Indies, 250-251; breaks arm, 261; Ruby Wedding, 273-274; awarded CBE, 278-279; *see also individual novels and plays*
Greece, 127
Greenwood, Joan, 26
Gregson, John, 90, 175, 177
Griffiths, Derek, 239, 241, 244-245
Grossmith, George, 243
Grout, James, 64
The Guardian, 135
Guinness, Sir Alec, 7, 21
Gwatkin, Brigadier Sir Norman, 78-79, 228, 251

Hale, Binnie, 44, 45
Hall, Sir Peter, 43, 131, 265, 269, 270-272
Hallam, Greville, 103
Hamilton, Patrick, 85
Hammond, Kay (Lady Clements), 105, 252
Hampshire, Susan, 159, 235
Hancock, Chris, 103
Hanley, Jimmy, 16
Hannen, Nicholas, 62
Harbottle, Revd A. A. H., 258
Harding, Gilbert, 42
Hardwick, Sir Cedric, 30
Hargreaves, Brian, 257
Harley, Pam, 176

Harris, 'Percy', 194
Harrison, Rex, 12, 20, 122
Harrison, Stephen, 49-50, 85
Hart, Elizabeth, 133
Hartog, Jan de, 17-20
Harvey, Laurence, 74
Hauser, Frank, 85-87, 101, 103, 104-105, 109, 119, 123, 128, 136, 219, 265, 277
Hawkes, Jacquetta, 30-31, 227, 247, 268
Hawkins, Jack, 24
Haymarket Theatre, 71, 139, 167, 268, 277
Headfort Lady (Rosie), 77, 78-79, 106, 127, 228
Heath, Edward, 170-171, 200, 210, 230-231, 269
Heath, John, 257
Helpmann, Sir Robert, 129
Henson, Leslie, 64-65
Hepburn, Audrey, 9-10, 12
Hewett, Chris, 26
Hickman, Charles, 219, 233, 253
Hickson, Joan, 269, 272
Higgs, John and Elizabeth, 133-134, 279, 280
Hoare, Elspeth, 161, 189-190, 206
Hobson, Sir Harold, 39, 75, 114, 164, 206, 232, 268
Hodgkinson, Joe, 101
Holland, Vyvyan, 145
Holm, Ian, 64
Hong Kong, 124, 125-126
Hope Wallace, Philip, 39, 135
Howard, Sir Douglas, 23
Howard and Wyndham, 142, 143, 172, 191-192
Howerd, Frankie, 83, 186, 200, 246-247, 272, 277
Howes, Sally Ann, 254
Howlett, Noel, 150
Hulbert, Claude, 91
Hulbert, Jack, 144
Hunt, Martita, 49, 82
Huntington, Laurie, 35

Industrial Relations Act, 210-214
Ingram, Pamela, 159
Irvin, Sir Henry, 87, 111-112, 138
Italy, 133-134
ITV, 12, 99, 105, 114-118, 151, 168, 211

Jackson, Gordon, 87, 247
Jacobi, Derek, 264, 267
James, Marjorie, 77-78
James, Sid and Val, 178
Jeans, Ursula, 62, 145, 158

Jefford, Barbara, 87
John, Rosamund, 31-32
Johns, Glynis, 22
Johnson, Dame Celia, 16, 24, 91, 144, 185, 192-193, 269
Johnston, Sir John (Johnnie), 279
Jowett, John, 35

Kaufmann, George, 16
Keane, Molly, 275
Keith, Penelope, 87, 163, 277
Kelly, Barbara, 42
Kendal, Felicity, 87
Kendall, Harry, 91-92
Kennedy, John F., 133
Kerr, Deborah, 109
Kerridge, Mary, 271
King's Theatre, Edinburgh, 241
King's Theatre, Glasgow, 172
Kirkwood, Pat, 260
Knight, Esmond, 81
Kulukundis, Eddie, 199

Ladd, Alan, 7
Lang, Harold, 109-110
Laughton, Charles, 30-31
Law, Mary, 64
Lawrence, Gertrude, 228
Laye, Evelyn, 85, 253, 260
Leahy, Eileen (housekeeper), 99, 128, 181, 218
Lee, Jennie, 171
Leggatt, Alison, 194
Leggett, Sir Frederick, 118
Leigh, Vivien (Lady Olivier), 12, 40, 54, 55-56, 57-58, 59-61, 168, 174
Lennard, Kay, 9, 279
Lennard, Robert, 9, 26, 256, 279, 280
Leno, Charles, 85
Leonard, Hugh, 142
Lethbridge, Miss, 121
Levin, Bernard, 278
Lewis, Ronald, 38
Lillie, Beatrice, 25, 57
Littler, Sir Emile, 91
Livesey, Roger, 62, 113, 145, 158, 264
Lockhart, Freda Bruce, 22
Lockwood, Margaret, 139, 145
Löhr, Marie, 36
London Theatre Council, 13, 118
Longdon, Terence, 234
Lonsdale, Frederick, 91, 159, 162, 164, 166
Loraine, Lorn, 195
Love à la Carte, 85
Love Affair, 61, 64, 66-67, 68, 85, 282
Lumsden, Geoffrey, 271

Lunt, Alfred, 19
Lyric Theatre, Hammersmith, 113-114

McCallum, John, 119, 121, 122, 124, 268
McDonald, Murray, 143, 159, 162, 166, 219
Macdonalds, 257
MacEwan, Geraldine, 35, 163, 264
McFarland, Olive, 156
MacGrath, Leueen, 16
McGusty, Jenny, 239, 243
McKellen, Ian, 87, 265
McKenna, Virginia, 38, 272
Mackenzie, Compton, 76
McKern, Leo, 87, 275
Macmillan, Harold (Lord Stockton), 189, 249-250
McMillan, John, 82-83, 84, 138
Macowan, Michael, 268
MacShane, Ian, 181
McWhinnie, Donald, 166
Malaysia, 215-217, 276
Malleson, Miles, 26
Malta, 263
Mancroft, Lord (Stormont), 106, 136
Marcus, Frank, 164
Margaret, Princess, 103
Mark, Robert, 76
Marrakesh, 178-80
Marsh, Sir Edward, 8
Marsh, Ngaio, 77
Marten, Mary Anna, 253-254, 257
Marten, Toby, 253-254, 257
Mason, Brewster, 54
Mason, James, 12, 227
Matthews, A. E., 7
Maugham, Somerset, 8, 75, 102, 105-106
Mayo, Virginia, 11
Medwin, Michael, 143
Melford, Austin, 91, 185
Melia, Joe, 247
Melville, Alan, 227
Melvin, Bobby, 256
Men and Women of Today Club, 180
Merchant, Vivien, 181
Mercouri, Melina, 143
Merry family, 176
Messel, Oliver, 104
Michaels, Louis, 167
Michell, Keith, 55, 59, 64, 87, 129
Middleton, Guy, 91
Miles, Lord (Bernard), 63
Millar, Sir Ronald, 175, 254, 255-256
Millington, Rodney, 256
Mills, Hayley, 137, 205, 227
Mills, Sir John, 60, 230, 231
Mills, Lady (Mary), 60

Mills, Juliet, 64, 256
Minney, R. J., 272-273
Mirvisch, Ed, 268
Montague Meyer, Tom, 188-189, 190
Moorhead, Agnes, 30
More, Kenneth, 16, 163
Morell, André, 25, 115, 147, 148
Morgan, Terence, 82
Morley, Robert, 42, 184-185
Mortimer, John, 275
Mosco, Maisie, 182
Moyheddin, Zia, 119
Mullen, Barbara, 227
Munro, Nan, 133
Murder in Melbourne, 75, 94
Murder in Mind, 75, 123
Murder on the Stairs, 68, 75, 102
The Murder of Love, 75, 123, 168, 169-170
Murray, Barbara, 194
Murray, Braham, 235-236, 237-238, 240, 242, 249
Murray, General Sir Horatio, 69-70
Murray, Pete, 227
Murray Hill, Peter, 22
Musgrove, John, 44-45
Music Corporation of America (MCA), 126-127, 128

National Theatre, 138, 164, 174-175, 209, 268, 270-272
Neagle, Dame Anna, 145, 252-253
Neal, Patricia, 11
Neilson, Julia, 135
Neilson, Perlita, 113, 145
Nesbeth, Vernon, 239, 243
Neville, John, 166, 172, 182, 183, 191
New Shakespeare Company, 200, 219, 222-223, 278
News Chronicle, 12
Nicholls, Lord Harmar, 171, 209-210, 211, 212
Nicholls, Tony, 234
Nichols, Beverly, 276
Nicol, Ian, 218
Nimmo, Derek, 147-148, 231, 275-276
Niven, David, 13
No Quarter for a Star, 139
Nollier, Claude, 24
Norgate, Matthew, 22
Norman, Anne, 106-107, 159, 201, 219, 224
Norman, Antony, 106-108, 159, 201, 219
Norman, Lady, 107-108
Nottingham Playhouse, 172, 182, 183, 191
Nugent, Lord (Tim), 185, 228, 229

Nunn, Trevor, 43, 265
Nureyev, Rudolf, 176
Nutbeam, Mr, 258

Odell, Harry, 125-126
Ogilvy, Angus, 176
Old Vic, 200, 263-8
Olivier, Lord (Laurence), 7, 12, 21, 36, 40, 53, 54, 55-56, 59-61, 91, 111-112, 133, 138, 162, 174, 202, 206, 235, 264, 268
Orton, Joe, 181
Osborne, John, 66-67, 78, 85, 186
Oulton, Brian, 64
Overture and Beginners, 200, 231-232, 281
Oxford Playhouse, 85-87, 101, 104
Oxford University Law Society, 110-112, 130
Ozenfant, Amédée, 61

Pain, Peter, 155
Palladium, 50
Palmer, Lilli, 20
Panov, Valery and Galina, 233
Paton, Alan, 52
Patrick, Nigel, 141, 183, 203, 234-235
Payn, Graham, 195, 229
Peck, Gregory, 7, 10, 11
Perry, Clive, 241
Persian Gulf, 276-277
Philip, Prince, 277
Philippe, Gerard, 24
Philpotts, Ambrosine, 185
Phoenix Theatre, 261
Piccadilly Theatre, 104-105
Picturegoer Gold Awards, 6-7
Pius XII, Pope, 79
Play Company of London, 199, 205-206
Plays and Players, 164
Plouviez, Peter, 213
Plowright, Joan (Lady Olivier), 206, 277
Plowright, Oiver, 139
Podlashuk, Bernard and Fredagh, 51
Pollock, Ellen, 141
Preminger, Otto, 12
Priestley, J. B., 21, 30-33, 92, 113, 136, 158, 168, 169, 171, 188, 200, 227, 246-247, 252, 268, 271, 274, 282
Prince of Wales Theatre, 271
Pringle, Val, 239, 240, 244, 256
Profumo, John, 77, 78
Prospect Company, 175, 200, 263-268
Purnell, Louise, 264

Quayle, Sir Anthony, 53, 56, 61, 63, 131, 133, 235

Queen's Jubilee Medal, 200, 260
Quentin, John, 223

Rabagliati, Euan and Beatrix, 201-203, 219, 231
Raine, Gillian, 103, 129, 163
Ramsay, Peggy, 221
Randell, Ron, 256
Rank, 12, 25
Rank, Lord (Arthur), 12
Rattigan, Sir Terence, 41, 67, 231, 259-260
Rawlings, Margaret, 62, 95
Rawlinson, Dick, 35
Rawlinson, Lord (Peter), 155, 211
Ray, Andrew, 156
Raymond, Cyril, 91
Reagan, Ronald, 11
Redgrave, Corin, 212
Redgrave, Sir Michael, 8, 21, 26, 27-28, 235, 264
Redgrave, Vanessa, 212
Redman, Joyce, 53
Redonda, 92-93
Regent's Park Open Air Theatre, 200, 219, 222-223, 277-278
Relph, George, 38
Rendle Adrian, 263
Reynolds, Helen, 241
Rich, Roy, 69
Richardson, Sir Ralph, 7, 21, 224
Richfield, Edwin, 56
Ride on a Tiger, 199, 242, 253
Riley, Joan, 221, 224, 254
Riley, Norman, 258
Rix, Brian, 99, 143, 167
Roberts, Ewan, 234
Roberts, John, 183, 185, 192
Robertson, Toby, 43-44, 175, 263-268
Robinson, Clive and Vera, 125-126
Robinson, Sir Kenneth, 266
Robson, Dame Flora, 25
Roffey, Jack, 71, 139
Rogers, Paul, 62
Rose, Pam, 256
Rosehill, 104, 136
Ross, Charles, 81, 85
Ross, George, 219
Rothschild, Dr Miriam, 258
Routledge, Patricia, 163
Roux, M., 47
Roy, Harry, 14
Royal Shakespeare Company, 175
Royal Variety Performances, 50
Rutherford, Dame Margaret, 26, 44, 64-65, 282
Rye, Daphne, 137

St John, Christopher, 62-3
St Martin's Theatre, 133, 167, 184
Salberg, Derek, 63-64
Salew, John, 114
Sandison, George, 10, 115, 214
Sargent, Sir Malcolm, 121
Saunders, Sir Peter, 137, 138-139, 261
Scales, Prunella, 265
Scofield, Paul, 21, 61, 187, 229, 244
The Scotsman, 253
Scott, Sir Peter, 257
Seago, Edward, 48, 90, 179, 180
Sekers, Lady (Agi), 103, 104
Sekers, Sir Nicholas (Miki), 103-104, 136
Seyler, Athene, 62, 277
Shaftesbury Theatre, 114
Shakespeare, Mr and Mrs, 54
Shakespeare, William, 53-57, 136-137, 200, 222-223, 251, 263, 264-265, 277
Shakespeare Memorial Theatre, Stratford, 53-57, 60-61, 63
Sharp, Tony, 224
Shaw, Bernard, 30, 69, 85-86, 87-88, 102, 105, 106, 107, 122, 142, 158, 187, 203-204, 277, 282
Shelley, Norman, 62
Sherek, Henry, 64, 66, 69, 70
Shiel, David, 93
Shiel, M. P., 93
Shute, Nevil, 7
Sim, Alastair, 175, 176-177
Simpson, Leonard, 278
Sinatra, Frank, 35
Singapore, 94, 125, 216, 218
Singer, Campbell, 219
Sitwell, Dame Edith, 247
Sleep, Wayne, 222-223
Smith, Dodie, 95
Snowdon, Roger, 150
Society of Authors, 67
Society of West End Theatre (Managers), 105, 210, 237
Somers, Julie, 64
South Africa, 50-52, 67-68, 73-74, 99, 146-157
Spain, 22-23
Spenser, Jeremy, 103, 114
Springfield, Dusty, 147
Spurling, John, 143
Squire, Ronald, 164
The Stage, 101-102, 105, 209
Stais, John, 113
Stannard, Heather, 38
Stevens, John, 143
Stevens, Robert, 264
Stevens, Ronnie, 267

Stone, 'Rocky', 143
Strand Theatre, 7, 145, 176
Strasberg, Lee, 186
Sunday Times, 75, 232
Sutherland, Dame Joan, 129-130
Sutro, Alfred, 62
Sutro, John, 22
Suzman, Helen, 156
Symons, Julian, 95

The Tailor and Cutter, 50
Take Copernicus, 85
Tandy, Jessica, 19, 273
Taylor, Elizabeth, 12
Taylour, Lady Molly, 78
Taylour, Lord William, 78, 127
Tebbit, Norman, 211
Teeton, Annie, 183
Tempest, Dame Marie, 13, 211
Terry, Dame Ellen, 61-63, 87, 88
Terry, Fred, 135
Terry, Phyllis Neilson, 91
Tey, Josephine, 16
Teynac, Françoise, 43
Teynac, Maurice, 43
Thatcher, Margaret, 269
Theatre Investment Fund (TIF), 209-210
Theatre Royal, Norwich, 163
'Theatre under the Tories', 172-174
Thesiger, Ernest, 78
This is Your Life, 200, 201, 227, 256
Thorndike, Dame Sybil, 135, 137, 185, 186, 187-8, 231
Tickner, Martin, 199, 203-204, 229
The Times, 104, 164, 177, 193, 266-267
Times Educational Supplement, 268
Todd, Richard, 11, 145, 199, 256
Toye, Wendy, 15, 92, 194
Trades Union Congress (TUC), 212-213
Tredgold, Dr, 38
Trewin, John, 39, 64, 141, 164, 268
Triumph Productions, 173-174, 260, 267-268
Tucker, Anita, 239, 244
Turner, Bunty, 120, 122
Turner, John, 87
Turner, Maxwell, 110
Tutin, Dorothy, 26, 28, 275
Tynan, Ken, 26, 33, 40, 67
Tyzack, Margaret, 95

United States of America, 119
Uruguay, 22, 23-24
Ustinov, Peter, 269

van Thal, Herbert, 68, 215, 231, 257

Vanbrugh, Irene, 14
Vaudeville Theatre, 261
Venice Film Festival, 25
Venning, Una, 64
Verdict, 110-112
Verner, James, 235-236, 237, 240, 241-242
Verwoerd, Dr, 147
Voss, Stephanie, 75

Waley Cohen, Sir Bernard, 113
Walker, Hugh and Shirley, 176
Walker, Richard, 120
Wallace, Bryan, 22
Wallach, Ira, 183-184
Waller, Fats, 35
Walsh, Dermot, 43
Walton, Sir William, 247
Ward, Leila, 88-89
Ward, Vivien, 88-89
Warner, David, 186
Watergate Theatre, 26
Waters, Ronnie, 128, 236, 275
Watford, Gwen, 254
Watling, Deborah, 234
Watling, Peter, 8
Wauchope, John and Vanessa, 253
Webb, Alan, 54
Weldon, Duncan, 167, 199, 218-19, 221-222, 224-225, 226, 252, 254, 260, 267-268, 278-279
Welles, Orson, 25
West, Dame Rebecca, 95, 200, 230, 231, 234, 243-244, 249, 272, 274, 277, 278
West Timothy, 265
West Indies, 250-251

What's My Line?, 41-42
Whitemore, Hugh, 194
Wilde, Oscar, 20, 42, 73, 102, 144-145, 201
Wilding, Michael, 7
Willard, M., 80
Willes, Peter, 84, 105, 180-181, 194
Williams, Dorian, 77, 256
Williams, Emlyn, 60, 187, 235
Williams, Harcourt, 62
Williams, Molly, 60
Williams, Simon, 275
Williamson, J.C., 119
Wilson, Lord (Harold), 230, 273
Wilson, Lady (Mary), 200
Wilson, Sandy, 26
Winter, Jessie, 91, 185
Withers, Googie, 15, 119, 124
Witty, Dame May, 12, 211
Wolfit, Sir Donald, 69, 182
Woman's Weekly, 215
Wood, Christopher, 102-103
Woodward, Edward, 162
Wooland, Norman, 31
Wooster, Millie (housekeeper), 42, 76, 99
Worth, Irene, 87
Wymark, Patrick, 58
Wyndham's Theatre, 105, 113, 174
Wynne, Ken, 103
Wynne-Tyson, Jon, 93

Young, Francis Brett, 7
Yvonne Arnaud Theatre, Guildford, 159

Zachariah, George, 216
Zetterling Mai, 25, 90